The Long Journey of English

English is one of the most widely spoken languages in the world, with native-speaking communities at the furthest ends of the earth. However, just three thousand years ago the language which became English was not spoken anywhere in Britain. Trudgill, one of the foremost authorities on the English language, takes us on a remarkable journey through the history of English to show how it grew to become the global phenomenon that we know today. Over twelve concise, easily digestible chapters, he traces its development and global spread, starting with the earliest genesis of English five thousand years ago, exploring its expansion in the British Isles and finishing with an overview of how the language looks today, including its use in an increasingly digital world. Particular attention is paid to the native-speaker varieties of English from all around the world and the relationship between colonial varieties of English and indigenous languages.

PETER TRUDGILL is Emeritus Professor of English Linguistics at the University of Fribourg and Honorary Professor of Sociolinguistics at the University of East Anglia. He has honorary doctorates from the universities of Uppsala, East Anglia, La Trobe, British Columbia, Patras, Murcia and Lublin. Recent publications include *European Language Matters* (2021), *Millennia of Language Change* (2020) and *Dialect Matters* (2016).

GW00649814

The Long Journey of English
A Geographical History of the Language

PETER TRUDGILL
University of Fribourg

CAMBRIDGE
UNIVERSITY PRESS

Shaftesbury Road, Cambridge CB2 8EA, United Kingdom

One Liberty Plaza, 20th Floor, New York, NY 10006, USA

477 Williamstown Road, Port Melbourne, VIC 3207, Australia

314–321, 3rd Floor, Plot 3, Splendor Forum, Jasola District Centre,
New Delhi – 110025, India

103 Penang Road, #05–06/07, Visioncrest Commercial, Singapore 238467

Cambridge University Press is part of Cambridge University Press & Assessment,
a department of the University of Cambridge.

We share the University's mission to contribute to society through the pursuit of
education, learning and research at the highest international levels of excellence.

www.cambridge.org
Information on this title: www.cambridge.org/9781108845120

DOI: 10.1017/9781108954624

© Peter Trudgill 2023

First published 2023

A catalogue record for this publication is available from the British Library.

ISBN 978-1-108-84512-0 Hardback
ISBN 978-1-108-94957-6 Paperback

Cambridge University Press & Assessment has no responsibility for the persistence
or accuracy of URLs for external or third-party internet websites referred to in this
publication and does not guarantee that any content on such websites is, or will
remain, accurate or appropriate.

For Jean, with thanks for our own long journey together.

Contents

Figures and Maps

Figures

Maps

Acknowledgements

I would like to thank very warmly indeed the following people who have helped during the writing and preparation of this book: Bruce Austin, Geoffrey Benjamin, Tony Bradstreet, Kurt Braunmüller, Andy Butcher, Lyle Campbell, Magdalena Charzyńska-Wójcik, Denis Coghlan, Carol Geddes, Tom Geddes, Ives Goddard, Jean Hannah, Jack Hawkins, Annie Howes, Ellen Hurst, David King, Jacob King, Marianne Mithun, Hans Frede Nielsen, John Sandford, Peter Schrijver, David Taylor, D. J. Taylor, Stephen Trudgill, Theo Vennemann, Alastair Walker, David Willis and Ilse Wischer.

Prologue: A View from the Birthplace

I am sitting at my laptop, in the county of Norfolk in the east of England, about 16 miles (25 kilometres) from the North Sea coast, writing the beginnings of a book about English in English. That is a rather new thing to be able to do. And I do not mean because laptops are an extremely recent invention, although of course they are. And I do not mean because people of relatively humble origins like me have only quite recently known how to write, although that is true too.

What I mean is that the English language itself is rather recent. Human language is a phenomenon which is at least 200,000 years old, and maybe much more, but the English language has not been around for even as little as 1 per cent of that time. Five thousand years ago, there was no such language as 'English' – not even here in Norfolk which, as I shall argue later, is one of the places where English may have been born. Nowhere in the world 5,000 years ago was there a language which we would want to refer to today by the name of 'English'.

Nevertheless, there is an important sense in which the language in which this book is now being written did already exist at that time. Although there was no such thing as 'English' as such, there actually was a language which *became* English. And what this book is going to do is to tell the story of the journey that this language has made. And I am not using the term *journey* metaphorically. This is genuinely a *geographical* history of the language, so I really do mean journey in its concrete spatial, geographical sense of travelling from one place to another.

In this book, we shall be looking at the geography of what has happened to this *language which became English*, as well as to English itself, during the last five millennia. It is going to be a long journey, chronologically and spatially, which by the time we have finished will have taken us, over the course of 5,000 years, from the heart of the Eurasian land mass, via Norfolk, to the furthest ends of the earth.

1 Where It All Started: The Language Which Became English

Three thousand years ago, the language which became English was not spoken anywhere in Britain. You would have had to travel eastwards from Britain at least 500 miles or 800 kilometres across the North Sea in order to hear the forerunner of modern English being spoken. Sometime during the second millennium BC, that is, between 2000 and 1000 BC, the linguistic ancestors of modern English speakers were to be found in southern Scandinavia – in southern Sweden and on the Danish islands, in the region where the cities of Copenhagen, Ystad and Malmö are situated today.

It is nevertheless true that the English dialect I grew up speaking in the county of Norfolk, on the other side of the North Sea from Denmark, really is a direct descendant of that ancient language of southern Scandinavia – a descendant which has been passed down directly from one generation to another over very, very many centuries.

We have no idea what the speakers of that ancient language called it – if they called it anything at all – but modern linguists refer to it as 'Proto-Germanic', where *proto* means 'earliest, original'. Not much less than two hundred generations later, my native language is called 'English' by its speakers. But there is a direct line of transmission from the one language form to the other. Proto-Germanic no longer exists, but it has not died out.[1] It has simply become transformed, gradually over the millennia, into English. And not just into English but also into Scots, Dutch, Flemish, Afrikaans, North Frisian, East Frisian, West Frisian, Low German, High German, Swiss German, Luxemburgish, Yiddish, Swedish, Danish, Norwegian, Icelandic and Faroese – the other sister languages of English in the modern Germanic language family.

Some Proto-Germanic words, as reconstructed by experts in the history of Germanic, are to different degrees still recognisable, with a bit of thought, to English speakers today: *andi* 'in addition', *biridi* 'is carrying (bearing)', *ek* 'I', *fader* 'father', *hwat* 'what', *hwehwlaz* 'wheel', *jungaz* 'young', *isti* 'is', *mek* 'me', *samdaz* 'sand', *sangwaz* 'song', *tanthu* 'tooth', *that* 'that', *under* 'among', *wulfaz* 'wolf', *wurmiz* 'worm'. But over the course of the millennia, the language that was spoken in southern Scandinavia has in general changed so much, as languages do, that if we could hear it today it would be unrecognisable and incomprehensible.

---

[1] Some writers use the term 'Pre-Proto-Germanic' for the language as we suppose it was spoken before about 500 BC.

Living as they did on the shores of the Baltic Sea and the Kattegat, we have to assume that these Proto-Germanic-speaking people were rather happy messing about in boats. But we are not at all sure about exactly how they came to be located in that area. Most of the journey undertaken in order to arrive in that location must have been by land, because it is certain that the language they spoke originally came from somewhere further – probably very much further – to the east, somewhere in the middle of the Eurasian land mass. This is because Proto-Germanic descended from an even older language which we now call Proto-Indo-European.

Indo-European

The modern Germanic languages form one of the branches of the Indo-European language family. This is the family which nearly all modern European languages belong to, together with most of the languages of Iran, Afghanistan and the northern South Asian subcontinent.

Exactly where the Proto-Indo-European language was first spoken is the subject of much debate. One piece of evidence which linguists have employed in an attempt to locate the original homeland is *shared vocabulary*. If it can be shown that all or many of the modern Indo-European languages have words in common which refer to natural phenomena that are geographically restricted in their distribution, then that would give us some strong evidence. For example, the Germanic, Baltic and Slavic languages all have words descended from the Proto-Indo-European root *laks*, meaning 'Atlantic salmon' *Salmo salar* – the modern German word is *Lachs* – suggesting that the parent language must have been spoken in a region where these salmon are still found today, namely north-central Europe. There is, however, a big problem with this approach: there is no guarantee that the shared word applies in all cases to the same referent – in this case, to the same species of fish. A chastening example is provided by the English word *robin*, which applies to two entirely different species of bird, in Europe and in North America respectively: the word is shared, but the referent is not.

In fact, however, many archaeologists and philologists today believe that if we suppose that the Indo-European *Urheimat*, the original homeland, was located somewhere in the area between modern eastern Ukraine and western Kazakhstan, we might not be going too far wrong. This area was the part of the vast Eurasian Steppe which is sometimes known as the Western Steppe, with *steppe* (originally a Russian word) meaning a relatively level, treeless, mainly grassland plain. The Western Steppe stretches from the mouth of the River Danube, where it debouches into the Black Sea in the Bulgarian–Romanian borderlands, through Moldova and eastern Ukraine, and then eastwards across the lower Volga regions of Russia and on to western Kazakhstan, passing to the north of the Caucasus mountains (see Map 1.1).

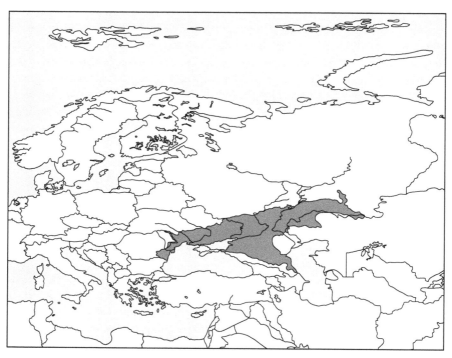

Map 1.1 The Pontic–Caspian Steppe

This particular part of the Eurasian Steppe is perhaps more widely known as the Pontic–Caspian Steppe. In Ancient Greek, πόντος, *pontos* meant 'sea', but *o Πόντος, o Pontos*, 'the Sea', was typically most often just used to refer specifically to the Black Sea, which lay at the western end of the Western Steppe, with the Caspian Sea being situated at the other, eastern end.

It is generally supposed that this Proto-Indo-European language, the ultimate linguistic ancestor of English, was a single rather homogeneous language up until about 4000 BC, after which it underwent geographical expansion and broke up into increasingly different dialects and, eventually, different languages, of which Germanic was one.

This is what happens to languages. It is a natural characteristic of human languages that they change through time – that is quite simply how they are – and it is also very characteristic that they change in different ways in different places, so that a single language can over time break up into several different languages.

But then there is the very intriguing question: what about *before* Indo-European? Where did Indo-European come from, and what ancestral language did it descend from itself?

One possibility is that Proto-Indo-European was in some way related to Proto-Uralic. This was the parent language of the modern Finno-Ugric languages such as Sami, Finnish and Hungarian, as well as of the Samoyedic languages of Siberia. This Indo-Uralic hypothesis makes good geographical sense, given that one homeland which has been postulated for Proto-Uralic lies in the region of the Ural Mountains. The southern end of this mountain range meets the north-eastern end of the Pontic–Caspian Steppe in north-western Kazakhstan. And it has been argued by scholars, including the eminent linguist Johanna Nichols, that the homeland of Pre-Proto-Indo-European indeed lay in Central Asia, perhaps in about 7000 BC, and that its speakers then moved westwards across the steppe, eventually arriving at the north-eastern edge of the Black Sea.

Connections with a Proto-Northwest-Caucasian language may also be possible, although linguistic similarities between these language groups seem more likely to have had to do with contact and borrowing than with a genetic relationship implying descent from a common ancestor.

LANGUAGE NOTES

Caucasia is situated between the Black Sea and the Caspian Sea and is no more than 350 miles (560 kilometres) across at its narrowest point, the zone being mostly taken up topographically by the Caucasus mountain range. The modern Northwest Caucasian linguistic family consists of a small group of languages, including Abkhaz, Abaza and Circassian, which are spoken in small areas of Caucasia.

Proto-Germanic

The time depths we are dealing with here are enormous, and it will probably always be difficult to be at all confident about the nature and origin of any Pre-Proto-Indo-European language there might have been and its possible relatives. But we are on somewhat surer ground with Proto-Indo-European itself and its descendants. We can suppose that it took the Indo-European dialect which became Proto-Germanic at least 2,000 years to make its way from the Pontic–Caspian Europe–Asia borderlands to its first known homeland in southern Scandinavia. This was a journey of very approximately 1,500 miles or 2,400 kilometres.

But how did this Indo-European dialect itself get to the Malmö–Ystad–Copenhagen area? The most obvious explanation has to be that some of the people who spoke Indo-European migrated westwards across what is now Russia into north-western Europe – and we do suppose that that is what actually happened (see Map 1.2). There were after all several groups of speakers of other Indo-European

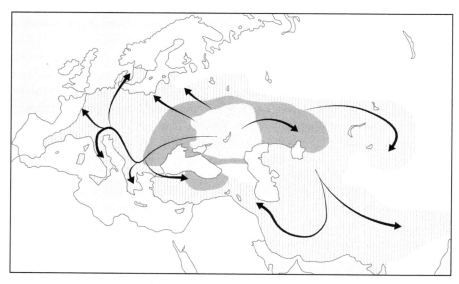

Map 1.2 The geographical diffusion of Indo-European

dialects who had made their way westwards at around the same time. For example, to the south of the Germanic speakers, on the northern European mainland, there were speakers of the Proto-Celtic dialect of Indo-European, which can perhaps be dated to around 1500 BC. At around this same period, moreover, to the south of the Celts, and probably still at least mostly to the north of the Alps, there were speakers of Proto-Italic, the group of dialects ancestral to Latin and hence to the modern Romance languages.

To the east of Germanic and Celtic, occupying territory to the south-east of the Baltic Sea, were speakers of Proto-Baltic, the language ancestral to Latvian and Lithuanian, with the closely related Proto-Slavic language immediately to the south of them, while further south the proto-language which became Greek was penetrating downwards into the southern Balkans.

Elsewhere, Anatolian languages such as Hittite were being spoken in Asia Minor from around 1600 BC. And Proto-Indo-Iranian, the proto-language ancestral to Kurdish, Persian, Punjabi, Hindi and Bengali, was spoken in the region where Russia and Kazakhstan now meet. Indo-European speakers moving east also took Tocharian into Xinjiang, the now mainly Turkic Uighur-speaking area of China.

Demic versus Transcultural Diffusion

The term 'demic diffusion', from Ancient Greek δῆμος, *demos*, 'people', refers to the spread of cultural phenomena, including language, through migration, such as we are postulating here. But it has to be remembered that languages can also, to an extent, move without any people actually moving themselves. Languages can spread from one place to another by means of a gradual process whereby people adopt the language of their neighbours and abandon their own. This kind of transcultural diffusion occurs as a result of the acquisition of cultural phenomena from nearby groups without any actual migration taking place. For example, a useful invention like the bow and arrow might be copied from neighbours and spread in that way. A lot of the movement of Scots into the Gaelic-speaking areas of Scotland seems to have been of this type; and so does some of the spread of English into Cornwall (we shall discuss both of these processes later in the book). Another classic example is the way in which the French Flemish language border in northern France has very slowly shifted eastwards, along the coast of the English Channel and inland from there, over the last 1500 years. In AD 700, Boulogne, Etaples, Montreuil, Calais and Lille were all Flemish/Dutch-speaking. Over the centuries, first Boulogne, then Calais and then Dunkirk switched from speaking Flemish to speaking French; and now Flemish in France is increasingly confined to a relatively small area around Hazebrouck close to the Belgian border. The main driver for this process was once again transcultural diffusion rather than demic diffusion: a language moved without any significant movement by people.

Similarly, the Romansh language is now confined to some of the south-eastern valleys of Switzerland, but the geographical base of the language has been gradually shrinking for many centuries. In AD 1000, the language was spoken from the shores of Lake Constance, which now forms part of the border between northern Switzerland and Germany, to areas which are now part of northern Italy and to territory which now includes Liechtenstein and the Vorarlberg and parts of the Tyrol of Austria. In the last 1,000 years, the Romansh-speaking territory has shrunk very considerably. There has been, it is true, in-migration of Swiss German speakers into the area, but the reduction in size of the Romansh territory has also been due to the encroachment of German. Individual Romansh speakers living near to German-speaking communities, as a result of geographical proximity leading to frequent contact, interaction, trading and intermarriage, started employing the language of their neighbours more and more often and gradually abandoned their ancestral tongue. The current geographical distribution of Romansh sees it confined for the most part to two major areas, one in the mountain valley of the River Inn and the other in the high valley of the Anterior Rhine. The two areas are now language islands, having become separated from one another over the centuries by the gradual spread of Swiss German, through transcultural diffusion, outwards from the largest town in the area, Chur.

Demic diffusion – the geographical spread of languages via the spread of people – can very often lead to *language contact*, as languages move into new locations and meet up with other linguistic varieties which are already *in situ* and which, perhaps, then die out. Technically, the term 'language contact' refers to situations where two or more groups of speakers who do not have a native language in common come into social contact with one another. Communication between the groups may be difficult in the short term, but in the long term it can lead to the different languages influencing one another as a result of bilingualism on the part of (all or some of) the speakers involved. It may also lead to *language shift*, as communities who speak one of the languages shift to the other. And if *all* the speakers of one of the languages eventually switch to the other, then the result will be *language death*, the complete dying-out of the language.

Germanic

The Proto-Germanic language which came to be spoken in the southern Scandinavian homeland (see Map 1.3) was linguistically rather odd when compared to many other members of the Indo-European language family, in the sense that it had a number of idiosyncratic features in its vocabulary, grammar and pronunciation. These idiosyncrasies, aspects of which can still be found to this day in modern English, are thought of by many linguists to be the result of contact with other languages.

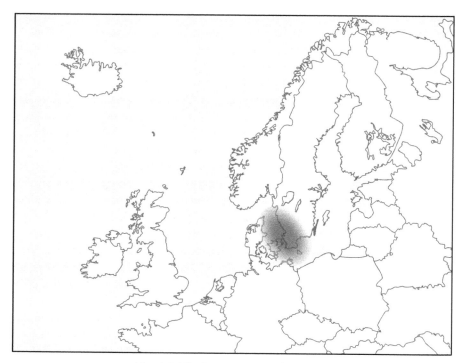

Map 1.3 The Proto-Germanic homeland

This contact may have occurred during the long journey of the language westwards from the Indo-European heartland, in which case it could have been contact with a language which no longer exists and which we have no knowledge of. One specific suggestion, however, is that the contact could have been with a language which we do have some knowledge of, namely Proto-Finno-Samic, the non-Indo-European parent language of modern Finnish, Estonian and the Sami (Lappish) languages of northern Scandinavia. Map 1.4 shows what Dr Petri Kallio has suggested was the most probable location of speakers of Finnic and Samic (also spelt Saamic) in the period before 2500 BC; and it can be seen that this location means that it is very possible that contact between Finno-Samic speakers and Indo-Europeans on their way westwards to southern Scandinavia could indeed have occurred. Suggestions like this are bound to be somewhat conjectural as the time depth we are dealing with here is so great that it is more or less impossible to find conclusive evidence. But the least we can ask of such suggestions is that they should be feasible and make sense, which this one does. It may not be correct, but it is not obviously wrong.

A number of writers, in fact, have argued that some of the major changes in the phonology – sound system – which occurred in the transition between Indo-European and Germanic were, at least in part, the result of Indo-European speakers

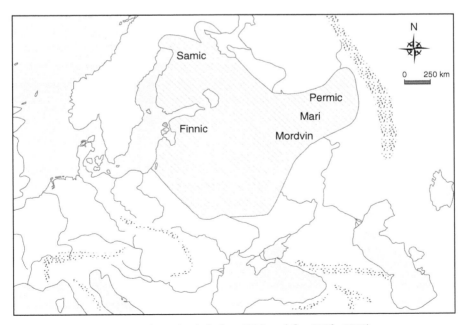

Map 1.4 Finno-Samic before 2500 BC (after Wiik, 2003)

coming into contact with Finno-Samic speakers, with some of these then learning a variety of Indo-European as a foreign language. The suggestion, as proposed by Professor Kalevi Wiik amongst others, is that eventually some of these Finno-Samic speakers shifted to speaking Indo-European altogether, with resulting 'substratum effects', as their Finno-Samic influenced their Indo-European in a way which we know is typical of people speaking a foreign language.

Substratum here is being used as a geological metaphor referring to the fact that the earlier language (Finno-Samic) forms a kind of layer which still 'lies beneath' the newly acquired language (a variety of Indo-European), with some of its words and/or pronunciations and/or grammatical features having been transferred to that new language as a result of the process of learning the foreign language.

In the pronunciation of Indo-European, for example, the main stress could fall on any syllable in a word of more than one syllable and was therefore unpredictable. In Proto-Germanic, on the other hand, the location of the word-stress was predictable: it was always on the first syllable. This is something which, fascinatingly, still survives two-and-a-half millennia later in modern English: all of our original Germanic words such as *finger*, *elbow*, *butter* and *seven* have this first-syllable stress pattern, unless the first syllable is some form of prefix, as with *before*, *asleep*, *forget* and *mistake*. There are also now, of course, a large number of modern English words which do not have this first-syllable stress pattern, but these are items which have been borrowed from French or other languages, such as *romance*, *genteel*, *divine* and *oblige*.

The significance of this typical Germanic stress pattern is that languages in the Finno-Samic family are also characterised by having a totally predictable word-stress – and the word-stress is always on the first syllable. This is still true of modern Finnish, for instance: the capital city of Finland is called *HEL-sinki* in Finnish. The suggestion is then that the presence of identical first-syllable stress patterns in both Germanic and Finno-Samic is not a coincidence.

LANGUAGE NOTES

An important set of distinctive sound changes which helped to take Germanic away from the other Indo-European languages goes by the name of the *First Germanic Sound Shift*. One aspect of this shift involved the sound changes /p/ to /f/ and /k/ to /h/. This is why we find innovative /f/ in English *foot*, West Frisian *foet* and Norwegian *fot* as opposed to the original Indo-European /p/ in French *pied*, Portuguese *pé*, Greek πόδι and Lithuanian *peda*; and innovative /h/ in English *hound* and German *Hund* 'dog' as opposed to the original /k/ in Latin *canis*, Gaelic *cù*, Welsh *ci* 'dog'. This First Germanic Sound Shift, which is also known as Grimm's Law after Jacob Grimm (1785–1863), the philologist who first promulgated this 'law', is another of the changes which some writers have argued to have been brought about as a result of the influence of Finno-Samic speakers (Wiik, 2003).

It has also been hypothesised that language contact and language shift could have occurred, instead of or as well as en route, in the southern Scandinavian homeland of Germanic itself. One obvious assumption is that this could have occurred when Indo-European people from the east arrived in southern Scandinavia, and its speakers came into contact there with people who were already living in the region. Contact would have been between a particular incoming Indo-European dialect, on the one hand, and some indigenous, pre-Indo-European language, on the other.

Professor Peter Schrijver has also shown rather convincingly that there are many other ancient parallels between developments in the sound systems of Germanic and Sami, which he outlines in some detail. His explanation for this, however, is not that Sami itself was the original underlying indigenous language. As can be seen from Map 1.4, the Samic homeland was not situated in southern Scandinavia. Rather, Schrijver argues, there was some common substratum language which is now lost that underlies both Sami and Germanic. Schrijver makes some carefully worked-out suggestions about what the sound system of that language would have been like, but he does not venture an opinion as to what the language itself might have been.

The people who spoke this earlier indigenous language, whatever it was, seem not to have left or died out altogether: modern genetic evidence suggests that a large proportion of the eventual Germanic speakers were genetically not of Indo-European origin. What could have happened, though, was that the indigenous people gradually abandoned their native language and shifted to Indo-European; and in so doing, the suggestion goes, they influenced that particular variety of Indo-European to a rather considerable extent, with Proto-Germanic being the result.

This story of an indigenous language dying out as a result of contact with Proto-Germanic, but leaving traces of itself behind it, is one which was to continue to be associated with the descendants of Proto-Germanic, notably English, for the next 4,000 years and is still continuing to this day. The shift in modern times from Irish Gaelic to English in Ireland, for example, has led to the growth of a variety of English in Ireland which has clearly been influenced by Gaelic, as we shall discuss later in this book.

Professor Theo Vennemann has a suggestion about indigenous languages whose speakers might already have been in residence in western Europe when the Indo-Europeans first arrived, though not necessarily in southern Scandinavia. These, he conjectures, were members of the Vasconic language family. To explain the term *Vasconic*, we have to go back much further in time. The scenario which Vennemann describes is that, during the last Ice Age, the only area of western Europe where human habitation continued to be possible was the Franco-Cantabrian Refugium. This was an ice-free area which stretched from the Asturias region of northern Spain into Provence in southern France. As the Ice Age was ending, perhaps around 8000

BC, there was then a gradual repopulation of the north-western part of the European continent as people followed the receding ice northwards. This repopulation, as climatic conditions became more favourable, started in southern France, which was the only area north of the 'Great Divide' – the barrier to northward migration formed by the Pyrenees and the Alps – where it had been possible for human beings to survive during the glacial period.

Vennemann supposes that the people who were involved in this migration out of the Refugium were speakers of Vasconic. This language was the ancestor of modern Basque and Aquitainian. Basque is still spoken today by about 700,000 people in parts of what was the Franco-Cantabrian Refugium – northern Spain and south-western France. The Basque-speaking region is about 100 miles (160 kilometres) from east to west and 30 miles (50 kilometres) from north to south. It no longer includes the cities of Bilbao (Basque Bilbo), Bayonne (Baiona) and Pamplona (Iruñea), all formerly Basque-speaking, but it does include the city of San Sebastián (Donostia). Basque's close relative, Aquitainian, was spoken further north in south-western France, in the region to the south of Bordeaux, until the early Middle Ages but then died out. Aquitainian was shown to have been a close relative of Basque through brilliant historical linguistic work carried out by the Basque linguist Koldo Mitxelena and published in 1961.

Basque is the only language to have survived in western Europe from the time before the arrival of the Indo-European speakers: it is the single truly indigenous language of western Europe.

LANGUAGE NOTES

There is a strong suggestion that the Iberian Romance (Catalan, Spanish and Portuguese) words for 'left' (as in the opposite of *right*) have been borrowed from Basque. The word in Catalan is *esquerra*, in Spanish *izquierda* and in Portuguese *esquerda*. This is utterly unlike the words in the most closely related languages: Latin *sinister*, Italian *sinistra*, French *gauche*. The modern Basque word, on the other hand, is *ezker*. If it were to be decided that the borrowing had gone the other way – from Iberian Romance into Basque – which is perfectly possible, we would be left with the puzzle of where exactly *izquierda* and so on had come from.

Gradually then, Vennemann suggests, Vasconic came to be spoken in much of western, central and northern Europe, with its speakers spreading north and east into previously uninhabited areas as more ice-free space became available. Eventually, over the course of the centuries, a number of different Vasconic dialects and languages would have developed in western Europe, as the region was repopulated.

Hypothetically, this state of affairs then continued for a few thousand years until the arrival of the Indo-European languages from the east. The first language-contact events which then took place in western Europe could have been between speakers of Vasconic languages and the first Indo-European speakers, as these arrived during the late Neolithic and/or early Bronze Age. The date of the Indo-European arrival in western Europe has not been established with any degree of certainty, but some scholars favour a date of around 3000 BC.

If Vennemann's vision is correct, then during the second and first millennia BC there would have been considerable language contact between Vasconic and the westward-moving Indo-European languages in mainland Europe. Once again, however, because of the enormous time-depth, this is conjecture – and therefore controversial. But it is a sensible conjecture, given that Basque is the only pre-Indo-European, pre-Finno-Ugric language we know to have existed in Europe. And Vennemann does in fact argue that there actually is some linguistic evidence for contact between ancient forms of Basque and Indo-European, one piece of which I present here in the Language Notes.

LANGUAGE NOTES

Vennemann's evidence for contact between Vasconic and western European Indo-European includes a number of what he argues to be Vasconic substratum features in the Indo-European languages of north-western Europe which are, crucially, absent from other Indo-European languages spoken further east which would not have come into contact with Vasconic.[2] One of these is *vigesimality*, that is, counting with 20 as a basic unit. This was unknown in Proto-Indo European but is found even today in certain of the Romance, Celtic and Germanic languages of western Europe. The French counting system includes numbers such as *soixante-dix* 'sixty-ten' = 70, *quatre-vingt(s)* 'four twenties' = 80 and *quatre-vingt-dix* 'four-twenty-ten' = 90.[3] In Welsh, 20 is *ugain*, 30 is *deg ar hugain* 'ten on twenty', 40 is *deugain* 'two twenty', 60 *trigain* 'three twenty', 80 *pedwar ugain* 'four 20'. In Danish – one of the languages which Proto-Germanic became – the numbers for 50, 60, 70, 80 and 90 are *halvtreds, tres, halvfjerds, firs* and *halvfems*. *Tres*, 60, is an abbreviation of *tresindstyve*, which means 'three-times-twenty'. The *halv* in *halvtreds* means 'half', and the whole word is derived from a form which meant 'half-of-twenty-less-than-three-times twenty'. The other forms are similarly derived from 'half (of 20) less than 4 × 20', '4 × 20' and 'half (of 20) less than 5 × 20'. In modern Basque, 20 is *hoge*; 30 is *hogeita hamar*, which means 20 + 10; 40 is *berrogei*, which is 2 × 20; 50 is *berrogeita hamar* (2 × 20 + 10); 60 *hirurogeita* (3 × 20).

---

[2] Mailhammer, 2011.
[3] Many varieties of Belgian and Swiss French do not use all or even any of these vigesimal forms.

Regularisation

Certain other linguistic idiosyncrasies of Germanic, as has been pointed out by Professor Kurt Braunmüller, can be viewed as *simplifications* or *regularisations*. Again, we can see a role for language contact here. Small children are very good indeed at learning languages, but human adults lose this remarkable ability as they get older; and so it is typical of adults to make things easy for themselves, in informal language-learning situations, by getting rid of irregularities and complications which make a language difficult to learn, remember and control, and which can be dispensed with without any undesirable consequences.

The effects of these simplifications still survive in modern English. One example is the development of an entirely new way of forming the past tense of verbs in Proto-Germanic. This can be seen from the way in which we form the past tense of a majority of verbs in English, such as in *love* − *loved*; or in Danish *elske* − *elskede* 'love − loved'; or in German *liebe* − *liebte*: an ending containing a -*t* or a -*d* sound is added to the basic form of a verb. This -*t*/-*d* ending probably developed historically, a very long time ago, out of the past-tense form of the Proto-Germanic verb meaning 'to do', which has come down into English as *do*, into Dutch as *doen* and into German as *tun*. A Proto-Germanic phrase such as *lubo dede* 'love did' became a single word, *lubodede*, and was then shortened to *lubode* 'loved'; *habde* became the past tense of *have* 'had'; and *sagde* was 'said'. This method of adding the word for 'did' to the ends of verbs was much easier to learn and remember, if you were a foreign language-learner, than the original Indo-European method of forming past tenses by changing vowels in a rather unpredictable way from one form to another, as is still the case with some verbs in English such as *sing* − *sang*; *blow* − *blew*; *see* − *saw*.

Vocabulary

But even if contact with Vasconic or some other unknown language might help to explain some of the things which need to be explained about the peculiarities of Germanic, such as Grimm's Law and the simplifications, it cannot explain everything. Another of the important peculiarities of Germanic is that, at least according to some researchers, Proto-Germanic had a vocabulary which contained a surprisingly large non-Indo-European element. Professor Jack Hawkins reports that one-third of Proto-Germanic words are not of Indo-European origin and that they "belong to the core of the basic vocabulary", involving common items such as those to do with maritime travel such as *sea, ship, strand, ebb, steer, keel, boat, sail, north, south, east, west*; military activities such as *sword, shield, helmet, bow*; and fauna such as *eel, carp, calf, lamb, bear, stork* and very many others.

Professor Hawkins has no suggestion as to which language these words might have been borrowed from, but Professor Vennemann does. The vocabulary does not seem to be Vasconic, and Vennemann claims that the language in question may in fact have been a member of the Afro-Asiatic language family. Ancient members of the Afro-Asiatic family included Ancient Egyptian, which we have records of from about 3400 BC; Akkadian (recorded from around 2500 BC); and Phoenician (from about 1000 BC). Modern varieties of Afro-Asiatic include the North African Berber languages such as Tamazight, Aramaic, Amharic (the major language of Ethiopia), Somali, Hausa (West Africa) and Arabic. The now extinct language of the Canary Islands, Guanche, may also have been Afro-Asiatic.

Vennemann's view is that seafaring Afro-Asiatic-speaking people sailed north from the Mediterranean along the Atlantic coastline to the British Isles (much as the Afro-Asiatic-speaking Phoenicians are said to have done, from their bases in North Africa, during the first millennium BC), and then travelled on to southern Scandinavia, where they arrived some time before 2000 BC, and colonised the Germanic people who were already there. He also argues that they brought their megalithic culture with them – they could have been the people, he suggests, who put up the large standing stones which can be found all along the Atlantic coastline of Europe, notably in Ireland and Scotland. He conjectures that in the areas which they colonised, they formed a minority ruling class; and it is not a coincidence, Vennemann suggests, that Germanic words with a possible Afro-Asiatic origin include items such as English *sword*, German *Schwert*; and English *weapon*, German *Waffe*; as well as German *Adel* 'nobility' – the word was *æðel* in Old English. Again, this view is necessarily conjectural, and therefore controversial. Some scholars have disputed Vennemann's putative Afro-Asiatic etymologies for these Germanic words, and some have indeed proposed Germanic etymologies for them.

Another attractive hypothesis which has also been developed by Professor Schrijver could account for at least some non-Indo-European substratum vocabulary items in a number of different European languages, including Germanic. This is the Hatto-Sumerian hypothesis, which derives from analyses of two of the ancient languages of the Eastern Mediterranean, Hattic and Sumerian. These are both usually classified by linguists as being *isolates* – languages which have no known relatives. Hattic was a pre-Indo-European language which was spoken in central Asia Minor, before it was eventually replaced by Hittite and other incoming Anatolian Indo-European languages. Sumerian was spoken in Mesopotamia (contemporary Iraq), where it was eventually replaced by the Semitic language Akkadian. But Professor Schrijver's research has now shown that there is a good chance that these two languages were actually related to each other. He has also argued that Minoan, the pre-Indo-European language of Crete, might well be descended from the same language grouping. Although the so-called Linear B inscriptions in the Minoan language have not as yet been fully deciphered by any means, there are indications that tie it, too, into a Hatto-Sumero-Minoan language grouping.

Archaeologists are rather well agreed that agricultural Neolithic culture was spread from Anatolia north-westwards into the Balkans, and then further on into central Europe, by demic diffusion – specifically by migrant farmers gradually expanding the area of land under cultivation. We would expect therefore that this Neolithic expansion would have been accompanied by the spreading out from Asia Minor of genes into Europe, and there is in fact good genetic evidence for this spread. But Schrijver argues, too, that the expansion also involved the spread of the Hatto-Sumero-Minoan language or languages into Europe. If this is so, we can suppose that, as Indo-European-speaking peoples spread westwards into Europe some millennia later, there would indeed have been considerable language contact between the two groups of languages, before Indo-European eventually totally replaced Hatto-Sumerian. Again, this is conjecture but is not obviously wrong.

Summary

We can say with some degree of certainty that the ancestor of modern English, Proto-Germanic, was originally a dialect of the Indo-European language which travelled from the borderlands of Asia and Europe to southern Scandinavia. It also seems rather likely that Proto-Germanic was significantly linguistically influenced at some stage by contact with another language or languages. And it is by no means impossible that much or some of that influence was exerted by Finno-Samic. It is also not unreasonable to suppose that the language ancestral to modern Basque might at one time have been spoken over a wider – and possibly much wider – area of western Europe than it is at present. And it does seem quite likely that the language of the people who first brought Neolithic agriculture into Europe spoke a language which had its origins in Asia Minor. But, as to the rest, the truth is that, as yet, we really do not know – and maybe we never shall.

FURTHER READING

Anthony, David. 2007. *The horse, the wheel, and language: how bronze-age riders from the Eurasian steppes shaped the modern world*. Princeton: Princeton University Press.

Bammesberger, Alfred, & Theo Vennemann (eds.) 2003. *Languages in prehistoric Europe*. Heidelberg: Winter.

Fortson, Benjamin. 2010. *Indo-European language and culture: an introduction*. Oxford: Wiley-Blackwell.

Hawkins, John. 1990. Germanic languages. In B. Comrie (ed.) *The major languages of Western Europe*. London: Routledge, 58–66.

Sanders, Ruth. 2010. *German: biography of a language*. Oxford: Oxford University Press.

Trudgill, Peter. 2020. *Millennia of language change: sociolinguistic studies in deep historical linguistics*. Cambridge: Cambridge University Press.

2   The Journey Begins: The First Movement South

The speakers of the language which was later to become English must have been rather comfortable in their Swedish/Danish home because they stayed settled in that rather small area of southern Scandinavia for many centuries. But then, perhaps around 1500 BC, some of them started setting off on the journey that was eventually to lead Germanic-speaking people all the way to England – and then far beyond.

Their journey began with a movement southwards out of their original homeland into what is now Germany. The journey they took would have been down along the Jutland peninsula of Denmark, but probably also across the Baltic Sea: Rostock in what is now Germany is only 22 nautical miles (40 kilometres) from the Danish island of Falster; and Rødbyhavn on the Danish island of Lolland is only 16 nautical miles (30 kilometres) from the German mainland north of Grossenbrode.

As a result of this initial migration, by about 1200 BC Germanic-speaking people were occupying the whole of Jutland, as well as a small area of northern Germany from the mouth of the River Elbe (where modern Hamburg now is) to the mouth of the Oder in the region of modern Stettin/Szczecin, now on the German–Polish border (Map 2.1).

Two hundred years later, the journey had continued, and Germanic had expanded further to the west and south. By 1000 BC, the language was spoken all along the coastline of what is now Germany from the mouth of the River Ems, close to the modern Dutch–German border, as far as the River Oder, and then as far inland as the regions where the modern cities of Hanover (German *Hannover*) and Berlin are now found.

The Dispossessed

As they travelled south, these speakers of the ancestor of English came into contact with speakers of another Indo-European language who were already settled in central Europe, having undertaken their own long migration from the *Urheimat* on the Pontic–Caspian steppe. These were the Celts, the first identifiable Indo-Europeans who can actually be pinpointed as being in western Europe through archaeological evidence. The evidence suggests that the modern Celtic languages descend from an Indo-European proto-language, Proto-Celtic, which had become located in central Europe by at least 1300 BC. The Proto-Celts themselves are often, though by no means universally, identified with the archaeological *Urnfield* culture

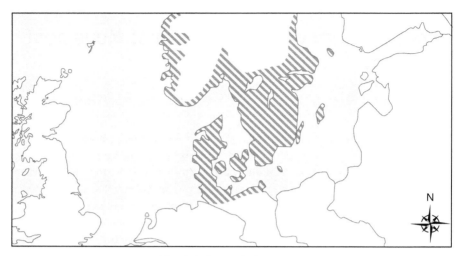

Map 2.1 Germanic in 1200 BC

which is dated 1300 BC to 750 BC. This cultural area was located in an area stretching from western Hungary through what is now Austria and southern Germany into eastern France. According to Professor Donald MacAulay:[1]

> The earliest named Celts (in Greek and Latin sources) are associated with two major Central European Iron Age cultures, the Hallstatt, dated to the seventh century BC, and La Tène, dated to the fifth century BC. The archaeological evidence suggests a cultural continuity backwards through the late Bronze Age Urnfield Culture *with no material evidence that the Celts were newcomers to the region.*

At the point of their greatest expansion, Celtic languages were spoken over a great deal of Europe, from the British Isles and Portugal in the west to the Balkans in the east, and from Germany in the north to Spain and northern Italy in the south. The Galatians of central Asia Minor, the recipients of the biblical Epistle of St Paul, were also Celtic speakers.

But now, with the southward movement of Germanic speakers, Celtic was experiencing the beginnings of a very long period indeed of gradual geographical contraction. The linguistic replacement of Celtic by Germanic in central Germany was the start of a 3,000-year-long retreat by Celtic in the face of the Germanic and Romance languages which continues to this day, with Breton, Welsh, Cornish, Irish Gaelic, Manx and Scottish Gaelic, on the western fringes of Europe, being the only survivors into modern times of the once very widespread Celtic language family.

---

[1] MacAulay (1992: 1; my italics).

The Battle of Noreia

The Teutones were a Germanic tribe who are believed by some scholars to have originated in the district of Thy, around Thisted in Northern Jutland, Denmark. They are known to have emigrated south, together with the Germanic Cimbrians also from Jutland, and to have fought against the Celtic Scordisci, perhaps by the Danube in what is now Hungary. By about 110 BC, they were engaging in hostilities with the Celtic Taurisci in what is now Carinthia, southern Austria/northern Slovenia. The Taurisci appealed to the Romans for help, but they too were eventually defeated by the Germanic tribes at the Battle of Noreia, in a location unknown to us but also somewhere in southern Austria.

Whatever form the original contact between the Germanic- and Celtic-speaking peoples took socially, politically, militarily and/or culturally, it eventually led to the shrinkage of the Celtic-speaking area. By 750 BC, Celtic had receded from the northern part of its territory, and Germanic had advanced as far south as the Münster area of Germany, as well as westwards into what is now the Netherlands, perhaps as far as Groningen; and, with a more dramatic push to the east, across the Oder as far as Danzig/Gdansk and Bydgoszcz in what is now Poland.

The North Sea–Baltic Dialect Continuum

By about 500 BC, a thousand years or so after the initial southward Germanic migration out of Scandinavia started, further Germanic expansion had taken place towards the south, towards the east and as far west as the North Sea coast. As a result, by the 400s BC there was now a long west–east line stretching across Europe which had Germanic to the north of it and Celtic to the south. The line started on the North Sea coast, probably somewhere in modern Belgium, crossed the Rhine somewhere near Koblenz in Germany, travelled on into northern Czechia and passed close to Katowice in southern Poland before reaching the banks of the River Vistula/Wisla/Weichsel to the north-east of Cracow/Kraków. The Vistula, which flows on northwards to the west of Lublin and then through Warsaw to Gdansk, probably constituted the eastern limits of Germanic dialect territory in the fifth century BC.

One last linguistic trace of the long-term Celtic occupation of the newly Germanic-speaking area to the north of the North Sea–Oder Contact Line can be seen in a number of the Proto-Celtic place names which they left behind. The name of Bonn, the former capital of the Federal Republic of Germany, is thought to be from Celtic *bona* 'base, bottom', which still survives in modern Welsh as *bôn* 'base, trunk, stump'. And the name of nearby Remagen, which, like Bonn, is situated on the Rhine, is formed from a second element derived from Celtic *magos* 'field, plain' (modern Welsh *maes*), preceded perhaps by Celtic *rigi* 'king, chief' (Welsh *ri*,

Scottish Gaelic *rìgh*). The Dutch city of Nijmegen, also situated on a branch of the Rhine, may take its name from the same *magos* element, preceded by Celtic *nowijo* 'new' (Welsh *newydd*, Irish Gaelic *nua*): it was called Noviomagus in Latin.

Germanic was now therefore spoken over a very extensive area: the distance from the North Sea coast of what is now Belgium to the River Vistula is about 800 miles (1,300 kilometres). We can therefore expect that there would gradually have developed a continuum of Germanic dialects stretching from Holland and Belgium in the west to eastern Poland in the east.

All languages change through time — which is why we would not be able to understand Proto-Germanic if we could hear it today. But they also change in different ways in different places. This is what gives rise to different regional dialects. And these dialects normally form a continuum: geographically neighbour- ing dialects differ from one another only minimally — but the further you travel away from any given starting point, the more different the dialects will become. All dialects on the continuum are intelligible to speakers of immediately neighbouring dialects, but the greater the distance between the locations where the dialects are spoken, the more difficult comprehension will become (Map 2.2).

The English language eventually developed out of the North Sea Germanic or Ingvaeonic/Ingvaeonian dialects which were spoken towards the western end of the North Sea–Vistula continuum which also gave rise to Frisian and Old Saxon (one of the ancestors of modern Low German). Dutch grew up out of Weser-Rhine

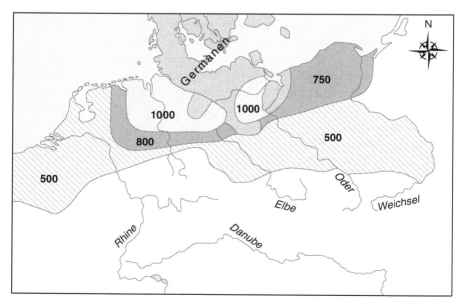

Map 2.2   The North Sea–Baltic dialect continuum

Germanic or Istvaeonic dialects spoken further inland, while German developed out of the Elbe Germanic or Irminonic dialects in the centre.[2] Descendants of these languages from the western and central parts of the continuum today form the West Germanic branch of the modern Germanic language family.

The Goths

The eastern end of the dialect continuum, centred on Poland, became the homeland of a set of dialects which in time developed into the East Germanic language subfamily. The speakers of these dialects eventually migrated south and east out of Poland towards the Balkans, probably initially setting off in around 100 BC.

There is then good evidence that, after the East Germanic peoples started migrating towards the south, the continuum dialects which had stayed where they were continued to remain in contact with the Germanic dialects to their north, in Denmark and beyond, and that these jointly developed together for some generations as a single language which we can call Proto-Northwest Germanic. The linguistic evidence in favour of this hypothesis lies in a number of linguistic changes which took place in North Germanic and West Germanic but which did not take place in East Germanic. It seems likely, however, that Proto-Northwest Germanic did not last for very long as a unitary language, since there seems to have been sufficient dialect divergence by about AD 450 for us to be able to talk legitimately of a split into separate North Germanic and West Germanic languages by about that time.[3]

LANGUAGE NOTES

One linguistic change which indicates the possibility of an earlier Northwest Germanic proto-language was the North and West Germanic change of /z/ to /r/ between vowels. This led to a set of /z/ ~ /r/ alternations, with some of them still surviving into modern English. The alternation between Standard English *I was* versus *we were* is due to this change of /z/ to /r/ in the form ancestral to modern *were*. Modern Dutch similarly has *was* 'was' *waren* 'were'. And in Proto-Scandinavian, the original *was/wa:zun* 'was/were' had become *was/wa:run* by about AD 550. East Germanic Gothic *wisan*, on the other hand, retained *s* throughout the verb paradigm: *was, wast, was, wesum, wesuð, wesun*.

Many East Germanic groups eventually became highly mobile, moving south-westwards out of the Balkans and conquering parts of the Roman Empire, including

---

[2] The terms 'Ingvaeonic', 'Istvaeonic' and 'Irminonic' come from the names given to Germanic tribal groupings by the Romans.

[3] Kuhn (1955–6).

Rome itself, Spain and Portugal and North Africa. We know the names of some of these groups: Burgundians, Vandals, Rugians and Goths (Ostrogoths and Visigoths).

The Burgundians may have emigrated to the mainland of Europe from the island of Bornholm, now part of Denmark, which is about 19 nautical miles (35 kilometres) from the southern mainland of Sweden. The island was known in Old Norse (see the section 'The Vikings') as Burgundaholmr 'island of the Burgundians'. It has also been suggested that the Vandals are in some way connected with the Vendel area of Uppland, again in southern Sweden, although they first appear in the written record as being located in what is now southern Poland. And the Rugians have similarly been associated with island of Rügen, off the north coast of eastern Germany in the southern Baltic Sea, though it is also hypothesised that, prior to that, they lived in south-western Norway, in the area which is now known as Rogaland, where the town of Stavanger is situated.

The Goths are often argued to have had their ultimate origins on the Swedish island of Gotland, which is about 48 nautical miles (89 kilometres) off the east coast of southern Sweden, part of the original homeland of the Germanic proto-language. The Ostrogoths eventually occupied the area to the north of the Black Sea, including the Crimea. The Visigoths were located to the west of the Black Sea, north of the Danube, in the Roman province of Dacia.

Gothic is the only East Germanic language which we have any substantial records of. These are for the most part fragments of a Gothic translation of the Bible, mostly of the New Testament, which was made for Visigoths living in the Balkans, dating from the AD 300s. This makes these Gothic texts our oldest written records of any Germanic language, by 300 or 400 years. The biblical translation was written by Wulfila, also *Ulfilas* (c.310–83), who was the bishop to the Goths living north of the Danube, outside the Roman Empire. One of his most notable achievements was the development of a Gothic alphabet.

In AD 348, Wulfila obtained permission from the Emperor Constantine II to bring his Gothic Christian converts south across the river into the empire, to escape religious persecution. They settled in Nicopolis, in the Roman province of Moesia, now Nikopol in northern Bulgaria. Wulfila died about thirty-five years later on a visit to Constantinople.

It seems possible that Wulfila was able to make his translation of the Bible because he not only studied Latin but, more crucially, grew up bilingual in Greek and Gothic. He had been born into a community of Greeks who, during a Gothic raid on Cappadocia in central Asia Minor in AD 271, had been captured and carried off into Gothic territory in what is now Romania.

None of the East Germanic groups held on to their ethnolinguistic identity in the long term, and they mostly eventually shifted to Romance or West Germanic languages: there are no East Germanic languages spoken anywhere at all today. Some of the Visigothic rulers of the Iberian peninsula appear to have continued to speak their East Germanic language until the eighth century AD, when the Arab-

Berber invasion from North Africa brought their period of dominance to an end. But there is no evidence of the survival of Ostrogothic in Italy after the fall of the Ostrogoth kingdom to the Byzantine Empire in the AD 550s.

In the AD 800s, there were reports that Gothic was still being used in church services along the lower Danube. And it is also possible that a form of Gothic survived on the Crimean peninsula as late as the 1500s: a Flemish diplomat called Augier Ghislain de Busbecq collected some words and phrases in use there which were clearly Germanic, and quite possibly East Germanic. These included *apel* 'apple', *handa* 'hand', *reghen* 'rain' and *singhen* 'sing'. Particularly suggestive of East Germanic antecedents are cases such as Crimean Gothic *fyder* 'four' which, like Wulfila's Gothic *fidwor* 'four', retains the original -*d*- of Proto-Germanic *fedwor*, unlike West Germanic German *vier*, English *four*, and North Germanic Swedish *fyra* and Danish *fire*.

LANGUAGE NOTES

The Gothic numerals show a clear relationship to those of the modern Germanic languages, including English (we have no record of the Gothic word for thirteen): *ains, twai, þreis, fidwor, fimf, saihs, sibun, ahtau, niun, taihun, ainlif, twalif,* [13], *fidwortaihun, fimftaihun.* Amongst the pronouns, *ik* was 'I', *mik* 'me', *uns* 'us', *thu* 'thou', *jus* 'you (plural)', *si* 'she' and *ita* 'it'. In the following passage from the Gothic New Testament, together with the corresponding text from the King James Bible, items readily recognisable to modern English speakers are rather few: *was* is 'was'; the *barn* in barniskeins is 'child, bairn'; *aflagida* can be parsed as 'off-laid'; *nu* is 'now'; *saihwan* is 'to see'; *þairh* is 'through'; *þan* 'then':

Iþ þan was niuklahs, swe niuklahs rodida, swe niuklahs froþ, swe niuklahs mitoda; biþe warþ wair, barniskeins aflagida. Saihwam nu þairh skuggwan in frisahtai, iþ þan andwairþi wiþra andwairþi; nu wait us dailai, iþ þan ufkunna.

When I was a child, I spake as a child, I understood as a child, I thought as a child: but when I became a man, I put away childish things. For now we see through a glass, darkly; but then face to face: now I know in part; but then shall I know.

The Vikings

The third major branch of Germanic is formed by the North Germanic subfamily, which now consists of the Scandinavian languages Danish, Swedish, Norwegian, Faroese and Icelandic. These are the languages which descend from dialects spoken by those Germanic peoples who, when the southward expansions started, stayed behind in southern Scandinavia.

Speakers of these dialects subsequently also began migrations, however, spreading northwards and westwards into central and northern Sweden and Norway, and, in the fullness of time, out into the Atlantic. The age of Viking expansion, from the late AD 700s onwards, carried the language amazing distances away from its homeland.

Old Norse is the label often given to the North Germanic language of the Vikings. A western variety of Old Norse was originally spoken in what is now Norway, and an eastern variety in Sweden and Denmark. Old West Norse was transported by Norwegian Vikings into the vastness of the Atlantic Ocean, and is still there – in Iceland, settled in about AD 850, and the Faroe Islands. The modern Icelandic and Faroese languages have changed less than the contemporary continental Scandinavian languages, and even now retain many Old Norse features. They also remain quite similar to one another.[4]

It is just under 1,000 nautical miles (1,850 kilometres) from the west coast of Norway to Iceland, so it is no surprise that on their westward journey the Vikings settled first on the Faroe Islands, which are about 400 miles (640 kilometres) from the Norwegian coast. And it also makes good sense that, on their way to the Faroes, they stopped off on the Shetland and Orkney Islands: Shetland is no more than 220 miles (350 kilometres) from Norway. As we shall see again later, a linguistic descendant of Old West Norse called Norn was spoken on Orkney until the early eighteenth century, and it was still alive in Shetland in the late 1700s. West Norse was also spoken for many generations in Viking settlements in north-east Scotland (surviving in Caithness until the 1400s), the Hebrides, the Isle of Man, north-western England and coastal areas of Ireland.

There are still many traces of this language in place names in these locations. Caithness is from Norse Katanes, and Sutherland was Norse Suðrland, 'south land': this might seem to be a strange name for a place on the north coast of Britain, but the Vikings called it that because it lay to the south of the Viking settlements on Orkney. The name of the island of Barra in the Outer Hebrides is probably from Old Norse *Barr-ey*, 'bare island'. Ramsey, on the Isle of Man, comes from Old West Norse *Hrams-á*, 'ramsons (wild garlic) river' – in modern Norwegian it would be *Ramså*. Ambleside in the Lake District of England was West Norse *Ámelrsǽtr*, which literally translates as 'a summer pasture on a sandbank by a river'. And Waterford in Ireland comes from *Veðrafjǫrðr*, 'ram (or wether) fjord'.

West Norse was also spoken in Greenland from the late 900s, as a result of colonisation from Iceland. The northernmost Greenlandic settlement was Vestribyggð, 'western settlement', which was about 1,500 miles from Iceland. More than fifty inscriptions in West Norse have been found in Greenland, where Norse-speaking colonies survived for more than 400 years, dying out in the early

---

[4] A Faroese speaker once told me that when he first arrived in Iceland he could not understand what people were saying – but after four days he could.

1400s, with many people then returning to Iceland. No one is quite sure what happened to the colonists, but climate change, overgrazing and conflict with the Inuit have all been suggested as reasons for the abandonment of the settlements.

According to the Icelandic sagas, whose reliability we cannot be totally sure about, the Vikings also made three voyages from Greenland to North America and founded at least one settlement there: the very first European language ever to be spoken in the Americas was the North Germanic language of the Norsemen.

The first voyage reported in the sagas was led by Leifr Eirikson, the son of the founder of the Greenland settlements Eiríkr Rauði, Eirik the Red. Leifr landed with his followers in A D 1000 in a place which from the description in the sagas sounds like it must have been Baffin Island. They then moved on, probably to the coast of Labrador, and then overwintered in a place further south which they called Vinland, meaning 'land of vines'.

The second trip was led by Leifr's brother Þorvaldr (Thorvald), who also went to Vinland, where he and his men were able to make use of the buildings Leifr had constructed to spend the winter in. And it was now that a dramatic, extremely historic event occurred: Thorvald and his men met up with a group of Native Americans who were indigenous to the area.

This was a remarkable event in the history of the world, even if it is one which has been little commented on. When modern human beings first migrated out of East Africa, one major migratory stream headed east into Asia, and some of these eventually travelled across Siberia and the Bering Strait to the Americas. The other major stream headed up from Africa through the Middle East and eventually westwards into Europe. The arrival of the Viking people in North America in the eleventh century therefore saw the first ever contact between these two groups of humans. It was the first time in the history of the planet that the eastward and westward migration streams, after having circumnavigated the globe in different directions, had come into contact with one another, after 70,000 years. Sadly, the historic encounter did not end well. The Scandinavians killed eight men who approached them in canoes, but a ninth man was able to escape and return with more men, who attacked the Norsemen with bows and arrows, killing Thorvald.

These indigenous people may have been ancestors of the Beothuk of Newfoundland, or the Innu of Labrador, or the Micmac of the Canadian Maritime provinces. The Beothuk have, tragically, been extinct since 1829. They may perhaps have been speakers of an Algonquian language. The languages of the Innu and Mi'kmaq peoples, which do survive, are certainly members of the Algonquin family.

The third Viking expedition was led by an in-law of Thorvald, Thorfinn Karlsefini. This group, which included some women, also overwintered in Vinland, a number of them staying on into the next summer and beyond. They too met up with native peoples, but this time much more peaceably, with some trading taking place.

Remains of an eleventh-century Viking settlement have been found on the northern tip of Newfoundland at a site called L'Anse aux Meadows, which has been excavated and confirmed as Scandinavian by archaeologists. It lies about 550 nautical miles (1,000 kilometres) south-west of Greenland – and a very long way indeed from Norway. This was a minor settlement or way station, however, and not the site of the main Scandinavian Vinland settlement. No one is very sure where that main settlement was, but vines would probably not have grown much further north than the coasts of New Brunswick and the Gulf of St Lawrence. Some archaeologists and historians suppose that Vinland was somewhere in the Canadian provinces of Nova Scotia or New Brunswick, with one specific suggestion being that it was located at Chaleur Bay between New Brunswick and Quebec.

The Norsemen withdrew relatively soon from Vinland, however, as well as from the L'Anse aux Meadows site in Newfoundland. And it would be almost another 500 years before the voices of men speaking a European language, this time English, would be heard again on the American continent. That was not to be until 1497.[5] But it was once again to be in Newfoundland.

Old East Norse had a no less remarkable geographical history during the same time period as the Viking North Atlantic expansion. Old Norse speakers from Sweden and neighbouring areas sailed, traded and settled along the rivers between the Baltic (*Östersjön* 'the eastern sea' in modern Swedish) and the Black Sea; and they are generally held to have formed the core of a multi-ethnic state known to us as Kievan Rus, which covered much of what is now Ukraine, Belarus and western Russia. East Slavic, the language ancestral to Ukrainian, Belarusian and Russian, eventually became the dominant language there, but with Old Norse not perhaps totally dying out until the fourteenth century. East Norse speakers are also known to have travelled as far as the Caspian Sea, and across the Black Sea to Constantinople and perhaps even Baghdad. In Constantinople, they formed the central element of the Varangian Guard, an elite unit of the Byzantine army.

Contact with Celtic

Back in fifth-century BC Europe, there would have been long-term language contact between Germanic speakers and Celtic speakers at many points along the North Sea–Vistula line, often resulting in bilingualism and language shift. This contact and bilingualism have been argued by linguists such as Stephen Laker and Stefan Schumacher to have had important consequences for the vocabulary and grammar of Germanic.

A number of Germanic words are suggested to have been borrowed from Celtic at this time, including early Celtic *ambaktos* 'follower, servant' which corresponds to

---

[5] In 1492, Columbus did not venture beyond the Caribbean islands.

the now obsolete Welsh word *amaeth* 'farm worker'. It appears in Old English as *ambiht* 'servant, attendant', in Middle High German as *ambahte* 'office', in modern Dutch as *ambacht* 'craft, occupation' and in modern Norwegian as *embete* 'office, position'.

Another example is the early Celtic form which gave rise to Gothic *reiks* 'king' and has come down into German as *Reich* and Dutch as *rijk* 'kingdom'. We saw above that the early Celtic from *rigi* 'king' may have occurred in the German place name Remagen. It also produced Gaulish *rig, rix*, which we know mainly from personal names such as *Biturix* 'king of the world' and *Vercingetorix* 'superior king', the chieftain of the Gauls as they united to fight against Roman forces under Julius Caesar. As also noted, the modern Scottish Gaelic word for 'king' is *rìgh*.

Yet another suggestion concerns the Proto-Germanic word *lauða*, modern English *lead* (the name of the metal), which can be compared to Old Irish *luaide*, modern Irish and Scottish Gaelic *luaidhe*.[6] Other words borrowed from Celtic into Germanic include, in their biblical Gothic forms, *eisarn* 'iron' (suggesting perhaps that the Germanic peoples acquired iron-manufacturing technology from the Celts), *aiths* 'oath', *arbi* 'inheritance' (modern Danish *arv*), *freis* 'free', *lekijaz* 'doctor, physician' and *gislaz* 'hostage'. Don Ringe suggests that there is a preponderance of words in the borrowed vocabulary relating to social relations, political relations and warfare, suggesting he argues a higher level of culture amongst the Celtic than the Germanic peoples.[7]

One of the probable grammatical consequences of this Celtic–Germanic inter-action along the line of contact can be seen in the grammar of one of the descendants of Proto-Germanic, Old English (Anglo-Saxon). Old English had two copulas,[8] *wesan* and *bēon* – two different verbs for *to be* – with different meanings. These are illustrated in the contrast between the two Old English sentences *þu bist halig* 'you are holy' and *þu eart nu þæt ic wæs* 'you are now what I was' (the letter *þ* stands for the sound of <th> as in *thing*). In modern English, both *þu bist* and *þu eart* have to be translated as 'you are', but in Old English, as spoken in eastern Britain from about AD 400, they had interestingly different meanings. The *bist* in *þu bist* = 'thou bist' can technically be described as a 'habitual' verb form, indicating continuity – that is, the subject of the verb (in this case *God*) was habitually or permanently or inherently holy. The non-habitual verb *eart* in *þu eart* = 'thou art', on the other hand, did not imply continuity but was used for non-inherent, maybe temporary, situations: 'you are now (for the time being) what I was'. This can remind us of the grammatical situation in modern Spanish, where *está borracho* and *es borracho* both

---

[6] Green (1998).   [7] Ringe (2006).

[8] A copula is a "verb with little or no independent meaning whose function is to link elements of clause structure … to show that they are semantically equivalent". In English, "the main copular verb is be", as in "She is a doctor, They are happy" (Crystal, 1992: 85).

mean 'he is drunk', but non-habitual *está* means 'is (right now)' while habitual *es* means 'is (usually)': *es borracho* can also be translated as 'he's a drunk'.

LANGUAGE NOTES

The parallel paradigms of *wesan* and *bēon* in Old English:[9]

Indicative		Subjunctive		Imperative	
ēom	*bēo*	*sīe*	*bēo*	*sīe/wes*	*bēo*
fart	*bist*	*sīe*	*bēo*		
is	*biþ*	*sīe*	*bēo*		
sind(on)/	*bēoþ*	*sīen*	*bēon*	*wesaþ*	*bēoþ*
āron					

Infinitive

wesan   *bēon*

Professor Ilse Wischer points out that the distinction between habitual and non-habitual *be* was a purely West Germanic phenomenon: copula forms derived from an Indo-European **b-* root, such as *bēo*, were not found in North Germanic or East Germanic. According to Anders Ahlqvist, the Old English *ēom* declension of *wesan* was used only for non-habitual meanings, while the *b-* declension of *bēon* expressed the habitual; this system was precisely the one which was found in Celtic.[10] Stephen Laker points out that the present-tense paradigms of BE have two different stems in all the West Germanic languages.[11] Old Saxon had the present-tense singular 1st-person *bium* and 2nd-person *bist* from the one paradigm and 3rd-person *is* from the other. Compare this with the North Germanic system where Old Norse had *em, ert, er*, all from the same paradigm. Laker also argues that the two paradigms of *be* were originally functionally distinct in continental West Germanic generally, not just in Old English, but the functionality of the distinction had been lost by the time we get to the written historical record. This same situation is now found in modern English: we have the two separate stems, as in *am, be* and so on, but they are no longer used distinctively. If what Laker suggests is correct, then the semantico-grammatical habitual/non-habitual distinction was acquired as a result of contact with Continental Celtic even before West Germanic speakers crossed the North Sea to Britain.

The point is that Ancient Celtic had exactly the same grammatical distinction as Old English. Neither Proto-Indo-European nor Proto-Germanic had it, so it looks as if some varieties of Germanic acquired it from Celtic as a result of bilingual speakers transferring it from the one language to the other. This argument is strengthened by the fact that the distinction never developed in North Germanic or East Germanic, whose ancestral dialects were not spoken along the North Sea–Vistula

---

[9] Wischer (2011).   [10] Ahlqvist (2010).   [11] Laker (2002).

line. And the suggestion is that Old English inherited the habitual/non-habitual distinction from those varieties of Germanic which, centuries earlier, had been in long-term contact with Celtic along that North Sea–Vistula line. The Old English distinction has now disappeared from our modern language, but its Celtic counterpart continued to be maintained in Welsh at least until the 1400s, with *yw* being 'is (non-habitual)' and *byd* 'is (habitual)'.

LANGUAGE NOTES

Proto-Celtic had a habitual/non-habitual distinction in the copula. Henry Lewis and Holger Pedersen write that, in Proto-Celtic, copula verb-forms descend from two different older roots *es- and *bheu-, where *bheu- has* the habitual meaning and *es- the non-habitual.[12] In modern times, there are still in Irish two verbs 'to be' marking "a distinction which bears some resemblance to Spanish".[13]

Another obvious and intriguing question is, if Proto-Indo-European did not have the habitual/non-habitual distinction in the copula, then where did Proto-Celtic get it from in the first place? Vennemann has a specific suggestion. He suggests that it all has to do with Vasconic, which did, he supposes, have the grammatical distinction. We do not have any actual evidence of this because there are no significant written records of Basque from before the 1500s. But it is certainly the case that modern Basque can be regarded as having the same grammatical distinction: the Basque verb *egon* 'to be (in a location)' is used to express temporary states, while *izan* is 'to be (habitually)'.

The argument then goes that the Celts were the first Indo-Europeans to arrive in western Europe and, once they had arrived, they came into contact with Vasconic speakers who had already been there for very many centuries. Then, as a result of long-term contact, bilingualism and language shift, Proto-Celtic acquired the originally Vasconic distinction. This is certainly not impossible. The strongest claim would be that, while Proto-Indo-European had only one copula, Vasconic had two, and those Indo-European dialects which experienced long-term contact with Vasconic, that is, the dialects which became Proto-Celtic, acquired the two-copula system as a result. Some forms of Germanic then also acquired it indirectly through contact with Celtic. Vennemann calls this indirect influence *transitivity of contact*: Germanic, including Old English, was influenced by Vasconic because of having been in contact with Celtic, which had been in contact with Vasconic. The same thing could be hypothesised to have happened in the case of the Romance languages spoken on the Iberian peninsula: not only Spanish but also Catalan and Portuguese have the same grammatical distinction; they might have been directly

---

[12] Lewis and Pedersen (1937: 317).   [13] Ó Siadhail (1989: 219).

influenced by Basque or indirectly by varieties of Celtic which had been influenced by Vasconic.

Crucially, for Vennemann's argument, North Germanic and East Germanic, which were not spoken in western Europe, never acquired the grammatical distinction, as we just noted. And Romansch and Rumanian, the descendants of Latin which were spoken further to the east in Europe, where there would have been no Vasconic contact, do not have it either.

FURTHER READING

Cunliffe, Barry. 1997. *The ancient Celts*. Oxford: Oxford University Press.

Fitzhugh, William, & Elizabeth Ward (eds.). 2000. *Vikings: the North Atlantic saga*. Washington, DC: Smithsonian.

Heather, Peter. 1996. *The Goths*. Oxford: Blackwell.

Jarman, Catrine. 2021. *River kings: a new history of the Vikings from Scandinavia to the Silk Roads*. London: Collins.

Jones, Gwyn. 2001. *A history of the Vikings*. Oxford: Oxford University Press.

Williams, Thomas. 2017. *Viking Britain: a history*. London: William Collins.

3 Interlude: A View from the Celtic Island

In about 500 BC, when Germanic speakers first arrived on what is now the Dutch and Belgian coastline, along the eastern shores of the southern North Sea, the island across the sea to their west was not devoid of inhabitants. It was already occupied by a population of human beings who spoke Brittonic, one of the Celtic languages which, as we saw in Chapter 2, had originally been spoken over a great deal of mainland Europe.

The Celts in Britain

Recent archaeological and genetic research has been interpreted as indicating that Celtic-speaking people first started arriving in southern Britain in about 1400 BC and that cross-Channel migrations of Celts continued for some centuries.[1]

Britain seems in any case to have been an entirely monolingual Celtic-speaking island for at least a millennium before an army of invading Roman colonisers brought their Latin language with them to England in AD 43, during the reign of the Emperor Claudius. The Roman invasion force, led by Aulus Plautius, landed at Richborough near Sandwich in eastern Kent. An army of Celtic Britons, who had been taken by surprise by the invasion, attempted to halt them at a crossing on the River Medway by Rochester but were defeated, with the Romans subsequently moving on to the Thames where the invaders were joined by the emperor himself. He took control of a major battle there, which was again won by the Romans, who then marched on to what was probably the most important of the Britons' towns, Camulodunon (Colchester). This they took from the local Celtic king, Caratacus (Brittonic *Caradoc*), who then retreated to Wales. He fought a last, and unsuccessful, battle against the Romans in AD 50 at Caer Caradoc 'Fort of Caradoc' (modern Welsh *Caer Caradog*) in Shropshire.

There were subsequently several anti-Roman rebellions including, in AD 60, a large uprising which was led by the queen of the Norfolk-based Iceni, Boudica, who sacked Roman Colchester, Verulamium (St Albans) and Londinium (London). The Romans defeated her and her other British allies in AD 61 at a battle which is known today as the Battle of Watling Street: it is not known exactly where it took

---

[1] Patterson et al. (2021).

place, except that it was somewhere between London and Wroxeter along the line of the Roman Road which later generations took to calling Watling Street, the modern A5 highway.

It then took until about AD 90 for the Romans to subdue the whole of England and Wales. And they were never successful in seizing control of Scotland: in the end, they constructed the defensive line of Hadrian's Wall across the north of England from the Solway Firth to the Tyne which, from about AD 130, marked the northern frontier of Roman-controlled Britain and indeed of the Roman Empire itself. The Latin language therefore never had any real presence in Scotland.

The Celtic inhabitants of England, on the other hand, had not necessarily remained unfamiliar with Latin before AD 43. There is good evidence to indicate that at least some members of elite groups in southern England had acquired some knowledge of the language, after its arrival with the Roman legions on the northern coast of Gaul (no more than 18 nautical miles from England at its closest point), about ninety years before the colonisation of England.

Gold coins minted sometime between 40 BC and 20 BC, and discovered in Alton in Hampshire, have on them the name of the Celtic ruler who issued them, written as *Commios*, with the Celtic suffix *-os*. Coins issued by a ruler who appears to be his son, however, and dating to somewhere between 20 BC and AD 10, give the name of the son as *Tincomarus*, with the Latin *-us* ending.[2] Several other archaeological finds from around the same period also suggest a move towards the use of Latin for ceremonial purposes in this part of Britain around the beginning of the first century AD and point to a certain amount of familiarity with the language on the part of Celtic officials in the south-east of England.

Much of this language learning would presumably have happened as a result of trading and other contacts across the English Channel. The first Latin–Brittonic contacts that we actually have historical records of, however, are from the brief exploratory Roman expeditions to England led by Julius Caesar in 55 BC and 54 BC, the second of them taking Caesar and his armies across the Thames into Middlesex and possibly as far north as Hertfordshire.

According to the Dutch Celticist and Indo-Europeanist Professor Peter Schrijver, the linguistic consequences of Latin–Brittonic language contact in Britain after AD 43 differed greatly as between the lowland and highland areas of the island, with the outcome in the lowlands resembling the outcome in Gaul (northern France). The highlands were less fertile, and therefore less desirable to Roman colonists; and Roman rule there was more contested and less secure, so there was generally less of a presence of Latin.

The lowland Britain of the south and east was divided from the northern and western highland area along a line which can be drawn approximately, starting in the south of England, from Dorchester via Bath, Gloucester, Wroxeter, Leicester,

---

[2] Adams (2007: 577).

Lincoln, and York to Corbridge and Carlisle – the names Dorchester, Gloucester, Wroxeter and Leicester all contain the Old English element *ceaster* 'Roman station' from Latin *castrum*, plural *castra* 'fortified camp'.

Some of the modern English counties were thus divided between the two zones: the line ran through areas which are now modern Dorset, Somerset, Gloucestershire, Worcestershire, Shropshire, Staffordshire, Leicestershire, Nottinghamshire, Lincolnshire, Yorkshire, Durham and Northumberland.

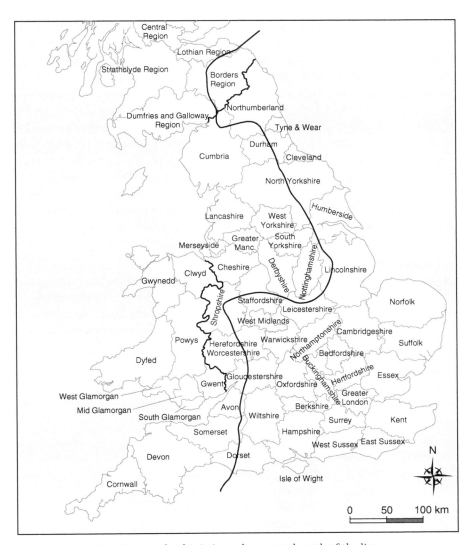

Map 3.1 Lowland Britain to the east and south of the line

Entirely on the highland side of the line were the counties of Cornwall, Devon, Herefordshire, Cheshire, Derbyshire, Lancashire and Cumbria as well as Scotland and Wales, and entirely on the lowland side were Norfolk, Suffolk, Essex, Cambridgeshire, Northamptonshire, Huntingdonshire, Bedfordshire, Hertfordshire, Middlesex, Surrey, Buckinghamshire, Oxfordshire, Berkshire, Warwickshire, Wiltshire, Kent, Sussex and Hampshire (see Map 3.1).

Professor Schrijver argues that, during the course of the four centuries of the Roman occupation, the lowland zone ceased to be a monolingual Celtic-speaking area.

Rather, as a consequence of the Celtic–Latin bilingualism which grew up over the decades, a specifically British, Brittonic-influenced form of vulgar (colloquial) Latin developed. This colloquial British Latin was extremely widely used both as a native language and as a second-language lingua franca by Romanised Celts, especially the upper classes, alongside Brittonic Celtic.

One important source of information about what this colloquial British Latin was like linguistically comes from archaeological discoveries of 'curse tablets'. One of the most significant finds involving these objects was the unearthing in Bath of 130 or so such tablets, dating to between AD 100 and AD 400. These tablets had been left in a spring sacred to the goddess Sulis in Bath, with pleas scratched on them asking her to bring afflictions down upon those who had stolen property and to have them return it. They were written by uneducated Romanised British people, in a British Latin which we can suppose would have been typical of the lower social class dialects spoken by Britons, whether as a first or second language.

LANGUAGE NOTES

The extent to which numerous Brittonic speakers must have learnt some Latin can be judged from the fact that about 800 different Latin words were borrowed into Brittonic rather early during the contact period. Many of these words have survived into Welsh and the other modern Brittonic languages. Here are just a few:

Welsh		Latin	Breton	Cornish
Awr	'hour'	*Hōra*	eur	owr
Barf	'beard'	*Barba*	barv	barv
Cadair	'chair'	*Cathedra*	cadoer	kador
Corff	'body'	*Corpus*	korf	korf
Ffenestr	'window'	*Fenestra*	fenestr	fenester
Llyfr	'book'	*Liber*	levr	lever
Nifer	'number'	*Numerous*	niver	niver
Parod	'ready'	*Parātus*	paret	parys
Pobl	'people'	*Populous*	pobl	pobel

cont.

Pont	'bridge'	**Pons**	pont	pons
Porth	'door, gate'	**Porta**	porzh	porth
Sôn	'mention'	**Sonus**	soun	son
Ysgrifennu	'write'	**Scrībere**	skrivañ	scrifa

Precisely how long contact between Latin and Brittonic lasted in England is not entirely clear. Imperial government from Rome was withdrawn in 410, but British vulgar Latin certainly continued to be spoken by Romanised Celts well after the beginning of the fifth-century Anglo-Saxon incursions had begun (see Chapter 4). Archaeological evidence indicates that a Romano-British lifestyle persisted in the west of England well into the fifth century.

Schrijver writes of Late Latin lasting well into the 600s, particularly in areas of the highland zone where large numbers of Latin-speaking refugees from the lowland zone arrived during the AD 400s, AD 500s and AD 600s, fleeing from (or at least moving out of) territory now occupied by the Germanic new-comers. If this scenario is correct, then Celtic–Latin contact, and hence mutual linguistic influence, could have lasted for as long as 600 years in England.

This British Latin was a language which, if it had survived, would probably have ended up being very much like Old French. In his book *Bilingualism and the Latin language*, Professor James Adams says that archaeological discoveries and linguistic analyses have shown that the Latin of Gaul and the Latin of Britain shared a common "northwestern character" and that certain Latin features which were found in the language as spoken in Gaul have been found in the Latin of England as well, and nowhere else. This was because "the common Celtic background, contacts across the Channel, and the remote-ness of Italy caused Gaul and Britain to develop their own linguistic features, embracing phonetic interference from Celtic and the adoption of Celtic loanwords".[3] It is certainly a possibility that, if it had not been for the Germanic invasions, people in England today would be speaking a form of French as their native language – if they were not speaking Welsh.

The Retreat of Brittonic

Any description of the geographical spread across Britain of the language which became English (see Chapter 4) is equivalent to a description of the geographical retreat of the Brittonic Celtic language which had preceded Germanic to the island by many hundreds of years.

---

[3] Adams (2003: 596).

We can perhaps think of this process of retreat as beginning with the declaration by the Roman legions in Britain of a Roman general as emperor of the western empire, in 407. Unfortunately for the future of Romano-British civilisation, this new emperor, Constantinus III, more or less immediately evacuated most of these troops from Britain to Gaul, leaving the island relatively unguarded. The Romano-Britons did subsequently appeal to Constantine's ultimately successful rival as emperor, Honorius, for military assistance, but he sent none; and in 410, he officially authorised the Britons to organise their own defence, effectively marking the end of Britain as a Roman imperial possession.

However, major permanent West Germanic settlements in England did not begin to develop in any significant way until somewhat later, in the middle of the fifth century AD. Exactly how this happened is not fully agreed upon, but it appears likely that an independent Romano-Celtic Britain continued to maintain some aspects of Roman language and civilisation for a number of decades after the withdrawal of Roman imperial government and administration from the island.

One possibility is that threats from outside England – perhaps raids by Picts sailing south from northern and central Scotland – led to invitations from the Romano-Celtic British to small groups of West Germanic peoples to cross the sea and come to assist them in the defence of the east coast, possibly in the late 420s. The Romans had certainly already been using Germanic mercenaries amongst their forces stationed in Britain. The Picts were a people who were speakers of the northernmost dialect of Brittonic Celtic,[4] but they had come to be regarded as a distinct ethnic group because over the centuries, in their homeland north of Hadrian's Wall, they had remained culturally uninfluenced by the Romans: they were still basically British rather than Romano-British.

One possibly genuinely historical Romano-British figure who emerged in this newly independent Britain as a leader – *king* might not be too inaccurate a term – is known to us as Vortigern, in Old Welsh *Guorthigern*. The modern Welsh form is *Gwrtheyrn*, from *gor-* 'over-, sur-' and *'teyrn'* 'ruler'.[5] He is often credited, or blamed, for having invited Germanic mercenaries from mainland Europe to establish garrisons in eastern England, to help defend the Romano-British people against the Picts.

This mercenary initiative was successful at first, but then it seems that, in the early 440s, some Germanic soldiers rebelled against their British hosts, ushering in a long period of fighting between the Brittonic Celtic and West Germanic people which led to general instability, a breakdown in the Roman estate system and, in the end, even an insecurity of food supply. For several decades, the Romano-Britons were on the defensive in many areas, with one sign of this turbulence being that many Brittonic speakers left England altogether and crossed the Channel

---

[4] Rhys (2015).   [5] Professor David Willis, personal communication.

from the English south-west to Brittany, where the Brittonic Celtic language Breton, a close relative of Cornish and Welsh, is still spoken to this day.

During the second half of the fifth century, under the leadership of a Romano-British war leader known to us as Ambrosius Aurelianus, the Celts then began to inflict defeats on the Anglo-Saxons. According to Bruce Mitchell and Fred Robinson's *A guide to Old English*, the Battle of Badon Hill, which was probably fought somewhere in the south-west of England – quite possibly near Badbury in Wiltshire – ended in a victory for the Brittonic/British Latin-speaking Romano-British forces over the Germanic-speaking Anglo-Saxons (probably predominantly Saxons, in this case), perhaps in about AD 500.

By the early AD 500s, the Romano-Britons had mostly subdued the Anglo-Saxons, who then remained for the most part confined, as a majority population, to Norfolk, Kent and Sussex. There were still plenty of Anglo-Saxons elsewhere, but they were in a minority: "their small size made them harmless, necessarily subject allies of the British."[6]

By AD 600, however, the situation of Brittonic was very much less secure, though it was still the dominant language in the highland western and northern areas of England. It was also dominant in most of Scotland, apart from the Anglo-Saxon south-east. The English (as we can now begin to call them) were still living in independent kingdoms cut off from one another by geographical barriers and by often hostile British Celts. But it is clear that in many areas the two ethnolinguistic groups did live together or alongside one another for very many decades, often peacefully.

The peacefulness of the coexistence should not be overestimated, however. We know that the Anglo-Saxons often enslaved Britons: the Old English word *wealh* or *walh* meant 'foreigner', 'Briton' and 'slave'. And there was certainly military conflict, as we have already seen, not least during the particularly turbulent second half of the fifth century, when the semi-mythical Romano-British figure Arthur is said to have been active.

Then, a second Anglo-Saxon revolt against the British began in the late 500s, and this was eventually to lead to Anglo-Saxon control of most of England and to the gradual domination by the West Germanic population of the Celtic population – some reports suggest that the last British military victory over the English was in 655.

By AD 700, Brittonic Celtic remained dominant in only two major areas of England: Cornwall and Devon; and northern Lancashire and Cumbria, stretching up into south-western Scotland, where the Brittonic kingdom of Rheged, perhaps centred on what is now Galloway, was situated. Archaeological remains have suggested that the site of Gatehouse of Fleet in modern Kirkcudbrightshire, in

---

[6] Morris (2004: 136).

Dumfries and Galloway, might have been the location of the administrative centre of Rheged.

There also appears to have been a Brittonic-controlled enclave for some while on the North Yorkshire Moors. And there was certainly also for several decades a Brittonic kingdom known as Elmet (Welsh *Elfed*) in what became the West Riding of Yorkshire (and including neighbouring areas of Derbyshire and South Yorkshire). This kingdom occupied forest areas around the valleys of the River Aire and the River Wharfe, with the main settlement perhaps being located on the site of modern Barwick-in-Elmet, which is between Leeds and York.

The main picture, however, was that the Britons in Cumbria/Rheged were now cut off from those in northern Wales by the English in Lancashire and Cheshire; and the Romano-Celts in Devon and Cornwall were separated from those in southern Wales by the Bristol Channel and the English in Somerset and Gloucestershire. The Brittonic language varieties which were spoken in the three now-separated areas of Britain eventually came to be known respectively as the Welsh, Cornish and Cumbric languages.

Welsh still survives rather strongly as a native language in much of Wales today. In the English south-west, however, Anglo-Saxons had taken over control of Devon by about 800, leading apparently to a further wave of emigration by Brittonic speakers to Brittany where, as we already noted, the Brittonic Celtic language Breton still survives. Cornwall, on the other hand, remained at least partly Brittonic-speaking for many centuries, at least until the 1700s, though over the centuries the language was gradually pushed back towards the far south-western edge of the county, as we shall see later.

Cumbric, the language of the *Hen Ogledd* or 'Old North', survived until around 1200, and maybe longer, before gradually ceding to English (in the south) and Gaelic (in the north). At its fullest extent, Cumbric was spoken in northern Lancashire, Westmoreland, Cumberland, Dumfries and Galloway, and there are still numerous Brittonic place names in this area today. The first element of *Carlisle* corresponds to Welsh *caer* 'fort' (as also in *Cardiff* and *Carmarthen*). Penrith is from the Brittonic for 'principal ford': modern Welsh *pen* is 'chief, main' and *rhyd* is 'ford'. And *Ecclefechan* (Dumfries) was the Cumbric for 'little church': modern Welsh *eglwys* is a feminine noun meaning 'church' and *fechan* is a feminine form of the adjective meaning 'small'.

The closest linguistic relatives of Cumbric, unsurprisingly, were the Brittonic dialects of northern Wales. Only three words of Cumbric as such are known to us: *galnys* 'blood money' compare with modern Welsh *galanas*; *kelchyn* 'tribute paid to a ruler on a royal progress' compare with Welsh *cylch* 'circuit'; and *mercheta* 'tax paid to a ruler on the marriage of a daughter' compare with Welsh *merch* 'girl, daughter'.

A special counting system is well known to have survived in Cumbria until recently and is clearly at least partly Brittonic in origin and might well therefore be a survival from Cumbric. The system is traditionally supposed to have been used by shepherds for counting sheep, and by knitters for counting stitches, but seems more often in recent times to have been employed by children playing games involving counting. The numerals vary from place to place, but one variant for the numerals 1–10 is: *yan, tan, tethera, pethera, pimp, sethera, lethera, nothera, dothera, dick*. The numbers from one to ten in modern Welsh are: *un, dau, tri, pedwar, pump, chwech, saith, wyth, naw, deg*. The correspondences between Welsh *pedwar* 'four' and *pethera*, between *pump* (pronounced 'pimp') 'five' and *pimp* and between *deg* 'ten' and *dick* are particularly striking. *Saith* does resemble *sethera*, but the former means 'seven' and the latter 'six'.

Very striking is the fact that the Cumbrian counting-system word for 'fifteen' is *bumfit*, which corresponds rather closely to Welsh *pymtheg*, and that *yan-a-bumfit* 'one +fifteen = 16' corresponds nicely to Welsh *un ar bymtheg*: the change from *pymtheg* to *bymtheg* is a word-initial grammatical mutation which is a common phenomenon in the Celtic languages, and it is interesting that the Cumbrian form appears to be derived from the mutated form. Welsh *pymtheg* is rather transparently derived from *pump+deg*, but the historical relationship between *bumfit* and *pimp+dick* is no longer so clear.

LANGUAGE NOTES

The numerals 1–10 in the Brittonic languages: modern Breton, reconstructed Cornish and modern Welsh:

Breton	Cornish	Welsh
unan	onan	un
daou	dew	dau
tri	tri	tri
pevar	peswar	pedwar
pemp	pymp	pump
chwech	hwegh	chwech
seizh	seyth	saith
eizh	eth	wyth
nav	naw	naw
dek	deg	deg

Further Pressures

To complete the overall picture of the geographical pressures on Brittonic Celtic, we also need to note, first, that at about the same time as Germanic speakers first started arriving on the shores of eastern Britain, speakers of another language started arriving in the western Highlands of Scotland. These incomers came from across the Irish Sea, from the northern regions of Ireland, and they spoke a Celtic language which we now call Goidelic or Gaelic. This gradually replaced Brittonic in most of central and northern Scotland, as we shall see later on in this book.

Secondly, rather later on, from the 800s onwards, Shetland, Orkney and the north-east of mainland Scotland started to be subject to raiding, and then settlement, by speakers of yet another language. The Brittonic-speaking Pictish inhabitants of the Northern Isles and the nearby mainland were replaced or absorbed by Vikings from Norway, who were speakers, as we saw in Chapter 2, of North Germanic Old Norse, who eventually took total control of these areas (see more on this in Chapter 5).

LANGUAGE NOTES

Brittonic Celtic and the closely related Gaulish of northern France are often referred to as P-Celtic, while the Goidelic Celtic languages, Irish, Manx and Scottish Gaelic, are often known as Q-Celtic. This is because of an early sound-change which took place in P-Celtic varieties whereby *kw-* changed to *p-*. In the Q-Celtic languages, *kw-* subsequently changed to *k-*, so there are now many corresponding pairs of words such as Welsh *pen* 'head' versus Gaelic *ceann* 'head'. The Cornish male personal name *Piran* corresponds to Irish Gaelic *Ciaran*. And Old Welsh *map*/modern Welsh *mab* 'son' corresponds to Gaelic *Mac* 'son'. *Ap*, a reduced form of Welsh *map* 'son', has produced a number of originally Welsh language surnames which are now found all over the English-speaking world, including Parry, Powell, Price, Uprichard/Pritchard, Probart, Pugh, Bevan and Bowen. Parry was originally *ap Harry* 'son of Harry'. The other names similarly indicated 'son of' Hywel, Rhys, Richard, Robert, Hugh, Evan and Owen respectively. The corresponding Gaelic form *mac* has been even more influential in the formation of scores of originally Gaelic surnames such as Macmillan, McDonald, Mackintosh, Mackenzie and very many more.

Latin and Brittonic

In his groundbreaking 1953 book *Language and history in Early Britain*, Professor Kenneth Jackson argued that nearly all of the many linguistic changes which converted Brittonic into the descendant Late British languages, Welsh, Cornish and Breton (and presumably Cumbric), took place between the middle of the fifth and the end of the sixth century; and that the evolution was so rapid that "we can be fairly sure that Vortigern around 450 could not have understood Aneirin around

600".[7] Aneirin was a sixth-century Cumbric poet known to us from his work *Y Gododdin*, which was probably written in about AD 600. The Guotodin or Gododdin were descendants of the Brittonic Celts of south-eastern Scotland and north-eastern England who were known to the Romans as the Votadini (see Chapter 4).

Peter Schrijver has suggested that at least some of the massive linguistic changes referred to by Jackson were the result of language contact, which had consequences in Britain not only for British Latin, as we just saw, but also, he argues, for Brittonic itself.

From a sociolinguistic point of view, we can suggest that it is not a coincidence that these rapid and massive changes in Brittonic occurred when they did. After the first Anglo-Saxon uprising in eastern England, much of fifth-century Celtic Britain became a socially rather unstable place. There were battles, destruction, flight, migration, emigration, enslavement, land-taking – in other words very considerable upheaval. This is certainly Jackson's interpretation of the relationship between the social and linguistic events: he says that periods of unusually rapid linguistic change are sometimes associated with great social upheavals, invasion and conquest.

Schrijver argues more specifically that what brought about the rapid linguistic changes in Brittonic was language shift, involving the large-scale adult second-language learning of Brittonic. But who was it, we might ask, at that period of history, who was learning Brittonic as a second language? Schrijver says that these second-language learners would have been the very large numbers of upper-class Romano-British refugees who fled from lowland England to the highland zone, to escape the same Anglo-Saxon revolt which also led to the flight to Brittany. These refugees were Romanised Celts who by now had become native speakers of Latin/British Northwestern Romance and who, on arriving in the still Brittonic-speaking highland north and west, were obliged to learn their ancestral but forgotten language as best they could. These refugees were so numerous that the effects of the changes they introduced into the grammar of Late British through their imperfect learning of it were in subsequent generations passed on even to the children of native speakers.

FURTHER READING

Clarkson, Tim. 2010. *The men of the North: the Britons of southern Scotland*. Edinburgh: John Donald.

Cunliffe, Barry. 2018. *The Ancient Celts*. Oxford: Oxford University Press.

Higham, Nicholas. 2007. *Britons in Anglo-Saxon England*. Woodbridge: Boydell & Brewer.

Mitchell, Bruce, & Fred Robinson. 2011. *A guide to Old English*. Oxford: Wiley-Blackwell.

[7] Jackson (1953: 690).

4 Heading West Again: The North Sea Crossing, 400–600

The North Germanic tribes who had initially stayed at home in southern Scandinavia would eventually set off across the Atlantic to Iceland, Greenland and Canada, as well as eastwards to the Black and Caspian Seas; and the Goths and others from the eastern end of the Rhine–Vistula line had already headed off towards the Balkans. Some of the Germanic peoples from the western end of the line, however, were now in motion themselves.

During the late AD 300s and early AD 400s – so about 1,000 years after the first arrival of the Germanic-speaking tribes on the eastern shores of the North Sea, and 300 years after the arrival of the Romans in Britain – boatloads of West Germanic Ingvaeonian–speaking people started crossing the North Sea to the eastern shores of Britain. Some arrivals had almost certainly come well before that because, as already noted, the Romans had been employing Germanic mercenaries in their garrisons in Britain since the second century AD.[1]

These Ingvaeonic Germanic people (see Chapter 2) were mostly members of the tribal groupings that we now refer to as the Jutes, Angles, Saxons and Frisians. They came mainly from coastal districts just across the North Sea from Britain. The Jutes had originally come from the furthest north, from northern and central Jutland. The Angles lived in areas to the south of them, in southern Jutland and Schleswig-Holstein. The Saxons had been located to the west of them, along the North Sea coastal areas of northern Germany, in the Elbe–Weser region of Saxony. And the Frisians came from Friesland, the area of coastline between the homeland of the Saxons and the mouth of the River Rhine in the modern Netherlands.

Though very short compared to the westward ocean crossings which the North Germanic Vikings would undertake four centuries later, these North Sea crossings would not necessarily have been very easy, depending on weather conditions; and journeys would have been of between 20 and 300 nautical miles, depending on how far north along the mainland coastline the travellers started. The major entry points into Britain for many of these peoples, as well as the south coast of England, were the rivers of the English east coast such as the Thames Estuary, and the estuary of the Rivers Stour and Orwell at Harwich.

By the end of the fifth century, West Germanic speakers seem still to have formed a majority population in only a few smallish areas of England. Kent, which was

[1] Nielsen (1998: 160).

reputedly settled mainly by Jutes, was the site of one of the earliest fifth-century West Germanic kingdoms on British soil. According to Bede, the Northumbrian monk who wrote *Historia ecclesiastica gentis Anglorum*,[2] it was the Jutes who settled not only in Kent but also on the Isle of Wight and in Hampshire. There is certainly archaeological evidence that the Isle of Wight and Kent were both settled by the same people, and their presence in Hampshire is confirmed by mediaeval place-name evidence. We know very little about the Jutes back in their Jutland homeland, but those of them who did not cross over to England seem later on to have merged with the Danes, as these North Germanic people migrated westwards across southern Scandinavia in the direction of the North Sea coast.

Many of the less densely wooded areas of Sussex had been settled by Germanic speakers by about AD 500, quite possibly by Saxons. Another area of major ffifth-century settlement was East Anglia. Some of the Eastern Angles, as they came to be known, entered Britain via the Great Estuary of eastern Norfolk which the Romans had called *Gariensis Ostium* 'mouth of the Yare',[3] and then sailed west along the Rivers Bure, Yare and Waveney. Others had entered via the Wash Estuary, and headed east along the Little Ouse and Lark.

The Angles seem mainly to have come originally from the area of Germany now known as Angeln. The Angeln peninsula is the part of eastern coastal Schleswig which lies between the Flensburg Firth, which today forms part of the border between Denmark and Germany, and the Schlei Inlet, which leads from the Baltic Sea down to the German town of Schleswig. Almost everybody from the peninsula appears to have emigrated to Britain. They settled in large numbers not just in East Anglia but also, during the later fifth century and the sixth century, in Middle Anglia, Mercia and Northumbria.

The East Anglian county of Norfolk is the area which today has the lowest level of survival of Romano-British place names, something which can be interpreted as being due to earlier and much heavier Germanic immigration to the region than to elsewhere in the English south-east. The Germanic kingdom of East Anglia is, too, the area where the largest concentration of early Old English runic inscriptions has been found.

In spite of the name, however, the East Anglian kingdom did have something of an ethnic mix. Several Old English place names confirm that British-speaking and Germanic-speaking peoples lived in some proximity to one another for some considerable time. The specific (first) element *Bret-* in the name of the two East Anglian villages called Brettenham (one each in Norfolk and Suffolk) indicates that these villages were inhabited by British, that is, Brittonic Celtic–speaking people. And the *Wal-* element in the names of places such as Walcott (Norfolk) and the two Waltons (Norfolk and Suffolk) also indicates the survival of Britons: *Wal-* came from

---

[2] *The Ecclesiastical History of the English People.*

[3] All that remains of the estuary today is Breydon Water, which is situated inland from Great Yarmouth. It is about 3 miles (5 kilometres) long and 1 mile (1.6 kilometres) across at its widest.

a Germanic form meaning 'foreigner' which survives in the modern English-language name of Wales.

Amongst the Germanic peoples of East Anglia, though, there were not only Angles, even if they were very much in the majority. The name of the Suffolk village of Saxham shows that, unusually for East Anglia, it was a Saxon settlement. And there were also Frisians: the Suffolk village names Friston and Freston signify 'village of the Frisians'. The American sociologist George Holman has argued that "Frisians invaded East Anglia in the fifth century" and that East Anglia "is culturally more closely related to Friesland than it is even to its nearest English relative, Kent".[4] There were also other Germanic peoples present: Swabia today is the part of Germany around Stuttgart, but some non-Ingvaeonian Swabians must have been part of the cross–North Sea migration because the name of the Norfolk town of Swaffham meant 'the home of the Swabians'.

In addition, Professor John Hines has argued that there is archaeological evidence to show that colonists from southern and western Norway also settled on the east coast of England from around 475, so the Germanic cultures arriving in East Anglia came from all round the North Sea, not just from Friesland, Saxony and Jutland but also from well up along the west coast of Norway, thereby opening up the way for later widespread Scandinavian influence on Anglian England.[5]

LANGUAGE NOTES

Before Christianisation and the introduction of the Latin alphabet into northern Europe, runes were used for the writing of a number of languages such as Old Norse, Old English and Gothic. From the first century AD, runic inscriptions were carved on wood, stone or bone, using a pre-Christian Germanic alphabet of between twenty and thirty letters. These were angular, straight-lined symbols, which made for easier engraving. The runic symbols were probably derived from ancient alphabets which had been used to write some of the different languages of the Italian peninsula.[6] One theory has it that the runic alphabet was developed by the Goths out of the Etruscan alphabet used in northern Italy, perhaps influenced by the Latin alphabet. The runic alphabet is sometimes known as the *fuþark* or *futhark*, after the sounds represented by the first six symbols. The Anglo-Frisian system is often also referred to as the *fuþork* or *futhork*, because of a phonological development – a sound change – which had taken place in Anglo-Saxon and Frisian but not in the other Germanic languages.

Apart from East Anglia and the Jutish areas along the south coast of England, there were certainly also other ethnic English communities scattered around in parts of Britain in the 400s, but they generally formed minority populations. According to Dr Robert McMahon, "the genetic evidence indicates that there was a significant movement of continental populations (males at least) into the

---

[4] Holman (1962: 181).   [5] Hines (1984).   [6] Barnes (2012).

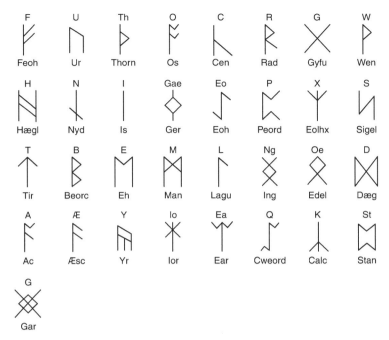

Figure 4.1 Anglo-Saxon runes

east and south of Britain around the 5th century, but for most of the country the incomers represented a relative minority".[7]

However, during the AD 500s, Ingvaeonian expansion into and across England continued, and a second wave of major Anglian kingdoms began to take shape. East Anglia came to be bordered on its west by the kingdom of the Middle Angles. Relatively little is known about this area, but it seems to have included parts of Cambridgeshire, Huntingdonshire and Northamptonshire and may have extended as far as the Chilterns. It was eventually incorporated into Mercia (see below).

And, away from the south-east of England, one other early area of Germanic occupation was the Anglian kingdom of Lindsey, to the north of Middle Anglia in what is now Lincolnshire. Lindsey had probably been settled via the Humber Estuary, and at its greatest extent it stretched from the mouth of the River Humber down to the Fens and inland as far as the River Trent. It was probably a successor state to the Romano-British polity which had been centred on Lincoln, one of the four main provincial Romano-British capitals;[8] and it also seems likely that it occupied the same territory as the modern Lincolnshire districts of East Lindsey and West Lindsey. The Roman missionary Paulinus of York converted

[7] McMahon (2011: 257).   [8] The others were London, York and, possibly, Cirencester.

Lindsey to Christianity in about 630. The Latin name of the settlement was *Lindum Colonia*, which the Romans derived from the Brittonic Celtic *lindon* 'lake'. The word has become *llyn* in modern Welsh and *lynn* in modern Breton.

To the north of Lindsey was the kingdom of Deira, on the northern side of the Humber. It included the Holderness and the Vale of York areas, and eventually stretched as far north as the River Tees. The first Anglian ruler of Deira who we have records of was Ælle, who came to power in about 560. The major centre of Deira was the former Romano-British town known as *Eburacon* in Brittonic and *Eboracum* in Latin, modern York. Deira appears also to have been settled originally via the Humber Estuary[9] and the River Derwent. The name *Deira* is probably also Brittonic in origin, from the Celtic root *daru* 'oak', compare with modern Welsh *derwen* 'oak'. Brittonic *derua* 'oak' is certainly also the source of the name of the River Derwent.

Then, later in the sixth century AD, another Anglian kingdom developed to the north of Deira, though initially separated from it by a zone which remained under Celtic control. This was Bernicia, which is believed to have been founded by Angles from Deira who bypassed the Brittonic-controlled area by arriving by sea. Its centre was Bamburgh, on the coast of what is now Northumberland, with another major settlement at Yeavering, about 20 miles (32 kilometres) inland, on the edge of the Cheviot Hills. The name *Bernicia* is probably also of Celtic origin. In the end, Bernicia stretched northward from as far as the River Tees. The first king of Bernicia who we know of was Ida, who was in power from about 550.

Inland from Lindsey, the area which became the important kingdom of Mercia also now started to be settled by Anglians, who moved initially along the River Trent into southern Derbyshire and Staffordshire, extending also to Leicestershire, Nottinghamshire and northern Warwickshire. Mercia subsequently also incorporated the territory of the minor kingdom of Hwicce, which had covered parts of Worcestershire, Gloucestershire and Warwickshire. The name *Mercia* probably derives from the Old English word for 'border' (see Chapter 5), and the kingdom did indeed occupy the frontier area between the districts of Germanic settlement and the non-germanicised Celtic tribes to their west. The first known king of Mercia was Creoda, who appears on the scene in about 580, having constructed a fortress at Tamworth, now in Staffordshire.

Eventually, it was the Angles who gave their name to the whole of England – as well as to the language which this book is written about, and written in. But it was the Saxons rather than the Angles who gave their name to the areas of southern England known as Wessex, Sussex, Middlesex and Essex, the labels referring respectively to the West, South, Middle and East Saxons. The early Saxon kingdom of Essex lay to the south of East Anglia and also included eastern Hertfordshire and Middlesex and perhaps also initially part of southern and southwestern Suffolk.

---

[9]   Downstream from the confluence of the Rivers Trent and Ouse, the name of the combined waterway changes to the Humber.

The major Saxon kingdom of Wessex started taking shape rather later, initially probably through the westward movement of people who had travelled southwards from the Wash, along the upper Thames Valley, spreading out from Dorchester as a focal point. By the end of the sixth century, Saxons had pushed the territory of Wessex on into the southern Cotswolds and the lower valley of the River Severn, reaching as far as the Bristol Channel by the AD 590s. This arrival of Germanic-speaking people on the west coast of Britain marked the beginnings of the permanent geographical separation of the Brittonic people of southern Wales from those of Somerset, Devon and Cornwall which we noted in Chapter 3 and opened the way up to Welsh and Cornish becoming different, if closely related, languages.

In the early seventh century, Anglian Bernicia and Deira were merged under King Æthelfrith, through a dynastic marriage, into the larger realm of Northumbria. Northumbrians then began to cross the Pennines to the west and appear to have extended the area under their control as far as the Irish Sea coast of southern Lancashire by about 650. Once this had happened, the Brittonic people of northern Wales were separated from those of the Lake District, the far north-west of England and the south-west of Scotland (see Chapter 3), eventually leading to the perception of Welsh and Cumbric as being different languages.

The Battle of Catraeth

The Battle of Catraeth was fought at the very beginning of the seventh century between an attacking Brittonic Celtic army and a Germanic Anglo-Saxon force, which had fighters from both Bernicia and Deira, defending the Anglian stronghold of Catraeth. This may well have been modern Catterick in North Yorkshire, although we are not sure. The assaulting Brittonic forces were under the leadership of the Edinburgh-based Gododdin but also contained warriors from Gwynedd in North Wales and from all over the *Hen Ogledd* 'the Old North' – the still Brittonic-controlled areas of Scotland and northern England. The battle was commemorated by the famous Brittonic poet Aneirin, who was probably based at the royal court of the Gododdin in Edinburgh, in his epic poem *Y Gododdin*, which describes the total defeat of the Celts by the Angles. Almost all of the Britons were killed.

Also during the seventh century, the kingdom of Mercia under King Penda (who died in 650) and his successors expanded to cover much of the Midlands of England. As part of this process, it eventually absorbed Middle Anglia and Lindsey. This led to a situation which later writers referred to as *The Heptarchy*,[10] the division of Germanic-speaking Britain into seven kingdoms: Northumbria, Mercia, East Anglia, Essex, Kent, Sussex and Wessex (Map 4.1).

---

[10] From Ancient Greek *heptá* 'seven'.

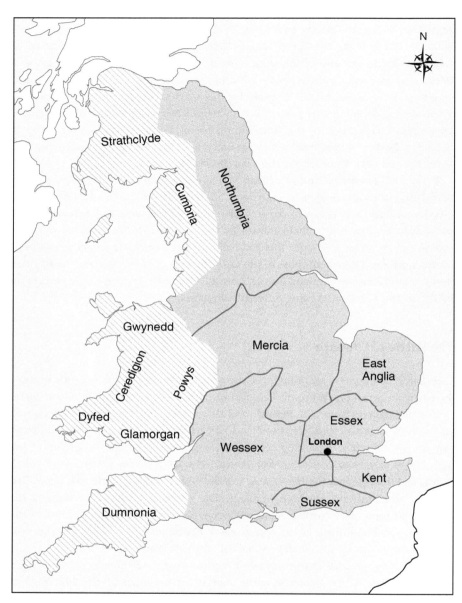

Map 4.1 The Anglo-Saxon kingdoms *c*.650

Western, central and southern Scotland were originally no less Brittonic-speaking than England, but after the Battle of Catraeth certain areas of Scotland became anglophone even before much of England did: Æthelfrith of Northumbria died in 616, but by about 630 his kingdom had been expanded by his successor Edwin as far north as the Firth of Forth in what is now Scotland.

Cumbric did, however, remain dominant in the south-west of Scotland, in the Brittonic Kingdom of Strathclyde (which was perhaps a successor state to Rheged), with some writers suggesting that Brittonic was still being spoken in the south-west as late as the twelfth century, as we noted in Chapter 3. And in the rest of Scotland, the Goidelic Celtic language Gaelic – having arrived from its original homeland in Ireland in the fifth century and gained a foothold in Argyllshire – had gradually penetrated into most of the centre and the north of Scotland, as well as the Isle of Man, by AD 800.

There was also some rather short-lived Irish Gaelic settlement in Cornwall and Devon and, perhaps, parts of Wales. Onomastic evidence also suggests that there were settlements of Irish people in other areas of England rather remote from Ireland. For example, the name of the village of Scottow in North Norfolk descends from Old English *scot-hoh* 'ridge of the Scots', where *Scot* signified 'Irish'; and Scotton in Lincolnshire contains the same element.

The last two areas of England to come under Anglo-Saxon control during this period were Somerset and Devon, and Herefordshire and Shropshire.[11] Wessex had taken control of most of formerly Celtic Devon by about AD 925; and Brittonic Hereford and Shropshire were absorbed into Germanic Mercia by about the same time.

Dialect Mixture in Old English

As we have seen, southern and eastern England and south-east Scotland were settled by Germanic speakers who came from all along the North Sea littoral, ranging at least from Jutland to the mouth of the Rhine – Jutes, Angles, Saxons, Frisians. We have also seen that the Jutes settled in Kent and Hampshire; the Saxons predominated in Essex, Middlesex, Sussex and Wessex; and Angles predominated everywhere else. But we also saw that there is place-name evidence of Saxons and Frisians in the Anglian area, Anglians in the Saxon areas and so on.

There is some specifically linguistic evidence for this complexity of settlement patterns too. Professor Hans Frede Nielsen has argued that there must have been some considerable contact in Britain between West Germanic speakers from different parts of the continental homeland because it can be seen linguistically that Old English was the result of a mixture of West Germanic dialects from different parts of the Germanic-speaking area;[12] and Old English initially had a greater degree of

---

[11] The label 'Anglo-Saxon' is a well-established and convenient one even though it does appear to ignore the Jutes and the Frisians.

[12] Nielsen (1998: 78–9).

variability than the other Germanic languages where no dialect contact and dialect mixture had been involved.[13]

LANGUAGE NOTES

Even if we did not know from other evidence that southern and eastern Britain were initially settled to some extent by a mixture of peoples from different locations on the continent, there is dialectal evidence that that was the case. Old English had a striking number of alternative forms corresponding to the modern English word *first*, probably indicative of dialect contact and dialect mixture: the variability appears to be linked to origins in different geographical dialects from the European mainland. The different forms were *forma*, which was identical with Old Frisian *forma*; *ærest*, which resembles Old High German *eristo*; *formesta*, which resembles Gothic *frumists*; and *fyrst*, which looks very like Old Norse *fyrstr*. Old English also exhibited variation in all the areas where it was spoken in the form of the interrogative pronoun meaning 'which of two'. The form *hwæðer* seems to relate to Gothic *hvaðar* and West Norse *hvaðarr*, while the alternative form *hweder* corresponds to Old Saxon *hweðar* and Old High German *hwedar*.

The Ingvaeonians Who Stayed Behind: The Frisians

Meanwhile, back on the European mainland, Ingvaeonian dialects continued to be spoken along the coastline opposite Britain by speakers of North Sea Germanic varieties who had not made the crossing to Britain, notably Frisians.

If we were to ask where it was that English first came into being as a language, it would make sense to suppose that it initially developed its first distinctive linguistic characteristics within the West Germanic language family, to the extent that we can tentatively start calling it 'English', in the two main early stronghold locations: Kent/Sussex/Hampshire and East Anglia.

And if we were to ask *when* English first came into being as a language, we can answer this question from a social perspective by saying that it began to acquire a separate identity of its own once the speakers of West Germanic who had initially crossed the North Sea from mainland Europe first started to overwinter and then settle permanently in Britain. It was the permanent settlement of these people in eastern Britain which was eventually to lead to the break-up of Ingvaeonian into separate languages, and thus to the development of the English language.

---

[13] Trudgill (1986).

Linguistically, however, what the question is asking is, essentially: when did English first start breaking away from Frisian in terms of its linguistic characteristics? Frisian remains the closest linguistic relative of English, and some linguists have postulated a possible earlier common Ingvaeonian language which they label Anglo-Frisian.

The West Frisian language is still spoken today in part of the original Frisian homeland, West Friesland, the north-westernmost part of the Netherlands, and has long been recognised as a language similar to English: East Anglian fisherman used to have a rhyme which went

> "Bread, butter and green cheese
> Is good English and good Friese."

And Frisian seafaring folk too still have, or had until recently, a version of the same rhyme:

> "Bûter, brea en griene tsiis
> Is goed Ingelsk en goed Fries."

There is also evidence of early trading between Frisia and East Anglia with, for example, Ipswich Ware pottery from the period A D 650–850 being imported into Friesland. It is likely that communication between the Angles and the Frisians would not have been at all difficult at that time.

The earliest available records show that the Frisian people were originally concentrated along the coast of what is now the Netherlands, from the northern edge of the estuary of the Rhine in the region of modern Rotterdam, northwards as far round the coast as the estuary of the River Ems, close to where the Dutch–German border is now located. However, by the time the Anglo-Saxons had begun to spread out across Britain and were in the process of becoming the dominant ethnolinguistic group in lowland England, in around A D 600, their stay-at-home Frisian fellows had similarly expanded their own territory (Map 4.2). They had spread further along the coast, both to the south and to the north-east, and were now dominating the whole of the eastern coastline of the North Sea from approximately where Zeebrugge is now located, in modern Belgium, along the Dutch coast, and round to the mouth of the River Weser by Bremerhaven in modern Germany. The North Sea was sometimes referred to in that period as 'the Frisian Sea' or 'Mare Frisicum', indicating the significance and dominance of the Frisians as a seafaring people.

Thereafter, however, the fortunes of the Frisians were the reverse of those of the Anglo-Saxons. Instead of dominating, as their Ingvaeonian cousins were doing in Britain, back home on the European mainland they were increasingly being dominated. From about A D 700 onwards, the Frisians started coming under increasing pressure from another Germanic people, the Weser–Rhine Germanic-speaking Franks, who had originally occupied territory further inland to their east. The Frisian–Frankish Wars for control over the Rhine Delta lasted for several decades. In A D 734, the Frisians were defeated in battle by the Frankish military

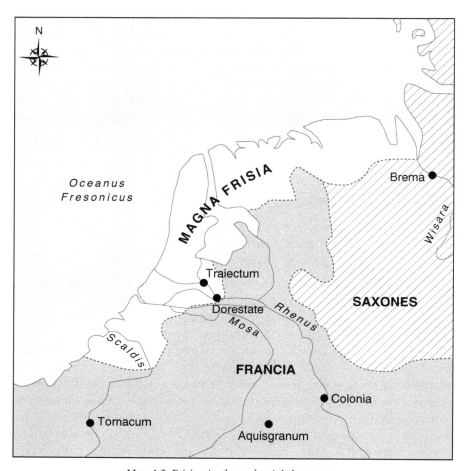

Map 4.2 Frisian in the early eighth century

leader Charles Martel 'the Hammer', who succeeded in extending the rule of the
Franks as far as the River Lauwers, now in the northern Netherlands. And by 800,
the Frisians beyond the Lauwers had also come under the control of the Franks
under Charlemagne.

This loss of political independence meant that, unlike in England, Friesland
never developed any major administrative centres. And the fact that the
Christianisation of Friesland was carried out in part from three different non-
Frisian bishoprics, Bremen, Münster and Utrecht, also meant that it did not develop
any major local ecclesiastical centres. Both these factors had a considerable impact
on the future of the Frisian language, particularly in terms of its future geographical
distribution as compared to that of English.

Under Charlemagne and his successors, the Frisian-speaking territories were initially allotted to the central division of the Carolingian Empire, Lotharingia, but in 870 they were transferred to the West Francian kingdom of the Western Franks, the forerunner of France. Soon afterwards, however, they were moved to the East Francian subdivision of the empire, the forerunner of Germany. This fluctuating status within the Carolingian – later, Holy Roman – Empire had the advantage for Friesland that it managed to restore a certain amount of the independence it had lost. And their watery terrain of marshes, peatbogs and moors afforded the Frisians good protection against influence and control from outside. For example, the mediaeval feudal system was never fully established in Friesland as it was elsewhere in the Frankish lands.

LANGUAGE NOTES

This brief word list gives an indication of the particularly close historical relationship between English and modern Frisian, as opposed to with the other modern West Germanic languages:

English	West Frisian	Dutch	Low German	German
day	dei	dag	Dag	Tag
cheese	tsiis	kaas	Kees	Käse
dream	dream	droom	Droom	Traum
ear	ear	oor	Ohr	Ohr
key	kaai	sleutel	Slödel	Schlüssel
nail	neil	nagel	Nagel	Nagel
rain	rein	regen	Regen	Regen
red	read	rood	root	rot
us	ús	ons	uns	uns
way	wei	weg	Weg	Weg
wet	wiet	nat	natt	nass

FURTHER READING

Barnes, Michael. 2012. *Runes: a handbook*. Woodbridge: Boydell & Brewer.

Higham, Nicholas, & Martin Ryan. 2013. *The Anglo-Saxon world*. London and New Haven, CT: Yale University Press.

Holman, Katherine. 2007. *The Northern Conquest: Vikings in Britain and Ireland*. Oxford: Signal Books.

Nielsen, Hans Frede. 1998. *The continental backgrounds of English and its insular development until 1154*. Odense: Odense University Press.

5 Anglo-Saxons and Celts in the British Highlands, 600–800

By AD 850, four centuries after its arrival on the island of Britain, the West Germanic language which we are now calling Old English was spoken everywhere in what is now England, even if by no means necessarily exclusively – with three geographically peripheral exceptions. These were the far south-west, where Cornish remained as a spoken language for almost another thousand years; the far north-west, from the Lake District northwards and continuing on into south-western Scotland, some of which remained Cumbric-speaking for perhaps another four centuries; and small areas of the English border counties of Shropshire and Herefordshire, which remained Welsh-speaking until the eighteenth century.

As we saw earlier, Scotland had originally been no less Brittonic-speaking than England; but certain areas of Scotland had become anglophone even before much of England: by AD 650–700, English had become dominant in the south-east of Scotland from the region around Edinburgh in the Lothians down to what is now the border with England. Cumbric, however, remained dominant in the south-west of the country, in the Brittonic kingdom of Strathclyde, the successor state to Rheged, with some writers suggesting, as we have seen, that Brittonic was in fact still being spoken in the south-west as late as the twelfth century.

But the major Brittonic-speaking area in Britain remained Wales. The linguistic border between England and Wales in AD 850 was essentially coterminous with the line along which the Anglo-Saxon westward expansion had halted. "Offa's Dyke" is what we today call the remains of the large earthwork wall, originally about 60 feet (18 metres) high, which originally ran from the estuary of the River Dee/ Afon Dyfrdwy, in the north, to the estuary of the River Severn/Afon Hafren near Chepstow/Cas-gwent in the south, passing through the English counties of Shropshire, Herefordshire and Gloucestershire as well as the Welsh counties of Flintshire, Denbighshire, Montgomeryshire and Radnorshire. It appears to have been as much a demarcation line as a defensive fortification, consisting as it did merely of a plain bank fronted on the Welsh side by a ditch.

Offa was the Anglo-Saxon king of Mercia from 757 to 796, and the dyke marks the border between the Brittonic-speaking kingdom of Powys and the Germanic-speaking kingdom of Mercia as of the end of the eighth century. Some of the lands east of the wall had only relatively recently fallen under Mercian control. In Old English, Mercia was called *Merce*, *Mierce* or *Myrce*, and Old English *mearc* or *mærc*, as we noted in Chapter 4, meant 'border'.

The Dispossessed

In the early centuries of the Germanic settlement of Britain, outside of the Anglo-Saxon strongholds of Kent-Sussex and East Anglia, many people of Germanic ancestry, as a minority in most parts of Britain, became bilingual in Brittonic Celtic and West Germanic; and it is evident that this had an important influence on the structure of the English language itself. For example, one of the major linguistic differences between English and the other Germanic languages is that English has an important grammatical distinction between 'simple' and 'progressive' verb forms. Progressive verb forms are formed with -*ing* participles, as in *I was walking, I am going, I will be doing*; as opposed to simple forms without participles *I walked, I go, I will do*. This innovation is very likely to be the result of influence from Brittonic or, as we can now call it at this period, Late British, which had a similar grammatical distinction. It is a typical *substratum effect* (see Chapter 1).

There are also Old English words which may have a Brittonic origin, a few of which are fairly well agreed upon. For example, *brock*, Old English *broc* 'badger', certainly has the same origin as Welsh and Cornish *broch* 'badger'. *Coomb*, Old English *cumb* 'hollow, deep valley', comes from the same Brittonic source as modern Welsh *cwm* 'valley': it is found in a number of modern place names in the English West Country, such as Branscombe and Salcombe, both in Devon. And *tor* 'high rock, pile of rocks', as in the well-known Glastonbury Tor in Somerset, is likely to be from the same source as Old Welsh *twrr* 'heap, pile'.

LANGUAGE NOTES

The English grammatico-semantic distinction is between progressive verb forms, as in *was walking, I am going, I will be doing*; as opposed to simple forms such as *I walked, I go, I will do*. A good explanation for why English has this distinction, while other Germanic languages generally do not, is that it is due to the effects of Brittonic–Germanic bilingualism, the point being that precisely this grammatical distinction was also observed in Brittonic. In the Brittonic of that period, progressive meanings were indicated by constructions following the pattern *BOT* + *yn* + *Verbal Noun*, where *BOT* stands for some form of the verb *bot* 'to be', *yn* was 'at' and verbal nouns were forms which had both noun-like and verb-like characteristics: Medieval Welsh *helu* could be translated into English as both 'to hunt' and 'hunting'. The suggestion is that bilinguals transferred this Brittonic progressive/simple verb distinction into Old English. Old English did not have a category of verbal nouns, and so speakers turned to present participles, corresponding to modern English -*ing* forms, to express the same meaning, as in the Old English sentence:

cont.

Hie thæt win drincende wæron

"They the wine drinking were"
They were drinking the wine

The modern Welsh would be:

Roedden	*nhw*	*yn*	*yfed*	*y*	*gwin*
Were	they	at	drinking	the	wine

Then, over the ensuing centuries, as Germanic demographic and political dominance increased, the linguistic balance flipped and it is rather certain that many people of British ancestry now became bilingual themselves. This form of bilingualism also had an influence on the English language itself – and a very significant one at that. There were, in particular, large differences between the grammatical structure of Early Old English and Late Old English, with the latter having considerably less grammatical complexity than Early Old English. This overall trend in the linguistic changes which took place between Old English and Middle English can technically be termed *simplification.*[1]

LANGUAGE NOTES

Early Old English was grammatically very different from the Middle English that it later became. Old English had three grammatical genders; three numbers; five cases; inflectional case-marking on nouns, adjectives, demonstratives and pronouns; strong versus weak nominal declensions; inflectional person-marking on verbs; and large numbers of irregular 'strong' verbs, which also made a distinction between the root vowels of singular and plural preterite forms, as in the verb *findan* 'to find':

	singular	plural
1st	*fand*	*fundon*
2nd	*funde*	*fundon*
3rd	*fand*	*fundon*

There were also large numbers of conjugations and declensions; and it had relatively free word order.

The adjective corresponding to *good* had the following weak forms:

	masc.	fem.	neut.	pl.
nom.	*goda*	*gode*	*gode*	*godan*
acc.	*godan*	*godan*	*gode*	*godan*

cont.

---

[1] The Middle English period is often defined as having lasted from *c.*1150 to *c.*1470.

gen.	*godan*	*godan*	*godan*	*godena*
dat.	*godan*	*godan*	*godan*	*godum*

There was also a set of 'strong' forms which were used in conjunction with indefinite forms of the noun phrase:

	singular			plural		
	masc.	fem.	neut.	masc.	fem.	neut.
nom.	*god*	*god*	*god*	*gode*	*goda*	*god*
acc.	*godne*	*gode*	*god*	*gode*	*goda*	*god*
gen.	*godes*	*godre*	*godes*	*godra*	*godra*	*godra*
dat.	*godum*	*godre*	*godum*	*godum*	*godum*	*godum*
inst.	*gode*	*godre*	*gode*	*godum*	*godum*	*godum*

Middle English, in contrast, had no grammatical gender; two numbers rather than three; three cases rather than five; and many fewer inflections, conjugations and declensions. There was also a reduction in case-marking and in subjunctive verb forms; and the distinction between the root vowels of the singular and plural preterite forms of strong verbs also disappeared, as did the strong/weak nominal declensions.

But why did simplification take place in English at this time? A rather obvious answer lies in the phenomenon of adult language-learning: small children up to the age of eight or so are brilliant at learning any language they are sufficiently exposed to; but adults have lost this ability. When learning a foreign language, adults typically make things easier for themselves by regularising irregularities and removing unnecessary complexities, so simplification is a well-known consequence of foreign-language learning: a typical example would be the use in 'foreigner English' of forms such as "That dog run very fast" where the *-s* of *runs* is omitted.

If we then ask who it was who was learning Old English as a foreign language at this time, the obvious answer is that it was people whose native language was Late British Celtic. Some writers have opposed this suggestion by arguing that Brittonic Celtic could not have been influential on Old English because it died out too early, the Brittonic-speaking population having fled, or been killed off, or assimilated. However, there is considerable evidence, as we saw in Chapter 3, that this was not the case. Celtic actually survived even in the lowlands of England for many centuries. Consider the following, from John Morris's *The Age of Arthur*:

spoken Welsh was common in the 7th century [. . .] British monks probably preached in Norfolk, and also in Hertfordshire, about the 590s; their activity implies a considerable population who understood their language.[2]

And:

---

[2] Morris (2004: 314).

near Peterborough, Guthlac was troubled about 705 by the still independent British of the Fenland, who were to retain their speech and untamed hostility into the 11th century.[3]

And also:

the population of the English kingdoms in the seventh century consisted of an uneven mixture of men of mixed Germanic origins and of descendants of the Roman British, called Welshman, who are likely to have constituted the larger number in many regions.[4]

But Brittonic survived even more strongly and for much longer in the highlands of Britain – and especially in the remotest highland fringes: parts of Devon remained Brittonic-speaking until at least AD 1000; parts of Strathclyde (south-western Scotland) and Cumbria (north-western England) were Brittonic-speaking until AD c.1200; and so too were Wales and Cornwall, of course.

The Battle of Gafulford

A significant battle occurred at a place called Gafulford in AD 825. It was one of a series of armed encounters between Saxons and Britons which took place on or near the Devon–Cornwall ethnolinguistic frontier during the westward drive of the Saxons under King Egbert of Wessex. It is thought that Gafulford may have been modern Camelford, in eastern Cornwall, or Galford near Lewtrenchard in western Devon.

The Enslaved

Professor Hildegard Tristram has argued that, in some areas of the highland zone of Britain, speakers of the post-conquest Germanic dialects of Wessex, Mercia and the Anglian areas ruled over the native population of the Britons. These continued to speak Brittonic Celtic as their native language for maybe six or seven generations before they shifted to Old English. The distinguished toponymist Dr Margaret Gelling believed that it took more than 400 years for the shift from Brittonic to Old English to be completed, even in areas under Anglo-Saxon control, and she suggests that the process only ended around AD 900. So there were in fact several centuries during which Celtic could have exercised some influence on Old English.

In those highland areas where Brittonic survived the West Germanic takeover on a long-term basis, its speakers were in a very different type of contact situation with Old English speakers than had been the case in the early period before AD 600. Something like a caste system was probably in operation, and speakers of Late

---

[3] Ibid. Guthlac was a Christian hermit (and later saint) associated with Crowland in southern Lincolnshire.

[4] Ibid., 316.

British were often slaves. A number of writers have actually described the social situation as being one of 'apartheid'.

Residential patterns would also have been significant, with slave communities often living in separate villages. There is considerable evidence for this residential separation from place names: Professor Eilert Ekwall listed about fifty different places in England containing the Old English element *walh, wealh* 'Briton, serf', including Walbrook, Walburn, Walcot, Walden, Walford, Wallington, Walmer, Walshford, Walworth and Walton – there are as many as twenty Waltons with this origin.

Demography would also have been very important for these linguistic developments – in the English Highlands, there were relatively few native speakers of Old English around to act as linguistic models. Many historians and archaeologists argue that a Romano-British population of about two million was taken over by a much smaller Anglo-Saxon elite.

As far as the actual linguistic processes are concerned, Tristram says that if we assume that the Celts in the English Highlands slowly shifted to Old English between roughly 600 and 900, then linguistic contact and language acquisition would have had to be of the adult-learner type. She also suggests that for Britons acquiring Old English, especially in the highland zone, the first step would have been one of adult acquisition of Old English as a second language. The resulting simplified and regularised form of Old English would have increasingly been passed on to subsequent generations, with children learning the originally imperfectly acquired second language from their parents as their own first language. They then passed this on to their own children, and the simplified version of the language eventually became the dominant variety, not least because of the relatively small size of the Anglo-Saxon elite minority.

There is also a second anti-Celtic-influence argument which has to be countered. This is that the chronology does not work, because the important linguistic changes which occurred in Old English did not happen until centuries after the Celtic Brittonic language had died out in England. But this is to ignore one very important and, if we think about it, rather obvious point. Everything we know about what the Old English language was like we know from Anglo-Saxon writing: the only records we have, obviously, are written records. We know nothing about how Old English was actually spoken.

Bearing that in mind, we can now understand that what happened was that the Celtic-induced changes in spoken Old English actually took place very early on, at a time when contact with large numbers of Celtic speakers would have provided a very reasonable explanation for what happened. But we have no hard evidence for the existence of these changes until they started appearing in writing. The point is that fundamental changes occurred in the spoken language without making their way into the written language which now provides the only data that we have.

Crucially, the written evidence that survived came from the pens of a small upper-class Anglo-Saxon elite who preserved the knowledge of how classical Old English was supposed be written, long after the original form of the language had disappeared from everyday speech. We can compare this with the way in which in France, for example, knowledge of how Latin was supposed to be written survived amongst elite educated scribes long after massive linguistic changes had produced a situation in which the population as a whole were now not speaking Latin at all but its descendant, Old French.

Evidence of massive language change then appears rather suddenly in the written record after the social breakdown brought about by the bloody and enormously destructive Norman Conquest. William the Conqueror forcibly replaced the Anglo-Saxon aristocracy with Norman-French-speaking barons and clerics. This led to the disappearance of the elite scribal tradition of English writing, and from about 1100 onwards – and only then – forms that had been typical of spoken English for some considerable time started to appear in writing. It makes sense, then, to argue that many changes in Old English were the result of language contact, after AD 600 and mainly in the highland zone of England, between Old English speakers and speakers of Late British Celtic – who eventually shifted to Old English.

Old Norse

During the course of the ninth century, another language began to appear on the scene in both Friesland and Britain. The Frisians and the English were both subject to frequent raids and invasions by Old Norse–speaking Vikings from Denmark and Norway. In Friesland, however, there were no major permanent Norse settlements as there were in the English Danelaw and in Scotland and Ireland.

Large-scale Viking settlements took place in England during the ninth and tenth centuries, leading to many eastern and northern areas of the country containing a heavily Scandinavian or Scandinavianised population, as famously witnessed by the hundreds of surviving Norse place names. The number of Scandinavians who actually arrived and settled in Britain is unknown and the subject of quite a lot of controversy. But from about 890 onwards, much of eastern England became officially part of the Danelaw – the area which was signed over to the Danes by Alfred, the king of Wessex, basically because he had no choice other than to do this in view of the military realities (Map 5.1). Further north in England, and in Scotland, Scandinavian settlement was mostly carried out by people who had come from Norway.

The original parent language of Old Norse, North Germanic, was a close relative of West Germanic; and indeed many linguists agree, as we saw earlier, that there was an earlier language which was ancestral to both, Northwest Germanic, which would have split up into North and West Germanic around AD 450.[5] This makes it quite possible that English speakers and Norse speakers could still understand one another to some

[5] Kuhn (1955).

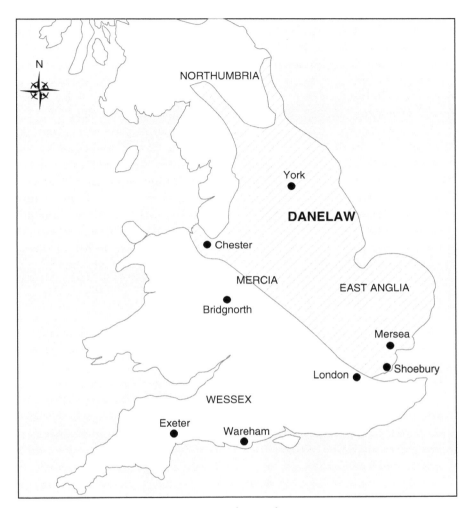

Map 5.1 The Danelaw

degree during the ninth, tenth and eleventh centuries, even without becoming particularly bilingual as individuals.

In spite of the fact that the Danelaw soon came back under English control (in 917), very large numbers of Danes still stayed on the island, and there was certainly considerable influence from Norse culture on English culture. There still remains the interesting question, however, of how much Old Norse was spoken in England, and for how long.

Scores of words of Scandinavian origin are still in general use in modern English wherever in the world it is spoken. A study based on the *Oxford English Dictionary* found approximately a thousand words of Norse origin. Something like a half are nouns such as *booth, cake, egg, law* and *skin*; a quarter are verbs such as *call, die, get, give, take* and *want*; and an eighth are adjectives such as *flat, ill, odd, ugly* and *weak*; as well as various other adverbs, pronouns, prepositions and particles, including *both, same, they* and *though*. In parts of Britain where Norwegian and Danish Viking settlement was heavy, an even larger number of words from Old Norse survive to this day in local speech, such as *cleg* 'horsefly', *lopp* 'flea', *flit* 'move house' and *bairn* 'child'.[6]

There are also many Old Norse–origin place names in parts of England and Scotland. For instance, *toft*, as in Lowestoft, meant 'plot of land'; and the Old Norse form *kirk* 'church' is also found in many place names such as Kirby and Kirkley. In eastern Norfolk on the former island of Flegg, for instance, there is an extreme concentration of place names ending in Old Norse *-by* 'settlement': Ashby, Billockby, Clippesby, Filby, Hemsby, Herringby, Mautby, Oby, Ormesby, Rollesby, Scratby, Stokesby and Thrigby. *By* is now the Danish and Norwegian word for 'town' and the Swedish word for 'village'. Place names in *-thorpe* originally indicated smaller outlying Danish villages dependent on a *by*.

LANGUAGE NOTES

Joseph Emonds and Jan Terje Faarlund claim that the Germanic language which eventually emerged out of language contact in early mediaeval England between Old English and Old Norse was in fact not Norsified English but Anglified Norse – a Scandinavian language heavily influenced by Old English.[7] Modern English, they argue, should therefore be considered to be a Scandinavian language. They argue their case using mainly syntactic data, citing the Norse character of a number of Middle English syntactic constructions as compared to Old English. They point out, for example, that Henk van Riemsdijk[8] makes the strong claim that the only languages in the world which permit grammatical constructions with fully developed preposition stranding[9] are, firstly, members of the North Germanic language family and, secondly, English: Danish *Reven ble skutt på* (Fox-the was shot at) is entirely paralleled by English 'The fox was shot at'.[10] According to Emonds and Faarlund, most languages disallow this construction completely; and West Germanic Dutch allows it only "under very restrictive condition" – which was also the situation in Old English. According to Jarich Hoekstra, it is also disallowed in Frisian.[11]

Eventually speakers of Old Norse did abandon it in favour of English – an English, however, which by then had as a consequence of English–Norse

---

[6] Durkin (2023).   [7] Emonds and Faarlund (2014).   [8] Riemsdijk (1978).

[9] In *The boy I gave it to*, the preposition *to* is said to be 'stranded' at the end of the sentence, as opposed to in *The boy to whom I gave it*.

[10] Holmberg and Rijkhoff (1998).

[11] Hoekstra (1995). For a discussion of the work of scholars who have suggested possible Brittonic influence on the development of English preposition stranding, see Roma (2007).

bilingualism/bidialectalism become considerably Norsified. In fact, 'abandon' might well not be the most appropriate word here at all. In view of the at least quasi-dialectal nature of the relationship between Old English and Old Danish, we would probably do better to think of the descendants of the Viking invaders as gradually modifying their Old Danish over the generations in the direction of Old English. Especially if Old English speakers, in bilingual towns like York, Lincoln and Norwich, also gradually modified their dialect in the direction of Old Norse, then there would have come a point where the two became no longer distinguishable.

King Canute

The Danish ruler King Canute was, at the height of his powers, king of England for nearly twenty years, as well as king of Denmark (from 1018) and Norway (from 1028). He had become England's ruler by invading the country in 1015 and finally taking control of the entire kingdom, through military might and political negotiation, in 1016. Widely known as Cnut the Great, he was a European figure of some considerable consequence: in 1027, he actually travelled all the way to Rome to attend the coronation of the Holy Roman Emperor, Conrad IV. Cnut probably grew up in Denmark, and it is certain that he spoke Old Danish, which was his father's language. He also wrote letters in Old English – though of course he might have had them written and/or translated for him. Cnut was the son of the Danish royal Sweyn Forkbeard, whose wife was possibly the daughter of King Mieszko I of Poland, and it is possible that he spoke Polish in addition to Anglo-Danish.

As we saw in Chapter 2, Old Norse speakers colonised not only parts of the British Isles but also Iceland, Greenland and, briefly, a small area of Canada. A look at a map of the North Atlantic shows that anyone sailing from western Norway to Iceland would be likely to stop off in the Faroes on the way. And the best route from western Norway to the Faroes would involve stopping off along the way in Shetland.

In fact, the Shetland and Orkney Islands were probably settled by Norsemen in the late AD 700s, the Faroe Islands in the early 800s and Iceland in the mid-800s. The original inhabitants of Orkney and Shetland were probably Picts, as discussed in Chapter 4.

The Nordic language that was spoken by the descendants of these eighth-century settlers in Shetland for more than a thousand years is now known to us as Norn. It was also spoken in Orkney and on the north-east Scottish mainland in Caithness. However, Norn did not survive as long in these places as it did in Shetland, probably losing its last native speakers in Caithness in the 1400s and in Orkney in the 1700s, though there is considerable controversy about how long the language survived –

and how 'Norn' it actually was in the mouths of it last speakers (see further Chapter 11).

THE KINGDOM OF THE ISLES NORSE GAELS

Scandinavians also colonised the Gaelic-speaking Hebrides and established sizeable settlements in Ireland, including Dublin, Waterford and Wexford. As these Scandinavian settlers intermarried with Gaelic-speaking people in Ireland and Scotland, and gradually adopted very many aspects of Gaelic culture, a group of people who are often described as the 'Norse Gaels' gradually emerged. From about ad 800, these Norse Gaels, part-descendants of the seafaring Vikings, came to control large areas of the Irish Sea, including the Isle of Man, as well as the seas off the coast of western Scotland, and they maintained that control until perhaps as late as the 1200s. The kingdom of the Isles, which included the Hebrides, the Kintyre peninsula, the Isle of Arran and the Isle of Man, was essentially a political entity founded by these mixed bilingual groups of Gaels and Norsemen. The same was true of the kingdom of Galloway, on the far south-western mainland of Scotland: the name Galloway derives from the Gaelic *Gall Ghaidheil* 'stranger Gaels'.

LANGUAGE NOTES

Scottish Gaelic has a number of words derived from Norse, such as *acair* 'anchor' from Norse *akkeri*; *bideadh* 'to bite' from *bita*; *dorgh* 'fishing line' from *dorg*; *nabaidh* 'neighbour' from *nabua*; *sgarbh* 'cormorant' from *skarf*; and *trosg* 'cod' from *thorsk*. Some Gaelic personal names have Norse origins, such as Ruairidh (Rory) from *Hrodrik* and Tormod from *Thormund*.

The Ingvaeonians Who Stayed Behind

During the AD 1000s and AD 1100s, Friesland came under different degrees of external control, and from different geographical directions, notably by the Saxon Counts to the east and the Counts of Holland to the south. By 1300, the Counts of Holland had established a degree of control as far as the Vlie, the seaway between the West Frisian islands of Vlieland and Terschelling. The West Frisians maintained a greater degree of freedom between the Vlie and the Lauwers, as did the East Frisians beyond the Lauwers, where attempts by the Saxon Counts to establish rule over the Frisians met with limited success, though during the 1400s the Frisian language gradually receded under the influence of Low German.

LANGUAGE NOTES

A modern West Frisian present-tense verb paradigm:

harkje	'to hark, listen'

ik harkje	I hark
do harkest	thou harkest
hy harket	he harketh
sy harket	she harketh
it harket	it harketh

wy harkje	we hark
jimme harkje	you hark
sy harkje	they hark

FURTHER READING

Gelling, Margaret. 1993. *Place-names in the landscape: the geographical roots of Britain's place-names*. London: Dent.

Hadley, Dawn, & Julian Richards. 2021. *The Viking Great Army and the making of England*. London: Thames & Hudson.

Holman, Katherine. 2007. *The Northern Conquest: Vikings in Britain and Ireland*. Oxford: Signal.

Mitchell, Bruce, & Fred Robinson. 2012. *A guide to Old English*. Oxford: Blackwell.

Morris, Marc. 2021. *The Anglo-Saxons: a history of the beginnings of England*. London: Hutchinson.

6 And Further West: Across the Irish Sea, 800–1200

By the year 1100, seven centuries after the arrival of West Germanic dialects in Britain, Wales still remained solidly Brittonic-speaking, and would continue to be so for several hundred years – with one exception, which is something of a geographical surprise. A perusal of a map of modern Wales will show that the majority of the places in the country bear unmistakably Welsh-language names: Aberystwyth, Caernarfon, Ffestiniog, Llanelli, Machynlleth, Pwllheli, Ystradgynlais.[1]

But if we look at the names of the towns and villages in the far south-west of the country, in the historical county of Pembrokeshire which was originally part of the Brittonic-speaking kingdom of Dyfed, we find a rather different picture. Here, there are place names such as Tenby, Milford, Upton, Templeton and Wiston, which are clearly not Welsh: there are dozens of places in England called Upton; and there are scores of place names in England ending in -by, -ford and -ton.

The fact is that modern Pembrokeshire is divided into two cultural zones by a boundary known as the Landsker or Lansker Line. The name might be of Scandinavian origin – land was the Old Norse for 'land', and skera meant 'to cut' – although it is not clear how such a name might have come about. Areas to the north of the line, with Welsh-language place names, are mainly still Welsh-speaking to this day, while the rather sharply delineated area to the south, with the English-language place names, is English-speaking. And not only are the people of this part of south Pembrokeshire and the immediately neighbouring area of south-western Carmarthenshire English-speaking today; they have actually been anglophone for very many centuries. The genuinely special linguistic and cultural character of this southern area is demonstrated by the fact that it is sometimes known as 'Little England beyond Wales'. As Map 6.1 shows, the Gower Peninsula of Glamorgan also falls into this centuries-old English-speaking zone.

The modern local English accent bears a rather close resemblance to the accents of the English West Country, rather than to other accents of Welsh English, even though Little England beyond Wales is quite a long way from England: from Pembroke to Bristol is about 140 miles or 230 kilometres.[2] The accent is rhotic – the r's in words like *girl* and *farm* are pronounced. And, unlike any other accents in

---

[1] The meanings of such Welsh names are often still transparent to native speakers: Aberystwyth 'mouth of the River Ystwyth'; Pwllheli 'briny pool'.

[2] Australian and North American readers should note that 230 kilometres is a long way in Britain.

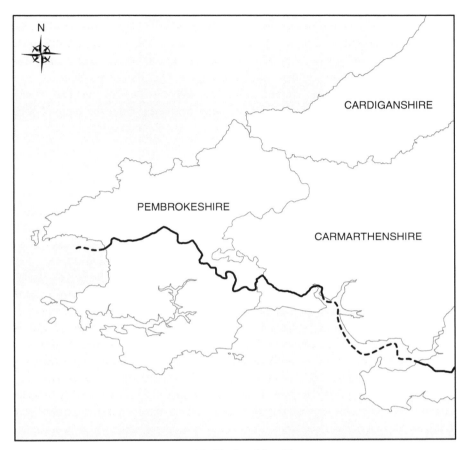

Map 6.1 The Landsker Line

southern Wales, local people pronounce words like *butter* and *up* with the vowel of *foot*, just as people from the North of England do.

The most usual explanation for this phenomenon focusses on the acts of King Henry I of England, who was the fourth son of William the Conqueror. In the wake of the 1066 invasion of England, the Normans began military incursions into Wales, and by 1094 they had gained control of large areas of the country. They found it difficult to maintain this control, though, and by 1101 had lost much of it again. The efforts of the Normans continued, however, and as part of his anti-Welsh campaign King Henry established a Flemish settlement in southern Pembrokeshire, in 1108. The course of the Landsker Line, which still delineates the anglophone region, does not follow any obvious physical or topographical features, so it is supposed that it was probably imposed politically and militarily, by the Anglo-Norman monarchy, with any original Welsh-speaking inhabitants being expelled.

The twelfth-century Flemish/Dutch and English languages would have been somewhat similar language varieties, but it is probable that the real reason why the area in the end became totally English-speaking was because the 'Flemish' colony from the very beginning actually contained large numbers of people who had come from England – which would also explain why there are still settlements there with names such as Picton, Upton and Wiston. But the survival of this cultural and linguistic boundary for so many centuries, from the days of King Henry I till the twenty-first century, is a remarkable phenomenon.

A Momentous Event

After arriving in Britain in about A D 400, the language which became English remained where it was for 700 years without ever leaving the island. Now, for the first time, this began to change. In a momentous event for the linguistic history of the world – as we can now see – the first instance of the spread of English beyond the island of Britain took place in 1169. This spread was, unsurprisingly, across the sea to the nearby Gaelic-speaking island of Ireland: at its closest points, Ireland is not much more than 10 nautical miles (19 kilometres) from Scotland across the North Channel, and about 27 nautical miles (50 kilometres) from Wales across the Irish Sea. However, it was the harbours of English-speaking Pembrokeshire, to the south of the Landsker Line, which formed the jumping-off point for this first significant linguistic crossing of the Irish Sea, and so the actual maritime journey was more like 50 nautical miles (90 kilometres).

This expansion of the English language beyond Britain occurred, ironically enough, because of the activities of the Normans. It was these conquerors of England who led the expedition to Ireland from the Flemish/English-speaking area of south-western Wales. They were themselves aristocratic speakers of Anglo-Norman (Norman French). Importantly, however, they brought with them on their expedition their English-speaking soldiers and retinues.

RICHARD QUOR DE LION

Richard the Lionheart, king of England 1189–99, may have had some competence in English, as he was born in England. But, like all the early kings of England from William the Conqueror onwards, he grew up surrounded by the Norman aristocracy, whose everyday language was Anglo-Norman (Norman French) (in which the name *Lionheart* would have been rendered as *Quor de Lion*). After he became king, Richard spent a total of only about six months in England, which presumably did nothing to improve his English-language skills. His native language was not even Norman French but Occitan, the language of southern France, spoken then and now in different regional varieties such as Provencal, Gascon and Languedocien. Richard's mother was Eleanor of Aquitaine, Aquitaine being the

cont.

area of south-western France where Bordeaux, Pau and Bayonne are situated. Richard not only spoke Occitan but also wrote poetry in the language. It was not for another 200 years that England acquired an English-speaking monarch. The first king since 1066 to have English as his mother tongue was Henry IV, king from 1399 to 1413.

The island of Ireland was at the time divided up into a number of kingdoms, the major ones being Ulster (*Ulaidh* in Gaelic), Meath (*Midhe*), Leinster (*Laighin*), Munster (*Mumhain*) and Connaught (*Connacht*). The king of Leinster was Diarmait Mac Murchada (known in English as Dermot Macmurrough). His entitlement to the kingship was disputed by other claimants, and in 1166 he was driven out of Ireland by rivals. King Henry II of England, the grandson of Henry I, then gave him permission to attempt to regain his kingdom by enlisting the military help of Anglo-Norman lords from southern Wales, notably the Earl of Pembroke, nicknamed 'Strongbow'.

In May 1169, Anglo-Norman forces landed at Bannow Bay on the south coast of County Wexford. Dermot Macmurrough, in cooperation with them, had very soon taken back control of Leinster; and the Normans began to undertake raids into the neighbouring Irish kingdoms. Strongbow went on to take military control of the bilingual Norse-Irish city-kingdoms of Dublin, Waterford and Wexford. This military operation had the backing not only of King Henry II but also of Pope Adrian IV, an Englishman who had been born in Hertfordshire and whose real name was Nicholas Breakspear.

In 1170, the High King of All Ireland, Ruaidrí Ua Conchobair/Rory O'Connor, led an Irish counteroffensive against the Normans, but in 1171 King Henry himself landed an army in Ireland in an attempt to establish control, not least over the unruly Anglo-Normans. A number of Irish kings formally submitted to Henry, possibly hoping that he would keep Norman expansion under control which, however, he had not done by the time he returned to Britain in 1172. Then, in 1177, Henry declared his ten-year-old son, the later King John, to be Lord of All Ireland and authorised the Anglo-Norman conquests to continue. In addition to Norse-Irish Wexford and Waterford (see Chapter 5) – both places which still today bear Scandinavian-origin rather than Gaelic names – and Dublin, there were subsequently also further Norman urban coastal settlements to the west, such as in Galway, Limerick and Cork.

Settlers from England now began to move into the Norman-occupied areas, and as more and more of them arrived, much of the eastern and south-eastern coastal areas of Ireland gradually became English-speaking, under an Anglo-Norman-speaking aristocracy. According to Professor Michael Samuels, the available dialectal evidence indicates that the English settlers came predominantly from the West Midlands and the south-west of England.[3]

---

[3] Samuels (1972: 108).

The Enslaved

During the first two centuries after the destabilisation of Romano-British England which had been brought about by the fall of the Roman Empire, Irish raiders began crossing the Irish Sea and kidnapping and enslaving Britons, their most famous victim being Saint Patrick. From the ninth century to the twelfth, Norse-Gaelic Dublin became a major slave trading centre, perhaps the biggest in Europe, leading to an increase in slaving raids into western Britain, especially Wales and Scotland, with slaves being sold as far afield as Iceland and Spain. Slavery was very much part of Viking society; and slaves appear to have played a big role in the settlement of Iceland: on the basis of genetic evidence, Gaelic women in particular are thought to have formed a significant proportion of the founding population, and it seems rather probable that not all of them were there of their own free will. An early Icelandic settler, Icelandic Hjörleifr Hróðmarsson, was killed in 875 by his slaves, many of them apparently from Ireland and Britain. The sale of slaves to Ireland was banned in England in 1102, and in 1171 the Council of Armagh freed all English slaves in Ireland.

The Dispossessed Fight Back

Interestingly, in spite of the military and political power that the Anglo-Normans exercised in Ireland, a long process of assimilation then set in during which the English- and French-speaking colonial minorities gradually became culturally more and more Irish and shifted to speaking Irish Gaelic.

One major factor leading to this setback for English was the plague known as the Black Death, which came to Ireland in 1348. Most of the descendants of the Anglo-Norman invaders and settlers lived in towns and villages, where they were less able to resist the infection. The Gaelic-speaking Irish tended to live in more scattered rural areas and survived at a much higher rate. After the plague had receded, the Gaelic people, and the Irish Gaelic language, came to dominate the island once more, with the Irish taking back control of large parts of Leinster, Connaught, Ulster and other regions (see more on this in Chapter 10).

Forth and Bargy

In one small area of the far south-east of Ireland, mediaeval English survived the Gaelic Resurgence and was not replaced by Gaelic. This was on the Forth and Bargy peninsula, to the south of the town of Wexford, where a continuation of this mediaeval English continued to be used until the nineteenth century. A dialect descended from the speech of the original twelfth-century English settlers was spoken in that area until the early 1800s and beyond. After the recolonisation of Ireland by the English Crown in the sixteenth and seventeenth centuries (see below), English gradually replaced Gaelic in much of Ireland once again, leading to the development of the modern Irish English we are familiar with today. But the inhabitants of that far south-eastern peninsula resisted the encroachment of this upstart modern form of English until the reign of Queen Victoria.

Their dialect was described by the philologist A. J. Ellis in his 1889 work *The existing phonology of English dialects*. He was never able to hear it spoken himself but, using written sources and reports from people on the spot, he did acquire enough information to be able to classify the dialect as grouping together with the dialects of the West Country and south coast of England.

One well-known characteristic of the pronunciation of the dialect was the use of *v* rather than *f*, *z* instead of *s* and *zh* instead of *sh*. We are familiar with this feature from stereotypical English West Country dialect pronunciations such as 'Zummerzet' for Somerset, as well as forms like 'vrom' (from), 'zixpence' (sixpence) and 'zhilling' (shilling). Records from Forth and Bargy show the same kind of thing, with spellings such as *vear* (fear), *zich* (such) and *zeven* (seven).

The dialect also preserved archaic grammatical features: the mediaeval-style English past-participle forms using a prefix - *y-drow* (thrown), *y-spant* (spent) and *y-go* (gone) – are reminiscent of Chaucer's *y-clad* (clad, clothed).

It also retained the verbal form *cham* 'I am'. This appears in Shakespeare's plays in dialogues involving country-bumpkin characters; and it survived in the dialects of the English West Country until quite recently. The word was derived from the mediaeval English form of *I*, which was *ic*, pronounced 'itch': *ic am* thus gave *'ch am*, just as modern *I am* has become *I'm*.

LANGUAGE NOTES

Word-initial fricative voicing was a sound-change affecting southern English dialects which reached its peak in the fifteenth century. In this change, /f, θ, s, ʃ/ changed to /v, ð, z, ʒ/ at the beginning of words, as in *finger* > *vinger*, *thing* > *dhing*, *sit* > *zit* and *shilling* > *zhilling*. Ultimately, this change spread into all of the dialects along the English south coast from Kent to Devon, and as far north as the West Midlands in the west and southern Essex in the east. In modern times, it survived only in the dialects of the English south-west, notably Somerset 'Zummerzet', where the Survey of English Dialects recorded forms such as *vurrow, vlea, vloor, vrom, Vriday*. The word *vixen* 'female fox' is a southern dialect form, with the change of /f/ to /v/, which has spread into General English, though southern *vox* has not. So is *vat* 'barrel, cask', which was *fæt* in Old English, corresponding to modern Norwegian *fat* and German *Fass*. It is possible that the southern dialect form *vat* became the general term in order to avoid confusion with the other English word *fat* 'plump, greasy'.

Elsewhere in Ireland, English, after having more or less died out, was gradually reintroduced after the reconquest of the island by the Tudor monarchy in the 1500s and the Stuart monarchy's 'plantation' of northern Ireland by Scottish and English settlers in the 1600s. Modern Irish English is thus not a descendant of the English which was originally brought over from Little England beyond Wales in the 1100, even though that did survive in Forth and Bargy until the nineteenth century.

LANGUAGE NOTES

Modern Irish English contains a number of features which result from the almost – but happily not total – language shift from Gaelic to English which took place on the island over the period from 1600 to 1900. One syntactic calque (loan translation), due to the transfer of a Gaelic feature into English, concerns the use in modern Irish English of the adverb *after*, followed by a progressive verb form, where a perfective verb would be used in most other English varieties: *I'm after seeing him* 'I have (just) seen him'.

A number of Irish Gaelic words have also survived in modern Irish English: *boreen* (from *bóithrín* 'small road') 'narrow rural road'; *colleen* 'young woman' (from *cailín*); *poteen* 'hooch' (*póitín*); *sleveen* 'sly person' (*slíbhín*); *tilly* 'additional free item given by a shopkeeper to a customer' (*tuilleadh* 'supplement'); *ommadhawn* 'fool' (*amadán*); *bosthoon* 'clown' (*bastún*); *spalpeen* 'rascal' (*spailpín* 'seasonal worker'); *kish* 'basket' (*cis*); and *slane* 'turf-spade' (*sleaghán*).

The Ingvaeonians Who Stayed Behind: The Emigrations

Back on the European mainland, the Frisians were also once again expanding their territory through migration, by land and sea. Migrations out of the Frisian homeland started in the AD 700s. The North Frisian islands including Sylt, Föhr, Amrum and Heligoland were, as far as we can tell, settled in the eighth century by emigrants from the original Friesland (Map 6.2).

It is probable that the Frisians had come to know of these islands as a result of their trading voyages northwards to Scandinavia. Runic inscriptions dating from the fifth and sixth centuries AD, which have been found along the Norwegian coast, contain a good number of personal names which are probably of Frisian origin, with trade being an obvious explanation for their presence. Some parts of western Norway in particular seem to have had closer contacts with Friesland than with other Scandinavian areas to the east. And archaeological finds in West Friesland have also provided us with evidence for trading contacts with

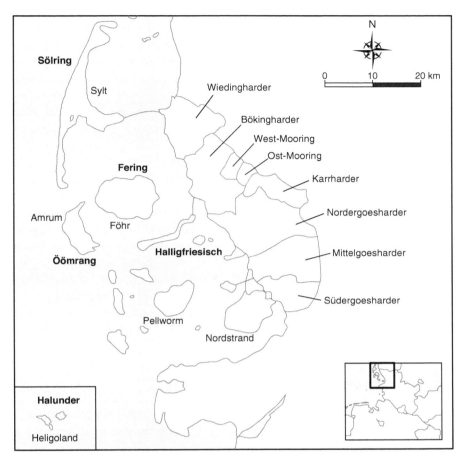

Map 6.2 North Frisian

Scandinavia. These include one silver clasp from seventh-century Denmark, another from Gotland and a Swedish bronze comb from the region of Uppsala.[4]

The mainland North Frisian settlements, along the west coast marshlands of Schleswig in what is now the far north of Germany, are believed to have been the result of a rather later emigration from the Frisian homeland, during the period 950–1200. The Frisians involved in these migrations may well have been invited to settle in the area by the king of Denmark. Dialectological evidence suggests that they probably originated from the East Frisian area around the mouth of the Ems.

---

[4] Jellema (1955).

Reflecting these two different waves of settlement of North Friesland, there are still considerable differences today between the island and mainland dialects of the modern North Frisian language; and there is a good deal of interest in where exactly in Friesland the two waves of migrants did originally come from. The evidence is both archaeological and linguistic. The dialectological data is complex, but there is a strong suggestion that the mainland North Frisians came originally from the area around the estuary of the River Ems, between Eemshaven in the province of Groningen in the Netherlands and Emden in Lower Saxony, Germany.[5] It is more difficult to determine on linguistic grounds where the first wave of settlement, to the islands, originated, not least because at that earlier time dialectal differentiation between the different areas of the Frisian homeland was not so great as it was later.

Subsequently, in the years before 1250, the Saterland area of Lower Saxony between the modern Dutch border and Oldenburg was also occupied by emigrants who had come from the eastern part of the Frisian homeland and spoke East Frisian dialects. Saterland was an area consisting of sandy heath surrounded by the marshes which were associated with the River Leda. The East Frisian dialects have since died out in their homeland and now survive only in Saterland.

These waves of emigration eventually led to the modern situation where there are now three Frisian languages: West Frisian; North Frisian; and East Frisian or Saterlandic, as we shall discuss further later.

LANGUAGE NOTES: NORTH FRISIAN GRAMMAR

Some North Frisian dialects have an interesting grammatical distinction between two different definite articles corresponding to English 'the'. In the Mooring dialect of the Bökingharde area, the two sets of forms are:

masc.	di	e
fem.	jü	e
neut.	dåt	et
pl.	da	et

The usage of the two definite articles is quite complicated, but basically the articles *e* and *et* are used to refer to something which is unique such as *e moune* 'the moon' and *e wjaard* 'the truth'. They are also used to refer to something which is close by. The definite articles *di*, *jü*, *dåt* and *da* are used to refer to things which are distant or not unique. For example, 'I have spoken to the village-mayor' can be translated in two ways:

cont.

[5] Århammer (2001).

(1) ik hääw ma e bürgermäister snaaked

and

(2) ik hääw ma di bürgermäister snaaked

literally

 'I have with the mayor spoken'

In sentence (1), the mayor is the mayor of your own village, but in sentence (2) he or she is the mayor of some other village. If some outsider entering a village were to ask, *Huar wenet di bürgermäister?* 'Where does the mayor live?', this could only produce the response 'Which mayor do you mean?'.

FURTHER READING

Davies, Robert. 2000. *The age of conquest: Wales 1063–1415*. London: St. Martin's.

Flechner, Roy. 2019. *Patrick retold: the legend and history of Ireland's patron saint*. Princeton: Princeton University Press.

Kostick, Conor. 2013. *Strongbow: the Norman invasion of Ireland*. Dublin: O'Brien.

Mallory, James. 2013. *The origins of the Irish*. London: Thames & Hudson.

Walker, Alastair. 1990. Frisian. In C. Russ (ed.) *The dialects of modern German: a linguistic survey*. London: Routledge, 1–30.

7 Atlantic Crossing: On to the Americas, 1600–1800

In 1600, English had rather fewer than 4 million native speakers and was still a minor language on the world scale. It had no particularly important role as a foreign or second language anywhere outside the British Isles and was spoken as a native language in only a very small area of the globe – it was almost entirely confined to parts of a rather small island on the western edge of Europe.

English was at the time basically just the native language of the indigenous population of (nearly all of) England and of the south and east of Scotland. As we have seen in earlier chapters, it was still absent from much of Cornwall and from Welsh-speaking parts of Shropshire and Herefordshire; most of Ireland was still Goidelic Irish Gaelic-speaking; nearly all of Wales was still Welsh-speaking; the Highlands and Hebridean Islands of Scotland spoke Gaelic; Orkney and Shetland spoke Scandinavian Norn; and the Isle of Man was Goidelic Manx-speaking. The Channel Islands still had Norman French.

During the course of the 1600s, however, this situation changed dramatically, and the original southwards and westwards expansion of Germanic, which had begun 2,000 years earlier in northern Europe, as described in earlier chapters, now regained a new impetus. There was an explosive expansion of the English language into and across the Atlantic Ocean, a process which was to lead to the eventual death of a very large number of the indigenous languages of the Western Hemisphere.

During the 1600s, something like 350,000 people left the British Isles for the Americas. Some of this expansion of English into the Western Hemisphere was the outcome of large-scale, planned and often official attempts at colonisation. Other English-speaking settlements just happened, as a result of haphazard settlements by refugees, pirates, runaway slaves, sailors, shipwrecked mariners and passengers and military deserters, as for example from the English army of Oliver Cromwell which had captured Jamaica from the Spanish in the 1650s.

As with everywhere else in the world to which English has expanded, the spread into the Atlantic was not just a simple geographical process. There were three factors involved: the arrival of native English speakers from elsewhere, that is, directly or indirectly from the British Isles; the extermination (deliberate or not) and/or expulsion of the indigenous peoples by the new arrivals; and, where indigenous peoples were not exterminated or expelled, the process of *language shift*, as discussed earlier, whereby indigenous peoples gradually abandoned their native languages and adopted English instead. These were the same processes which had been taking place ever since the assimilation and germanicisation of the original Brittonic-speaking population of England after they had come into contact with the Anglo-Saxons; and indeed these same processes were also precisely those which had also occurred many centuries before that, in continental Europe, in the face of the original southward Germanic expansion out of southern Scandinavia.

North America

The history of linguistic anglicisation in the Western Hemisphere is a complex one, involving considerable competition between European powers for colonial possessions, the main competitors being the Spanish, Portuguese, Swedish, Danish, Dutch, French and English (later British).[1]

In what is now the USA, the Dutch had established several colonial trading enterprises in the late sixteenth century. Eventually, in 1623, the Dutch West India Company took over the area that had previously been exploited by the New Netherland colony, which comprised areas of what is now the USA in Connecticut, New York, New Jersey and Delaware. They then founded Fort Orange (Albany, New York) and New Amsterdam (New York City).

Subsequently, in 1637, the New Sweden Company established a colony to the south of the Dutch-controlled area, in what is now Delaware. In 1655, the Dutch seized control of New Sweden but then in 1674 ceded both colonies to the English, who nevertheless allowed individual Dutch and Swedish colonists to remain on their lands. The Dutch language survived in much of the area for many decades: the US President Martin Van Buren (1782–1862) initially grew up monolingual in Dutch, in Kinderhook (Dutch *Kinderhoek*) in New York State; and there were still a few Dutch speakers left in 1910.

Jamestown

The very first location in which any sizeable group of native speakers of English became successfully established outside the British Isles was the Jamestown settlement, in what was also to become the United States of America. It was founded on 14 May 1607, as a private venture by the London Company under Captain John Smith, with a charter granted by King James I of England. Astonishingly enough, the Company's main goals were not only to find and extract gold and silver to carry

---

[1] In 1707, England (plus Wales) and Scotland, hitherto separate countries, became the United Kingdom of Great Britain; and the English and Scottish parliaments were replaced by a single Parliament of Great Britain.

back to England but also to locate a river route to the Pacific Ocean to facilitate trading with the Far East: it seems as if the people involved had little idea of how wide the North American continent actually was.

This westward journey of the English language to Jamestown was much longer and more arduous than any of the previous sea crossings which the language had made from continental Europe to Britain, or subsequently from England to Ireland: the distance from London to Jamestown is about 3,200 nautical miles (6,000 kilometres). The Company's three ships sailed out of London towards the end of December 1606 and after a four-month-long voyage landed with more than a hundred anglophone settlers in the Americas, on 26 April 1607, not finally determining the site for their settlement until two and a half weeks later.

The Jamestown colony very nearly failed. In the August of 1607, very many of the Jamestown colonists died from dysentery and other diseases; and then in the autumn of 1609 the indigenous American people began a campaign to starve the English out of the settlement. They stopped bartering with them for food and attacked any men who went out hunting. The coming winter came to be known as the 'Starving Time'; and by the time the spring of 1610 arrived, large numbers of the colonists had perished. A decision was in fact then taken to abandon the colony, but fortuitously further ships suddenly arrived from England bringing many more colonists and supplies and, in the end, the colony did survive. A temporary peace was also achieved with the Native Americans.

A young Native American Virginia Algonquian girl called Matoaka, aged about eleven, spent quite a lot of time in the English colony and is known to have played with the children. She had also begun to learn English and eventually became an important emissary and interpreter between the two communities. In 1613, when she was about sixteen, during hostilities between the two groups she was kidnapped and held as a hostage by the settlers. She was converted to Christianity and married a settler, John Rolfe, in 1614. Matoaka, who was also known as Pocahontas, then gave birth to a son, Thomas Rolfe, in early 1615. Later that year, the couple and the baby made a trip to London, staying for a while also in Heacham, Norfolk, Rolfe's family home.

They set out to sail back to Virginia in the spring of 1617, but tragically Matoaka died when they had sailed only as far from London as Gravesend. Thomas returned to Virginia as an adult in about 1635 and remained there for the rest of his life, seemingly maintaining some kind of relationship with his mother's Virginia Algonquian people. Presumably, however, there was no way in which he could have retained any of her native language.

This (ultimately) successful English colonisation in Virginia had been preceded by a number of failed attempts elsewhere, notably the well-known unsuccessful colonisation twenty years previously of Roanoke Island (now in North Carolina), which had been organised by Sir Walter Raleigh in the 1580s. In 1587, the governor of the Roanoke colony had returned to England seeking various forms of assistance, leaving 117 colonists behind. Delayed by a number of factors, including the Spanish Armada of 1588, he was not able to return to America until 1590, when he found that the colony had been abandoned.

It is not known what happened to the colonists, but one theory is that they may have become assimilated with a group of local Native Americans. Certainly, there were many cases of individual Europeans who did become assimilated into indigenous communities, to different degrees. Sometimes this was part of a deliberate policy to produce interpreters: at the age of fourteen, Thomas Savage was sent from Jamestown to live amongst the Virginia Algonquians, and within a year he was instrumental in negotiating the peace between them and the English. Another English boy, Samuel Collier, was sent to join him, but he then ran away to go and live with another tribe on the Potomac river, staying with them for more than a year.

The Dispossessed

The first linguistic casualties of the expansion of English out of the British Isles were the languages of North America. In what are now Canada and the USA (including mainland Alaska and the Aleutian Islands), there were about 300 languages at the time of first European contact. Now, well over 100 of these languages have disappeared and, according to Professor Marianne Mithun, another quarter, about 75, "are remembered by only a small number of elderly speakers".[2] Only Navaho today has as many as 100,000 speakers, in the south-west of the USA. According to Professor Mithun, nearly all of the remaining 100 or so North American languages are likely to be gone by the end of the twenty-first century. If this miserable scenario is correct – and there is no reason to suppose that it is not – then, from the time of the first anglophone settlement in Jamestown it will have taken a mere 500 years for English to have killed off (nearly) all the indigenous languages of Canada and the USA.[3]

Jamestown was located near modern Williamsburg, in what is now Virginia, in an area inhabited by Native American tribes of the Powhatan Confederacy who spoke an Eastern Algonquian language now known to linguists as Virginia Algonquian. Eastern Algonquian languages were originally spoken along much of the east coast of North America, including as far south as what is now coastal North Carolina.

The Virginia Algonquian language itself, which had perhaps 20,000 speakers, was spoken in Tidewater Virginia along the lower courses of the James River and other nearby rivers to the north which drain into the lower Chesapeake Bay on the west. Like many Eastern Algonquian languages, Virginia Algonquian eventually

---

[2] Mithun (1999: 2).   [3] French and Spanish have of course also been involved.

died out when the community, under various different pressures, shifted to speaking English.

In the early years of the Jamestown settlement, the English settlers were very dependent on the Virginia Algonquian-speaking people for food; and they appear to have learnt quite a lot of words from the language, unsurprisingly including words for potential foodstuffs such as *hominy* 'ground maize kernels' from Virginia Algonquian *uskatahomen, persimmon* (from *pushemins*), *opossum* (from *opassom*), *raccoon* (< *rarowcun*) and *terrapin* (< *torup*). Some reports suggest that more words have been borrowed into English from Virginia Algonquian than from any other Native American language: other words include *hickory* (< *pawcohiccora*, which actually meant the 'milk' made from hickory nuts), *moccasin* (< *mockasins*) and *tomahawk* (< *tamahaac*).

LANGUAGE NOTES

Algonquian languages are polysynthetic: words typically have a complex internal structure. The Virginia Algonquian noun *uskatahomen*, from which *hominy* is derived, is pronounced /askəhte:hamən/ and is made up as follows: /ask-/ 'raw, uncooked' + /-əhte:h/ 'to strike with a stick-like tool' + /-amən/ 'that (inanimate) which is', so it literally means 'that which is ground with a pestle while uncooked'.

Pidgin Languages

The word *tomahawk*, and other such words from Virginia Algonquian and other East Coast languages, did not pass into English directly but rather through pidginised versions of Algonquian languages. These had been developed by Algonquian-language speakers as they did their best to accommodate to stumbling attempts by Europeans to communicate in the indigenous languages. Some Europeans who learnt these pidgins believed that they really had become proficient in a particular local language when in fact they were very far from having done so: native people could still readily converse with each other without being understood by the incomers.

Pidgin Algonquian varieties were widely known in eastern North America, from Massachusetts in the north down to Virginia. We know of a Pidgin Massachusetts in New England, a Pidgin Mahican in New York State and a pidgin Virginia Algonquian. None of these varieties is particularly well documented, but the one we know most about is Pidgin Delaware, which was first referred to in a report from 1628.

Delaware as spoken as a native language comes in two main variants, Munsee and Unami. The homeland of the language lay to the north of the area where Virginia Algonquian was spoken, stretching from Delaware up through Pennsylvania and New Jersey to Manhattan and western Long Island. The pidgin version of the language was used in interaction with Dutch, Swedish and English speakers. Professor Ives Goddard, from the Smithsonian Institution in Washington, DC, in his paper 'The use of pidgins and jargons on the east coast of North America'[4] has described Pidgin Delaware as having a vocabulary which is almost entirely Delaware in origin – specifically from the southern variant, Unami – but with a few loanwords from Dutch. The grammar is also basically Algonquian but, as is typical of pidgins, the complex inflectional morphology of Algonquian languages has gone entirely missing.[5]

LANGUAGE NOTES

A *pidgin* is a variety of language without native speakers which arises in a language contact situation and which operates as a lingua franca. Pidgins are languages which have been derived from a source language through *pidginisation*, a process which consists of the admixture, reduction and simplification associated with imperfect adult second-language learning. *Admixture* involves the mixing of elements from one language into another. This typically happens where speakers are using a variety that is not their native tongue, and interference, such as the use of a foreign accent or the transfer of grammatical patterns from one language to another, takes place. *Reduction* refers to the process whereby large parts of a source language that are available to native speakers are lost or are not acquired by pidginising non-native speakers: source languages will have a larger vocabulary and a larger repertoire of styles, phonological units, syntactic devices and grammatical categories than pidgins. *Simplification* refers to an increase in regularity in a language variety, for example the regularisation of irregular verbs. It also refers to phenomena such as the loss of grammatical gender, the loss of case endings and an increase in transparency.

Bermuda

The second episode of successful anglophone colonisation beyond the British Isles also originally resulted from a long and difficult journey. It followed very soon after the Jamestown settlement – and because of the Jamestown settlement. It happened on the island – or rather archipelago – of Bermuda, which lies about 700 nautical miles (1,300 kilometres) east of Jamestown. It is not, as is sometimes erroneously thought, in the Caribbean but in the North Atlantic Ocean. The island was totally uninhabited at the time of the settlement, and so, for once, the arrival of the English language did not presage the death of an indigenous American language.

---

[4] Goddard (2000: 61–78).   [5] Goddard (1997: 43–98).

What happened was that the London Company of Virginia received a new royal charter in May 1609, and a fleet of nine ships with hundreds of new colonists sailed to further complement – and, as it turned out, to rescue – the original Jamestown colony, in the June of 1609. However, the fleet was caught in a hurricane en route, and many of the would-be colonists were shipwrecked on Bermuda. Most of them did eventually continue on to Jamestown but, information about Bermuda having been transmitted back to England, sixty English settlers were then sent by the newly formed Somers Islands Company to colonise the archipelago, in 1612. The name *Somers Isles* had been given to what we now call Bermuda in honour of Sir George Somers, who had been the Admiral in charge of the wrecked fleet and was thought to have done well in minimising the extent of the disaster.

African slaves began to be transported to the Bermuda colony as early as 1616, and their descendants now comprise about 60 per cent of the island's population. There are noticeable differences today between the English speech of Bermudian Blacks and Whites, the former being more Caribbean in character: it is thought that many of the slaves arrived from the West Indies rather than directly from West Africa.

The English spoken by the white population, on the other hand, is unambiguously a dialect of North American English. It can be grouped together with the dialects of the American Coastal South, especially the dialects of the Low Country of South Carolina and Georgia, though a grouping together with the dialects of the Virginia Tidewater and Piedmont areas might also be justifiable.[6] This raises the interesting question as to what the historical origins of these dialectal relationships might be; and it turns out that there was significant early emigration from Bermuda to the towns of Charleston, South Carolina and Norfolk, Virginia.

It cannot be a coincidence that these two US dialect zones are amongst the areas of the eastern seaboard of the USA which are closest to Bermuda: from Hamilton, Bermuda, to Charleston is around 770 nautical miles (1,425 kilometres), and to Richmond, Virginia, the distance is 698 nautical miles (1,290 kilometres). For Charleston, Michael Jarvis writes that "Bermuda's links with South Carolina date to the dawn of the latter's settlement" and that "Bermudians made up a large proportion of the colonies' early population". For Norfolk, Jarvis has it that Norfolk "came to rival Charleston as Bermudians' preeminent expatriate port" and "Bermudian emigrants were among Norfolk County's leading slaveholders". There were many "Bermudian Virginians" and "Bermudian Charlestonians".[7] It is likely that the English of the US Coastal South was rather more influenced by the English of Bermuda than the other way round.

Bermuda became an English Crown colony in 1684 and is today a self-governing British territory.

---

[6] Trudgill (2019).   [7] Jarvis (2010: 333).

Newfoundland

The third settlement of English-speaking people outside the British Isles occurred in 1610, in Newfoundland. Newfoundland had probably been the first place in the New World where English was ever heard, in the form of the fifteenth-century dialect of Bristol: the island was 'discovered' by an Italian known to the English as John Cabot,[8] who arrived in Newfoundland in 1497, sailing from Bristol in western England under the English flag and with at least some Bristolians on board. The Newfoundland Grand Banks fishing grounds had actually been known to Basque and Breton fishermen much earlier that that; and during the 1500s, English, French, Basque and Portuguese fishermen competed for access to the fishing grounds.

The 1610 settlement was at Cuper's Cove, now known as Cupids, on the Avalon Peninsula in south-eastern Newfoundland. It was organised by the Bristol Society of Merchant Venturers, which had been given a charter by King James I for establishing a colony on the island.[9]

The expedition sailed from Bristol with three ships and thirty-eight colonists, arriving in August 1610. This was no doubt also an arduous Atlantic crossing, but Newfoundland, which had of course already been visited by the Vikings (see Chapter 2), is much closer to Britain than Virginia or Massachusetts: the voyage from Bristol was about 1,900 nautical miles (3,500 kilometres).

This and other attempts at colonisation on Newfoundland were not well received by the English fishermen who were used to fishing there undisturbed, and their hostility led to many of the would-be permanent settlers at Cuper's Cove leaving. By 1634, the establishment of colonies in Newfoundland was also being opposed by the English Crown, and in 1699 Parliament actually prohibited settlement on the island except in connection with cod fishing. There has nevertheless probably been continuous English-speaking habitation on the island since 1610.

Newfoundland was an independent Dominion of the British Empire from 1907 and has been part of Canada only since 1949. It currently has a population of approximately 555,000. About 95 per cent of these are of a British and Irish origin, while fewer than 3 per cent are of French extraction. Most rural areas are inhabited either by people whose ancestors came as early settlers from the south-western English counties of Dorset and Devon or by people with origins in south-eastern Ireland, whose settlement dates back to the early 1700s.

The history of the anglophone settlement of Newfoundland goes a long way towards explaining the current linguistic situation. The phonology of modern

---

[8] In Italian, Giovanni Caboto.

[9] Cuper's Cove was thus the second *official* anglophone settlement in the Americas.

Newfoundland English is characterised by considerable social variation, by North American standards, and non-standard grammatical forms such as present tense -*s* for all persons (*I goes*, *they goes*) occur very frequently and high up the social scale. There is also considerable regional variation. Overall, varieties seem to be the result of a mixture of southern Irish English and south-western English varieties but in different proportions in different places. The capital, St John's, is particularly heavily Irish English–influenced.

Newfoundland is also one of the few places in North America where it can be said that conservative traditional dialects of English still survive. In communities where immigration from Dorset and Devon played an especially important role, older speakers may still have the initial fricative voicing typical of the older dialects of the south-west of England (see also Chapter 6), as in *five* /vaív/, *six* / zíks/. And a number of Irish English-origin syntactic features can be found in Irish-influenced areas, such as the signalling of habitual aspect by *do be* as in *they do be full* 'they are usually full'.

The Dispossessed

The indigenous people of Newfoundland who, as we noted in Chapter 2, may have been the first Americans ever to encounter Europeans, were the Beothuk. On geographical grounds, it would not be surprising if the Beothuk language was a member of the Algonquian language family; and there were similarities between Beothuk culture generally and those of known Algonquian-speaking groups. But we sadly do not know enough about the language to be able to tell for sure whether this was the case. Beothuk might perhaps have been an isolate – a language with no known relatives.

In any case, it is now too late to try and answer this question. Early contacts between the Beothuk and the Europeans were reportedly rather amicable, but during the 1700s conflicts developed, and the Beothuk were driven into the island's interior. They suffered from imported diseases which they had no immunity against; and, forced to dwell away from the coasts, they had no access to the marine food sources which they had formerly relied upon. By 1824, there were only fourteen Beothuk left, with the last of them, who died in 1829, taking the language with her. As with so many other languages of the east coast of the Americas, the arrival of English and other European languages brought about, in one way or another, the end of both the Beothuk and their language.

By the 1600s, groups of Algonquian-speaking Micmac (Mi'kmaq) are reported to have started crossing over from mainland Canada to the island of Newfoundland, a distance of about 9 nautical miles (17 kilometres) at its nearest point, and communities of Micmac are certainly living on the island today.

Plymouth, Massachusetts

The fourth instance of English-speaking colonisation beyond the British Isles was the well-known New England settlement of the so-called Pilgrim Fathers, in Plymouth, now near Boston. A group of Puritans had initially left England in 1608 and emigrated, first to Amsterdam and then to Leiden in the Netherlands, to escape religious persecution. Never entirely at home in an urban Dutch environment, however, and still not feeling entirely safe from British harassment, a group of them decided to sail for North America, and in July 1620 they set off from the port of Delfshaven in Rotterdam on the *Speedwell*. By arrangement, at about the same time another ship called the *Mayflower* set sail from the Thames, having been fitted out at Leigh-on-Sea in Essex, and the two vessels met up in Southampton Water off the English south coast and embarked on their ocean crossing together. Once out in the Atlantic, however, the *Speedwell* started leaking, and both ships had to return to England. Some of the *Speedwell* Puritans boarded the *Mayflower*, while others went back to the Netherlands. The *Mayflower* then finally sailed off on its own – from Plymouth, Devon, hence the name of the new colony – with 102 colonists on board, including 35 Puritans. They finally landed in North America in November 1620 (Map 7.1).

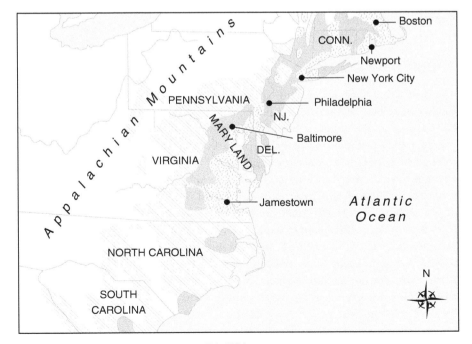

Map 7.1 USA east coast

The Dispossessed

The indigenous language of the area around the Plymouth colony was another Eastern Algonquian variety, Massachusett, which like so many others tragically became extinct, reportedly in the late 1800s. Massachusett speakers developed literacy in their native language during the seventeenth century, and more than 150 documents survive from the period 1660–1760. Words borrowed from Massachusett into English include *squash* 'vegetable marrow' from Massachusett *asquutasquash* 'uncooked'; *powwow* 'meeting, discussion' from *pauwau* 'American Indian priest'; and *squaw* from *ussqua* 'young woman'.

The English language, remarkably, had actually arrived in New England before the Pilgrim Fathers. In March 1621, a man walked out of the woods into the Plymouth colony and, having introduced himself as Samoset, asked the colonists for beer – in English. He had learnt the language by associating with fishermen and traders who for some years had been frequenting the coast of what is now Maine.

Another Algonquian English speaker, Tisquantum, became very important to the colonists as an intermediary and, crucially, interpreter. He came to be known to the Englishmen as Squanto; and he told a remarkable story. He had learnt English in London, which he had somehow escaped to from slavery in Spain. He had originally been snatched from the American shore in 1614 by an English sea-captain to be sold as a slave. Extraordinarily, he had then made his way back from London to Massachusetts. Sadly, he died only eighteen months after first making contact with the Plymouth colony.

North American English

The distinctive varieties of North American English which we are familiar with today owe their characteristics to six main factors. First, English in North America has adapted to new topographical and biological features unknown in Britain: for example, the word *robin* in North America refers to a bird which is different from its referent in Britain. Also, since the departure of English for the Americas, linguistic changes have occurred in Britain which have not occurred in North America: for example, the glottalling of intervocalic and word-final /t/, as in *better*, *bet*, is typical of British but not of North American English. Equally, since the arrival of English from Britain, linguistic changes have taken place in the Americas which have not occurred in Britain: the voicing of intervocalic /t/ and the flapping of intervocalic /d/ and /t/, as in *ready*, *city*, are typical of North American English, including Bermudian, but not British English. Fourthly, various forms of American English have experienced types of language contact with indigenous languages, such as Virginia Algonquian, which have obviously not been experienced by British English. Fifth, American English also experienced forms of language contact with other European languages in the colonial situation which were not experienced by British English: American English has borrowed lexical items such as *cookie* 'biscuit' from Dutch and *key* 'islet' from Spanish.

Finally, and perhaps most importantly, American English was subject from the very beginning to processes associated with dialect contact. Although the geographical and social origins of the English-speaking settlers were different in each American location, none of the early anglophone settlements on the east coast of what is now the United States was settled from a single location in England. Very early on, contact between different British dialects occurred in the American settlements, and indeed onboard ships on the long voyages across the Atlantic, and this led to the appearance of new, mixed dialects, none of which was precisely identical to any dialect spoken back in the homeland. The fact of modern regional variation along the east coast of North America is thus explained not only in terms of different linguistic changes having taken place in different areas during the last 400 years but also, more crucially, through the fact that the initial dialect mixtures – and therefore the outcomes of these mixtures – were different in the different places from the very beginning.

The Caribbean

It is a remarkable but little-known fact that by 1650 there were almost twice as many English-speaking settlers in the West Indies as there were in New England: 40,000 as opposed to 23,000. Between 1640 and 1660, nearly 70 per cent of the emigrants who travelled to the Americas from England settled in the West Indies.

The fifth English settlement in the Americas occurred in the Caribbean, also in the 1620s, when English colonisers settled in Barbados, which is about 230 nautical miles (430 kilometres) from the coast of Venezuela on the South American mainland. Barbados lies about 100 miles to the south-east of St Vincent and is the easternmost of the all the West Indian islands. For that reason, it was often the first landfall for sailing vessels arriving from Europe as well as from West Africa. A voyage from England to the island was a journey of about 3,500 nautical miles (6,500 kilometres), while from the West African coast the distance was 2,400 nautical miles (4,500 kilometres).

The word *Barbados* is the masculine plural of the Spanish and Portuguese adjective *barbado* meaning 'bearded', so signifying 'the bearded ones'. Spaniards appear to have first visited Barbados in the early 1500s. Appallingly, the Spanish then carried out such very frequent slaving raids on the island during the sixteenth century that those native people who had not been carried off escaped elsewhere to avoid enslavement, and there were eventually no inhabitants left. An exploratory English expedition in 1625 considered the possibilities of settlement on this now uninhabited island, and on 17 February 1627 the ship *William and John* landed from London with eighty English people on board.

San Andrés and Providencia, Colombia

The sixth successful English-speaking settlement to be established outside the British Isles – a fact which some people may find surprising – was in what is now the South American nation of Colombia, in 1630.[10] This was on the islands of San Andrés and Providencia, which are situated in the Caribbean Sea about 100 nautical miles (180 kilometres) off the Atlantic coast of Nicaragua and Panama but 380 nautical miles (700 kilometres) north-west of the mainland of Colombia.

This geographical anomaly has to be explained in terms of the history of these islands. They had long been a matter of dispute between Spain and Britain, and they were officially decreed to be Spanish rather than British in 1786. They then became part of Colombia when that country gained independence from Spain in 1822, at which time Colombia still included the area which has since become the nation of Panama. Panama seceded from Colombia in 1903, but San Andrés and Providencia did not secede along with it, and today they remain officially attached to a country which they are as geographically distant from as London is from Hamburg.

The original 1630 settlement of the islands was carried out by English Puritans who arrived both from Barbados and directly from England, and subsequently also by planters from Jamaica together with their black slaves. And the islands remain English-speaking to this day. The colony turned out not to be so successful as the Puritan settlement in Plymouth, and the Spanish seized control of it in 1641. But then, in 1670, English buccaneers – led by the infamous Welsh pirate Henry Morgan, who later (perhaps rather surprisingly) became Deputy Governor of Jamaica – took the islands back.

These same buccaneers were also very active on the Miskito (Mosquito) Coast of Nicaragua; and as a result of their buccaneering activity, the English government established a protectorate over the Miskito Indian territory, in the Caribbean lowlands of Nicaragua and neighbouring areas of Honduras and Belize. The Mosquito Coast's principal city is today called Bluefields. The nearby Honduran Bay Islands, Roatan and Utila, were also occupied by English-speaking buccaneers, in 1642, and many of the population today are still white anglophones.[11]

The legitimacy of the English, later British, Protectorate was contested by Spain and, in accordance with the terms of the 1786 Convention of London, Britain agreed to evacuate British settlers and their slaves from the Miskito Coast. However, Honduras was only officially ceded by the British to the Spanish in 1859, and even then British Honduras, now Belize, remained British and is currently an independent (British) Commonwealth nation.

One contemporary consequence of all of these settlements which is not widely appreciated is that a great deal of the Caribbean coastline of Central America, from

---

[10] Holm (1994).   [11] Davidson (1974).

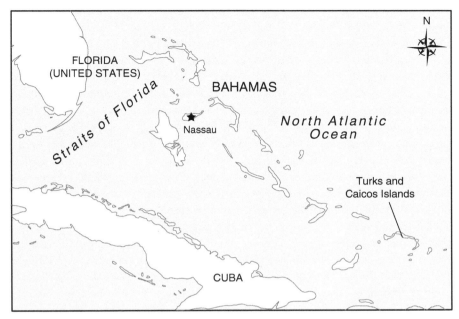

Map 7.2 Bahamas and Turks and Caicos Islands

Belize through Honduras, Nicaragua, Costa Rica and Panama,[12] right down to Colombia, is English-speaking to this day – Professor John Holm has edited a very interesting book on the English spoken natively in Central America (Map 7.2).[13]

Further Settlements

In the 1630s, English speakers also took control of the islands of Montserrat, Antigua and Barbuda in the Caribbean; and there was further anglophone settlement on the South American Caribbean coast in Surinam, which was already inhabited by indigenous populations speaking Arawakan and Cariban languages.

In 1640, the Dutch colonised the Caribbean island of Saba, but historical accounts make it clear that English was always the dominant European language there: an English-speaking clergyman was requested from the Dutch colonial authorities in 1659. Today, Saba, interestingly, remains a Dutch colony with an English-speaking population. The Dutch island colonies of St Maarten and St Eustatius also acquired English speakers.

---

[12] The anglophone communities of Costa Rica and Panama mostly arrived in the 1800s (see Chapter 8).
[13] Holm (1983).

The 1640s also saw English speakers settling in the Bahamas. The Bahamas today form an independent British Commonwealth state, consisting of about 700 islands to the south-east of Florida and the north of Cuba, with a population of about 270,000.

The English settlement initially occurred as a result of events on Bermuda, which was suffering from religious disputes. In 1647, Captain William Sayle, a former governor of Bermuda, decided to look for another island where religious dissidents could worship freely. The 'Company of Eleutherian Adventurers' was set up in London, and in 1648 Sayle left for the Bahamas with about seventy settlers (Bermudian dissidents and others from England). They had planned a plantation colony on the Bahamian island they called Eleuthera,[14] but this was largely unsuccessful, and a number of settlers, including Sayle himself, returned to Bermuda. Other Bermudian migrants continued to arrive, however, and the island of New Providence was settled from Bermuda in 1656.

The process of the linguistic anglicisation of the Americas continued throughout the seventeenth century, and by the end of the 1600s English had also become the dominant language on Anguilla, Jamaica, the Cayman Islands, the Virgin Islands and the Turks and Caicos Islands. Anguilla had been the home of Arawakan-speaking Native Americans and was colonised in 1650 by English settlers who previously been on St Kitts. There were no Arawak left by the time the English arrived, but there was a certain amount of conflict with indigenous peoples from neighbouring islands. Anguilla is today a British overseas territory or colony.

Jamaica was initially colonised by the Spanish, but in 1655 the English invaded and expelled the Spaniards. England was at that time ruled by the republican government of Oliver Cromwell, and the invasion was part of his plan to expand the number of English colonial possessions. The total number of actual settlers was rather small, but very large numbers of slaves were imported from West Africa, and their descendants today form the majority of the Jamaican population. English is the official language of the island, which became an independent nation in 1962, but the main native language is the English-based Jamaican Creole or Patwa. The linguistic repertoire of the Jamaican population comprises a whole continuum of varieties ranging from the basilectal creole, that is, the 'deepest' variant which is least like English, to acrolectal Jamaican Standard English.

LANGUAGE NOTES

A creole is a language which has undergone considerable pidginisation but where the reduction associated with pidginisation has been repaired by a process of expansion or creolisation, as a result of its having acquired a community of native

cont.

---

[14] *Eleutheria* is Greek for 'freedom'.

speakers and of being employed for an increasingly wide range of purposes. Creoles which have not undergone any decreolisation are not normally intelligible to speakers of the original source language. Some of the better-known creoles include English-based creoles such as the Sranan of Surinam, French-based creoles such as Haitian Creole and Portuguese-based creoles such as that of the Cape Verde Islands, but by no means all of them are based on European languages.

The Cayman Islands were also originally settled by the Spanish, but in 1670 the islands were ceded to England. Most of the anglophone settlers who then arrived were sailors, buccaneers and shipwrecked survivors, and there were also many African slaves. Settlers also arrived from Jamaica. The islands today constitute a self-governing British colony. About 20 per cent of the population are of European (mainly British) origin and 20 per cent of African origin, with the rest being of mixed ancestry.

The English language arrived in the Virgin Islands in 1672. The islands are today divided between two political units. The British Virgin Islands are a British colony. The American Virgin Islands were originally a Danish colony, but after a brief period of British control, the islands first reverted to Denmark and were then sold to the USA in 1917. The population of the islands is of both European and African origin, with the latter predominating.

Finally, the Turks and Caicos Islands became English-speaking in around 1678, when settlers arrived from Bermuda. The Turks and Caicos Islands today also remain a British colony.

By 1700, on the east coast of the future USA, there were now also the additional English-speaking colonies (to use the current names) of Maine, New Hampshire, Rhode Island, Connecticut, New York, New Jersey, Pennsylvania, Delaware, Maryland, North Carolina and South Carolina.

LANGUAGE NOTES: TAINO

We owe to the Taino language of the indigenous people of much of the Caribbean the word *maize*, from their word *mahiz*. Other English words which are probably of Taino origin include *barbecue*, *caiman* 'American crocodile', *canoe*, *cassava*, *cay* 'islet', *guava*, *hammock*, *hurricane*, *iguana*, *manatee*, *mangrove*, *maroon*, *potato*, *savanna* and *tobacco*.

The Dispossessed

We do not know exactly who the indigenous people of Barbados were, or which language they spoke. A good guess, however, is that they were the same people who

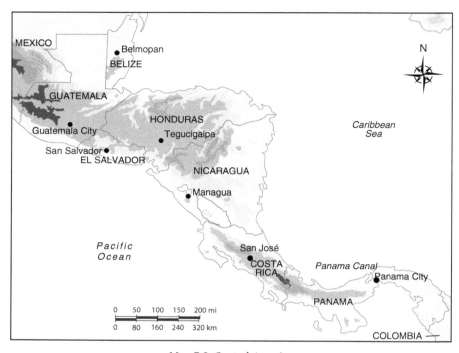

Map 7.3 Central America

inhabited the relatively nearby Windward Islands of the Lesser Antilles: Dominica, Saint Lucia, Saint Vincent, the Grenadines and Grenada – who we know more about because the indigenous populations were not so rapidly exterminated. Their language, then, would probably have been Iñeri, also known as Island Carib, a member of the Arawakan language family (Map 7.3).

In Jamaica, the Spanish were responsible for the extermination of the Arawakan-speaking Taino. The original inhabitants of the Bahamas, who were also Taino, suffered the same genocidal fate, also at the hands of the Spaniards. The Bahamas had been the location of Columbus's first landfall in the Americas, in 1492. After that, in another dreadful development, the Spanish carried off so many of the Bahamian Taino into slavery – some estimates are as high as 40,000 – that by 1520 there were only a handful left, with most of the islands then remaining uninhabited until the arrival of the English nearly 130 years later.

The Virgin Islands were also originally inhabited by Arawakan speakers, and they too were mostly killed, kidnapped or expelled by the Spanish. The Turks and Caicos Islands had originally also been inhabited by the Taino people, who died out because of the devastating effects of their contact with the Spanish.

LANGUAGE NOTES: GARÍFUNA

Before the arrival of Europeans, the Arawakan people of some of the Lesser Antilles in the Caribbean had been attacked and invaded by men from areas of the mainland of South America which are now French Guyana and Brazil. These incomers, who spoke Kalinago, a Cariban language, became the dominant group but nevertheless eventually shifted to speaking Arawakan Iñeri, probably because all or most of them were men, and their children grew up speaking the language of their mothers. Some Cariban lexical items did survive, however, as part of a special 'men's language', which was not in fact a language at all but simply a set of vocabulary items which were not used by women.

The Garífuna or Black Carib language is an Arawakan language which is spoken by approximately 190,000 people today in Belize, Guatemala, Honduras and Nicaragua. The ethnogenesis of the Garífuna (Garinagu) had occurred mainly on the islands of Saint Vincent and the Grenadines, when the indigenous people intermarried with escaped and shipwrecked slaves of African origin. However, the language was not spoken in its current location in Central America until the beginning of the nineteenth century, when the Garífuna were forcibly deported to Central America by the British. This expulsion began in 1797, though most of the arrivals occurred around 1832. The Garífuna language, then, is a variety of Iñeri derived from the Island Carib women's speech of the Lesser Antilles of 300 years ago.

The names *Carib* and *Garífuna* are both derived from the Proto-Cariban word *karípona* 'indigenous person', but the language itself is a member of the Arawakan language family, not Cariban.

It is not known if the Caribbean anglophone Colombian islands of San Andrés and Providencia had an aboriginal population or not. If there was an indigenous language, it might well have been Island Carib. There is a tradition, though, that the islands were at least visited by Miskito Indians from Central America.

The Native American Miskito language of the Caribbean coast of Honduras and Nicaragua is a member of the Misumalpan language family, and it still has perhaps 180,000 speakers in Nicaragua and Honduras. Modern Miskito has many long-standing loanwords from English, with Spanish lexical influence being very much weaker.

The Kalinago Genocide

It was Spanish speakers, as we saw, who were responsible for the disappearance of Island Carib from Barbados; but this was not true of the Caribbean islands of St Kitts and Nevis. In 1623, the English took possession of these islands, in cooperation with the French. The two islands then went back and forth between English and French ownership until 1783, since when they have constituted a British colony.

The Kalinago Genocide of 1626 was the genocidal massacre of 2,000 Kalinago Island Carib people on St Kitts by English and French colonialists. As more and more Europeans arrived, the Kalinago were understandably becoming increasingly unhappy about the growing number of English and French settlers on the island, and they were feared by the Europeans to be planning some form of action against them. In a pre-emptive move, the French and English invited the Kalinago to an ostensibly friendly gathering where they distributed alcohol. During the night, they then attacked the Kalinago village and killed 120 people in their sleep. The next day, thousands more were forced into an area now known as Bloody Point where about 2,000 of them were massacred, with piles of bodies being left behind. Any survivors were eventually expelled and removed to Dominica.

The Enslaved

The complex intertwining of the sociolinguistic factors involved in the spread of English during the seventeenth century can be vividly illustrated through the events in the Caribbean. Here, English obviously spread because of the arrival of anglophones from across the Atlantic, as well as the extermination and expulsion of indigenous populations – although much of that had happened, as we have seen, during the earlier period of Spanish colonisation. Importantly, though, language shift was also very much involved. This, however, was for the most part not a shift to English from the indigenous languages but rather from the many African languages brought by the very large numbers of slaves who the English and the other colonial powers cruelly transported across the Atlantic, and whose descendants now form a majority of the region's population. This shift led to the development and growth of English-based creoles. Some of these English-based creoles are linguistically so unlike English that to classify them as 'English' would actually be problematical. This is especially true of the creoles which are spoken by people of African origin in Surinam, including Sranan Ndjuka and Saramakkan (Map 7.4).

Sranan has more than 100,000 native speakers in coastal Surinam. The language is also known as 'Sranan Tongo', that is, 'Surinam tongue'; and it is used too as a lingua franca by those members of the population of the country who do not speak it natively. It is distinct from but has a number of resemblances to another Surinam English creole: Ndjuka. The first European settlement of Surinam was by Englishmen, as we have seen, but in 1667 it fell under Dutch control and remained a Dutch colony till independence in 1975. As a result, there has been little direct contact between speakers of these creoles and mainstream English. Sranan has

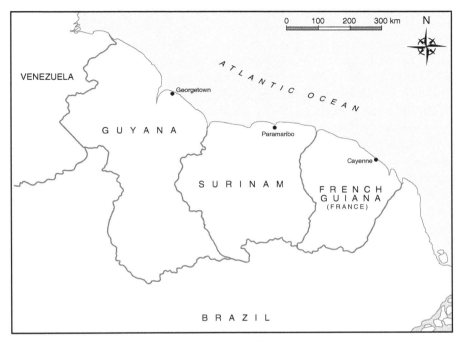

Map 7.4 Guyana and Surinam

therefore remained a 'deep' creole: because the official colonial language of the country was Dutch, Sranan has been very little influenced by English – unlike, say, Jamaican Creole. It has, however, borrowed a certain amount of lexis from Dutch.

LANGUAGE NOTES

An idea of the linguistic distance between Sranan and English can be gained from the following passage:

Lek fa Luki ben gwenti, fos sabaten a b'e krin hen kruyara, bika te a b'e go na doro, te neti hen krosi no ben mu doti. Den yonkman ben sabi now bub-bun, san ben de fu du nanga den mati, namku sens a grandinari-brad ben ori wan langa taki naga hen.

As was his custom, Luki cleaned his canoe in the early evening, for when he went out at night he did not want his clothes to be soiled. The boys knew full well what ailed their friend, especially since the elder of the church had chatted with him for a long time.

The origins of many of these words in English is clear enough: *krin* 'clean', *doti* 'dirty', *bika* 'because', *taki* 'talk', *neti* 'night', *krosi* 'clothes', *langa* 'long', *hen* 'him'.

White Anglophones in the Caribbean

There were also many places in the Caribbean where the transmission of English from one generation of native speakers to another took place in the more typical way, as is evidenced by the fact that, as is not particularly well known, the Caribbean contains a number of long-standing communities of white anglophones – as also in Roatan and Utila (see the section 'San Andrés and Providencia, Colombia') and the non-Caribbean Bahamas and Bermuda.

The linguistically important thing about these members of these communities, however, is not that they are phenotypically 'white' but that they are the direct cultural and linguistic descendants of immigrants from the British Isles and, as such, speakers of an English which, while clearly Caribbean in character, in some respects shows significant differences from the English/Creole of black West Indians, especially since residential and social segregation has been maintained in some places for hundreds of years.[15]

Of the Caribbean islands which have significant white populations today, direct white emigration to Barbados began, as we saw, in 1627; large numbers of these migrants were unemployed or otherwise impoverished people from England, many of them coming from or via London, Bristol and Southampton, who took positions as servants in these newly established colonies. Many of the English who arrived later in the 1650s were prisoners from the English Civil War or transported criminals. Irish immigration was also significant, particularly in the wake of Cromwell's 'harrying' of Ireland in the 1650s, when many of the arrivals were in fact political prisoners or prisoners of war.

The Dutch (but English-speaking) island of Saba was claimed by the Dutch in 1632 but settled by white anglophones coming from other islands, often as escapees from indentured labour, over a considerable period of time lasting until the 1830s. This isolated white community in Saba today forms about half the population of the island. Until quite recently, Montserrat had a population of whites who came originally from St Kitts: there was one community of Irish-origin Catholics and another of Scottish- and English-origin Protestants. Anguilla has a community of whites who arrived from other islands in the late 1600s. These were later reinforced by further inter-island immigrants who arrived around 1800. Some white communities also descend from people who were relocated from elsewhere in the Caribbean by government policy in the 1860s, as a response to what was perceived as the embarrassing poverty and unemployment of poor whites in a number of the original communities. One community arrived in St Vincent from Barbados, another in Bequia in the Grenadines and a third in Grenada.[16]

---

[15] Williams (2010).   [16] Holm (1994).

Summary

English in 1600 was confined entirely to the British Isles, mostly England. By 1700, it had spread as a native language to the following territories beyond the British Isles: Canada, Newfoundland,[17] USA, Bermuda, the Bahamas, the Turks and Caicos Islands, Belize, Honduras, Nicaragua, Colombia (San Andrés and Providencia), Surinam, Barbados, Montserrat, Antigua and Barbuda, Saba, St Eustatius, Jamaica, the Cayman Islands, Anguilla, the Virgin Islands and St Kitts and Nevis.

The Ingvaeonians Who Stayed Behind: The Frisians 1600–1699

As we have already noted, at its maximum mediaeval geographical extent – leaving aside the colonial North Frisian and Saterland areas – Frisian was spoken along the European coast from the region of Zeebrugge in Belgium in the south, where it bordered on Old Frankish, the ancestor (amongst other varieties) of modern Dutch, around to Bremerhaven in the north, where it met up with Old Saxon, the ancestor of modern Low German.

In the following centuries, as English expanded even to the extent of crossing the Atlantic, Frisian in its original homeland was undergoing the opposite process. It was experiencing gradual geographical contraction, squeezed in a kind of pincer movement between non-Ingvaeonian Frankish/Dutch, as this pressed westwards and northwards, and Ingvaeonian Saxon/Low German, as it moved westwards.

During the 1300s, the southern boundary of Frisian moved dramatically because of pressure from Dutch, travelling northwards for about 150 miles (250 kilometres) as far as the northern edge of North Holland. The regions where modern Dutch towns such as Rotterdam, The Hague, Amsterdam and Alkmaar are now situated had all originally been Frisian-speaking but now no longer were. The island of Texel, off the north coast of North Holland (and directly across the North Sea from Lincolnshire) initially remained Frisian-speaking, as did the other Frisian islands. However, the language then disappeared from the islands of Texel, Vlieland and Ameland; and by 1600 it had also been replaced on the mainland by Low German in the area between Bremerhaven on the River Weser and the River Ems: the area is still known as 'East Friesland' but has had no Frisian speakers for some centuries.

Across the border in the Dutch province of Groningen, the same process would eventually occur. The town of Groningen became part of the Hanseatic League in 1594 and, given that the language of the League was Saxon Low German, it is not perhaps a surprise that by 1700 Frisian had disappeared from the whole of the province of Groningen in favour of Low German/Plattdeutsch.

---

[17] Newfoundland did not become part of Canada until 1949.

FURTHER READING

Bailey, Richard. 2012. *Speaking American: a history of English in the United States*. Oxford: Oxford University Press.

Higman, Barry. 2011. *A concise history of the Caribbean*. Cambridge: Cambridge University Press.

Schneider, Edgar (ed.). 2008. *Varieties of English, vol. 2: the Americas and the Caribbean*. Berlin: Mouton de Gruyter.

Whittock, Martyn. 2019. *Mayflower lives*. London: Pegasus.

8 Onwards to the Pacific Shore

From St John's, Newfoundland, to Vancouver, British Columbia, is a distance of about 3,000 miles (5,000 kilometres). From Plymouth, Massachusetts, to San Francisco, California, is a distance of about 2,700 miles (4,300 kilometres). These are the distances which the English language covered on its westward expansion across North America, from the Atlantic Ocean to the Pacific, during the decades between 1700 and the late 1800s.

The Eighteenth Century

Canada

This westward expansion of the English language initially began with the taking over of lands, not only directly from native peoples but also from the French. The French colony of Acadie (English *Acadia*) had been founded as part of 'New France' on the territory of Eastern Algonquian–speaking Indians in 1604, three years before the Jamestown settlement. It comprised present-day New Brunswick, Nova Scotia, Prince Edward Island and parts of what is now the US state of Maine – Maine was probably originally named after the province of Maine in France.

After the war which was fought between France and Britain in North America between 1702 and 1713, 'Queen Anne's War', the Treaties of Utrecht led to the official transfer from French to British control of the Hudson Bay region of Canada, Newfoundland and Nova Scotia. New Brunswick was also officially transferred, but the French actually hung on to much of it, until they suffered another military defeat forty years later. Prince Edward Island was occupied by the British in 1758.

In the 1740s, as a counterweight to the continuing Catholic French influence in Acadia, the British founded the town of Halifax in Nova Scotia in 1749, with a population of about 4,000 mainly British Protestant settlers. During the 1750s, further English-speaking immigrants arrived in Acadia from the British Isles and New England, and French settlers, together with numbers of indigenous people, were expelled. Many of the French-speaking Acadians who were forced to leave Acadie did eventually return, but large numbers also emigrated to the French-controlled area of Louisiana around New Orleans where, under the label of *Cajuns* (from *Acadians*), they remain to this day.

Hostilities between the British and the French then flared up again in the form of the Seven Years War, which was fought worldwide between two coalitions of nations and empires, led by Britain and France respectively. It came to an end in 1763, with the British-led side emerging victorious. The longer but contemporaneous French and Indian War, which was fought in North America from 1754 to 1763 between the French and British colonies, was part of the same struggle, with the name reflecting the heavy involvement of indigenous peoples in the fighting on both sides.

The 1763 Treaty of Paris, which followed the end of these wars, finally settled most of the North American conflicts: France recognised the sovereignty of Britain over all of New France, that is, the areas of Canada formerly controlled or claimed by the French, including Acadia, Lower Canada (Quebec), Upper Canada (much of Ontario), Manitoba, Newfoundland and Labrador.

Excluded from this were the small islands of St Pierre and Miquelon, off the coast of Newfoundland, which remain a French-speaking colony of France to this day. Small communities of francophones still also remain in Newfoundland, Prince Edward Island and Nova Scotia; and about one-third of the population of New Brunswick are French-speaking (see below). Quebec, as is well known, remains officially French-speaking. And France also ceded sovereignty over the Caribbean islands of Grenada, Saint Vincent, the Grenadines and Tobago to Britain.

As a consequence of the 1763 treaty, a geographically very significant development occurred: Britain gained control of the Cape Breton Island area of Nova Scotia, which had remained in French hands until then. This meant that, for the first time, the English language had effected a complete takeover, as the dominant European language, along a very lengthy contiguous stretch of the east coast of the North American continent. There was now an English-language presence all along the coast from Newfoundland, in the north, right to Florida in the south, a distance of something like 2,800 miles (4,500 kilometres).[1]

The result of these moves was that, from then on, east of a line running south from Hudson Bay all the way to New Orleans, the English language now had little competition, except in Quebec, from any other European language. This geographical advance of English westwards from the Atlantic coast had taken 170 years and had covered an east–west distance of between 750 and 1,000 miles (1,200 and 1,600 kilometres) depending on latitude.

The English dialects spoken today in New Brunswick, Prince Edward Island and Nova Scotia differ rather considerably from one another, as well as from those of the rest of Canada on the other side of francophone Quebec.[2] This is for the most part

---

[1] Florida was subsequently returned to Spanish control in 1783 and reverted to the USA only in 1822.

[2] This is also true of the anglophone communities of the Magdalen Islands of Quebec – see Chapter 10.

due to the different patterns of settlement which occurred in the Maritimes, as English speakers moved into the previously French-dominated areas of Acadie, and then in the aftermath of the American War of Independence, also known as the American Revolutionary War, of 1775–83.

In Nova Scotia, about 35,000 American Loyalists – people opposed to American independence – arrived during and after the American War of Independence, and by 1800 refugees from New England formed about half of the population of the province. Irish people also arrived via Newfoundland or directly from Ireland. And Gaelic-speaking Scottish Highlanders settled in a number of areas of Cape Breton Island, and elsewhere in Nova Scotia, after the 1746 defeat of the Highland uprising against the Hanoverian monarchy and the infamous genocidal Highland Clearances (see Chapter 11).

More than three-quarters of the population of Prince Edward Island today are descendants of settlers from the British Isles: Highland Scots, Ulster Scots, English and southern Irish but, as in Nova Scotia, there are descendants of American Loyalists there too.

The first English-speaking settlers in New Brunswick travelled north from New England in 1762. And then, after the War of Independence, there was a much bigger influx of around 14,000 Loyalist Americans, who came mostly from the New York area. The English-speaking majority today – about two-thirds of the population, mostly in the south – thus consists largely of descendants of American Loyalists, together with the descendants of Scottish, Irish and English settlers who had arrived directly in the 1700s and 1800s. The province is today officially bilingual, and some places, notably the city of Moncton, are inhabited by people who are also very much bilingual themselves.

The English of younger educated speakers in some urban areas of the Maritimes today, such as Halifax, Nova Scotia, is not very radically different from the English of the rest of Canada. But in most places, especially in rural areas, Maritime English is still distinctively different, having a number of similarities to the English of Newfoundland, together with phonological features which appear to owe much to Irish English as well as to Gaelic.

The 1763 Paris treaty had also transferred Labrador from French to British control, but it was not until the late 1780s or 1790s that a small English-speaking community was established in the Lake Melville region of eastern Labrador; and settlement by English speakers did not really get under way until some forty years later. That was mostly on the south-east coast, with most arrivals coming from Newfoundland, Ireland and south-western England. The English spoken in Labrador today is typically of a Newfoundland type.

The first North American overland arrival of the English language at the Pacific Ocean occurred in 1793. A party led by a Scottish Hebridean islander from Lewis, Alexander Mackenzie, were the first people to cross Canada to the Pacific, reaching the coast of British Columbia in the July of that year. Mackenzie's book *Voyages from Montreal* relates the story of their journey. To get to the Pacific coast, they had travelled from Fort Chipewyan in northern Alberta, along the Peace River, and across the Great Divide, eventually finding the Bella Coola River which took them down to the North Bentinck Arm, an inlet of the Pacific Ocean.

Mackenzie and the cousin who travelled with him may well have spoken Gaelic as well as English, but the rest of the party consisted of indigenous people and French Canadians. When he was forced by hostile Wakashan-speaking people to turn back before reaching the open ocean, Mackenzie painted a message on a rock at Bella Coola which he wrote in English: "Alex MacKenzie from Canada, by land, 22nd July 1793." These words were later etched into the rock and can still be seen today.

The Bahamas and the Caribbean

In the Caribbean, meanwhile, the English language expanded once again onto the mainland of South America. After the earlier loss of Surinam to the Netherlands in 1667 (see Chapter 7), English planters began settling with their slaves in what is now Guyana,[3] formerly British Guyana, in the 1740s. Professor Derek Bickerton's 1975 book *Dynamics of a creole system* is a very interesting study of the Guyanese post-creole continuum.

A number of American Loyalists escaped to the Bahamas after the American War of Independence, and many of those from the American South took their slaves with them. This had the effect of doubling the white population and trebling the black population of the islands. A minority of the Bahamian population today are therefore descended from the seventeenth-century English pioneer settlers, whose arrival we noted in Chapter 7, plus American Loyalist refugees. The English of these white Bahamians thus has two main sources: the Bermudan English of the original settlers and the southern American English of the Loyalists. There was also some white immigration from the Miskito coast of Nicaragua, when this area was ceded by Britain to Spain in 1786 (see Chapter 7). Most of the population, however, are of African descent. Some black Bahamians are descended from slaves who arrived directly from West Africa, whereas others came originally from the American South or from the Caribbean. Black Bahamian English is closer to the English of the white people than varieties in the Caribbean are, but it is further from white varieties than the Black Vernacular English of the United States (see Chapter 6).

The nearby Turks and Caicos Islands are still a British colony consisting of two small groups of islands between the south-eastern end of the Bahamas and the north coast of the Dominican Republic. The population is about 14,000. As we saw in

---

[3] Official British control of Guyana dates to only 1814, however.

Chapter 7, the islands had been settled by Europeans in 1678, when Bermudans arrived and set up a salt industry. But like the Bahamas, the islands also received Loyalist refugees from the USA after the War of Independence, with some of them establishing cotton plantations employing slaves. In 1799, the Turks and Caicos were annexed by the Bahamas. After the abolition of slavery in 1843, the white plantation owners left the islands, leaving their former slaves in charge.[4] More than 90 per cent of the inhabitants are of African origin. The speech of the islands is often described as being very close to Bahamian English. In 1848, the islands were granted a separate British charter.

In the southern Caribbean, the British took over control of Grenada, St Vincent and the Grenadines from the French in 1783. And in 1797, the island of Trinidad was seized by the British from the Spanish.

LANGUAGE NOTES

A post-creole continuum is a social dialect continuum which results from language contact between a creole and its original source language, with consequent partial decreolisation of the creole. Varieties towards the 'top' of the continuum – acrolects – will have been decreolised in the direction of the source language much more than those towards the bottom – basilects – with intermediate mesolectal varieties having undergone intermediate degrees of decreolisation.

The USA

In the USA, there was the beginnings of a westward movement of British settlers into south-eastern Vermont, starting in 1724. And in the next decade, an extension of anglophone territory towards the south also got under way. The lands of the US State of Georgia had originally been colonised by the Spanish, but they later mostly withdrew, and English-speaking settlers started moving in from the Carolinas, with the British colony of Georgia, named in honour of King George II of Great Britain, being established in 1732.

In accordance with the Treaty of Paris 1763, Britain was also ceded Ohio, Indiana, Illinois, Michigan, Wisconsin and part of Minnesota, as well as the former French and Spanish territories along the northern shore of the Gulf of Mexico, now the Gulf shore of Alabama and Mississippi. Also in 1763, Spain ceded Florida to Britain in exchange for Havana, Cuba, which the British had taken during the

---

[4] The colony was placed under the control of Jamaica from 1874 till 1959 but became a separate British colony in 1962 when Jamaica became independent.

Seven Years War. In a further geographically significant development, British settlement in Tennessee began in 1772 and in Kentucky in 1774.

The Enslaved

One of the last instances of the geographical spread of the English language in the eighteenth century was a reversal of the centuries-long geographical pattern. This was for the first time a journey not westwards but eastwards back across the Atlantic Ocean.

The importation of West African slaves to the English-speaking regions of the Caribbean and North America had followed very soon on the arrival of the English language itself. The first African slaves arrived in Bermuda in 1616 and in the Virginia colony in 1619.

It is thought that around 12 million West Africans were forcibly transported across the Atlantic, to the Americas and the Caribbean, by the Spanish, Portuguese, French, English, Dutch, Danish and their successors such as the Americans and Brazilians, before the trade finally came to a halt. In 1790, the African-origin population of the USA alone was about 750,000, almost 20 per cent of the total population.

The eastward journey of the language back across the Atlantic resulted originally from a plan, which began to be implemented in 1787, to relocate some of London's 'Black Poor' to Sierra Leone on the West Coast of Africa. Many of these were Black Loyalists, American ex-slaves who had fought with the British Army during the American War of Independence. Some of them had arrived in London via Nova Scotia – where there are to this day still settlements of their descendants. Then, there was further repatriation of African Americans direct from the USA to Sierra Leone in 1792, when Freetown was founded by the Sierra Leone Company as a home for former American slaves. There was also settlement in Sierra Leone by Maroons, descendants of runaway slaves who had established free communities in the mountains of Jamaica. Many of these had also initially been transplanted to Nova Scotia.

LANGUAGE NOTES

Krio is an English-based creole language which is spoken natively in Freetown, the capital of Sierra Leone, West Africa, by about half a million people and as a lingua franca by several million second-language users in the country as a whole. People who have Krio as their native language are mostly descended from slaves who were repatriated from Jamaica and elsewhere in the Western Hemisphere, and the language bears a number of similarities to Jamaican Creole as well as to eighteenth-century African

cont.

American English. There is also a community of speakers of a variety of Krio in Equatorial Guinea, the former Spanish colony situated on the west coast of central Africa between Cameroon and Gabon, where it is known as Pichinglis, Pichi or Fernandino. It is spoken on the island of Ëtulá Ëria (formerly Fernando Po, now officially Bioko), where it was brought by Krio speakers who immigrated to the island during the nineteenth century. (The indigenous language of the island is Bube, a member of the Bantu language family.)

The Dispossessed

The years after 1700 formed the period when the process began of the killing off of indigenous North American cultures and languages on a very large scale, sometimes deliberately, sometimes through carelessness and indifference.

In Canada, the indigenous populations of Nova Scotia, Prince Edward Island and New Brunswick were, and are, Eastern Algonquian speakers. Except in western New Brunswick, these are predominantly Micmac; we have already noted that the Micmac language was also spoken in Newfoundland. Micmac is also spoken on the Gaspé peninsula of Quebec, and in Labrador, and is currently reported to have more than 10,000 speakers. Western New Brunswick, on the other hand, is the home of the Maliseet: the Maliseet-Passamaquoddy language is another Eastern Algonquian language which is spoken in New Brunswick by Maliseet and in eastern Maine by Passamaquoddy. There are fewer than 1,000 remaining native speakers.

Labrador is one of the areas of North America where indigenous languages have survived most strongly until today. In Canada as a whole, the population of indigenous people represents 5 per cent or less of the total (in the USA, it is less than 2 per cent). In Labrador, it is 22 per cent. But even here the picture is bleak. The indigenous population of Labrador consists of two main groups. The Innu speak Innu (Montagnais), a variety of the very extensive Central Algonquian language Cree, which today has about 1,500 speakers in Labrador and another 120,000 elsewhere in Canada. The culturally and linguistically very different Inuit are speakers of the Eskaleut (Eskimo-Aleut) language Inuktitut, which is today severely threatened in Labrador. There are also populations of mixed European and Inuit descent, often known as the Inuit-Métis, who have historically been Inuit-speaking. There are, that is, people of European origin in Labrador who speak Eskimo (see also Chapter 10).

In the USA, what is now the State of Vermont, and many other areas of New England, is part of the homeland of the Eastern Algonquian Abenaki people. Their language is reported to be tragically close to extinction today.

The languages of Tennessee and Kentucky are also not doing well. The local populations mostly spoke the Algonquian language Shawnee; the Iroquoian language Cherokee; Chickasaw, a Muskogean language closely related to Choctaw; and Yuchi, which may be related to Siouan. None of these languages is now spoken in Tennessee or Kentucky at all, because the peoples themselves were forcibly moved to Oklahoma (see the section "The Dispossession"). Cherokee does still have native speakers in North Carolina, but all of the languages are seriously or very seriously endangered: in 2016, Yuchi was reported to have only four native speakers left.

As far as the languages which have not already been mentioned here are concerned, one of the major indigenous languages of coastal Georgia, which was settled by English speakers in the 1730s, was the Muskogean language Creek (Muscogee), which is related to Choctaw, Apalachee and Koasati. Creek is reported today to have about 5,000 speakers in Oklahoma, where its speakers are now living as a result of the US government's Indian Removal Act (see the section "The Dispossession").

Elsewhere, the native population of the British Guyana colony were, as in Surinam, speakers of Arawakan and Carib languages. About 10 per cent of the current population of Guyana are of Amerindian origin.

The Nineteenth Century

In 1803, the Louisiana Purchase, according to which the USA 'bought' very large tracts of North American land from France, extended English-speaking control over North America an enormous distance towards the west. The area in question covered the whole of modern Iowa, Missouri, Nebraska, Kansas, Arkansas and Oklahoma; Minnesota beyond the Mississippi; large areas of North Dakota and South Dakota; those parts of Montana, Wyoming and Colorado which lay to the east of the Continental Divide;[5] the north-eastern part of New Mexico; and parts of Texas and Louisiana. In fact, of course, France did not truly 'own' or even control most of these areas, which were inhabited by Native Americans; so what the USA had purchased was the agreement of the French that, as far as they were concerned, the Americans were now free to proceed to invade those lands and dispossess the native people without any French interference, which is what they now began to do.

Indeed, it was not too long before the English language arrived overland even on the beaches of the Pacific Ocean, way beyond the territories ceded to the Americans by the French. The Lewis and Clark Expedition spent four months of the winter of

---

[5] This is the watershed in the Rocky Mountains between those waterways which drain into the Pacific and those which flow in the opposite direction.

1805/6 by the Pacific coast, on the southern bank of the mouth of the Columbia River, today the boundary between the states of Washington and Oregon.

Meriwether Lewis and William Clark were the leaders of an expedition commissioned by President Thomas Jefferson, who had read Mackenzie's *Voyages from Montreal*, and whose main objective was to do something which the Virginia Company had not even got close to doing, namely find a river route from the east right across to the Pacific coast. They were to travel across the newly acquired American territories, but then also beyond them into territories over which the Spanish, French, British and Russians also already had claims (Map 8.1). More than 200 years earlier, the English adventurer Sir Francis Drake, who was later the hero of the English campaign against the Spanish Armada in 1588, had landed in northern California in 1579 during his voyage circumnavigating the globe and had claimed it for England in the name of Queen Elizabeth I.

Lewis and Clark were greatly aided on their enormous trek by a young woman called Sacajawea, who travelled all the way with them from North Dakota to the Pacific and back. She was probably about sixteen and was a native speaker of Shoshone, a Numic language from the Uto-Aztecan language family, some of whose members are languages which are spoken as far south as El Salvador in Central America. She had grown up in a Shoshone community in the Idaho–Montana border area, but in 1800, when she was about twelve, she was kidnapped by a group of Hidatsa and held captive in their village in North Dakota. When she

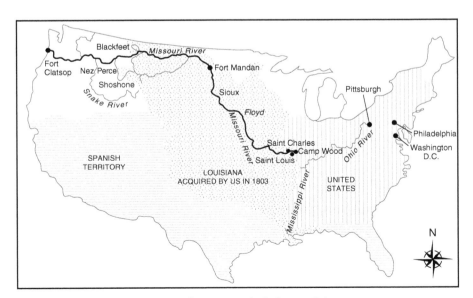

Map 8.1 The Lewis and Clark Expedition

was about thirteen, the Hidatsa then sold Sacajawea as a wife to Toussaint Charbonneau, a French Canadian trapper who was living in the village.

Having arrived on Hidatsa territory during the winter of 1804/5, Lewis and Clark hired the services of Charbonneau, not least because of the interpreting possibilities offered by Sacajawea. The language situation was complicated, but it seems to have worked. Sacajawea by that time spoke both Shoshone and Hidatsa, which is a Siouan language totally unrelated to Shoshone. Charbonneau spoke French and had also learnt some Hidatsa. One of the officers on the expedition, François Labiche, spoke French and English. So what would happen would be that Lewis and Clark would speak to Labiche in English; he would then address Charbonneau in French; Charbonneau would speak to Sacajawea in Hidatsa; and she would then speak Shoshone to the Shoshone speakers who they encountered as they travelled west. It is not absolutely certain what happened to her after the return of the expedition from the west coast in 1806, but there is some agreement that she may have rejoined the Shoshone, acted as an interpreter for them for many years and then been buried on the Wind River Reservation near Lander, Wyoming, where she is reported to have died, perhaps as late as 1884. There is certainly a monument to her memory on the Reservation today.

The first quasi-permanent anglophone settlement on the Pacific coast was founded a few years after the visit of Lewis and Clark. This was Fort Astoria, a fur-trading post belonging to the Pacific Fur Company, which was built in 1811, also on the south bank of the Columbia close to the Pacific, on the site of what is now the town of Astoria, Oregon. The Company was owned by a German called Johann Jacob Astor, who had emigrated to England as a teenager and then moved to the USA.

It had taken the English language 204 years to move from its first tenuous but ultimately successful toehold on the Atlantic coast in Jamestown to a similar toehold on the edge of the Pacific; but its arrival there had been greatly assisted by native speakers of Shoshone, French and German.

At the same time, English was also pressing westwards in Canada: the Anglo-Scottish philanthropist Lord Thomas Douglas founded the first English-speaking farming community in the Red River Colony, Manitoba, in 1812. The first British settlement on the west coast of Canada, however, did not come about until 1843, when Fort Victoria, later the city of Victoria, was founded on Vancouver Island.

LANGUAGE NOTES: MICHIF

From about 1820, there were, mainly in Manitoba and Saskatchewan, groups of Métis who spoke a fascinating language called Michif. The Métis were mostly descended from people who had fathers who were French-speaking fur-trappers and mothers who were native speakers of indigenous languages, notably Cree. The linguistic result was

cont.

a language which is a mixture in more or less equal parts of French and Cree. There are still speakers in Manitoba and Saskatchewan, though most of them are now in North Dakota.

One of the most remarkable things about Michif is that most of its nouns are French, with French-style grammatical gender and grammatical agreement between nouns and adjectives, while its verbs – which can be highly complex – are Cree. For example, *la fam miciminêw li pci* means 'The woman is holding the child'. *La fem* is in origin French *la femme* 'the woman', with the feminine form of the definite article *la* 'the'. *Li pci* is French *le petit* 'the small (one)', with the masculine definite article *le* and the masculine form of *petit*. *Micimiêw* is Cree and means literally 'holds (s)he-him/her'. Verbs in Algonquian languages have verb suffixes which show both what the person of the subject is and the person of the object. The suffix *-êw* in *micimin-êw* marks the fact that the subject of the verb is in the third-person singular (so *he/she*) and that the object is also in the third person (*him/her*).

In the Caribbean, after many conflicts between the British and the French, the islands of Dominica and St Lucia finally passed to Britain in 1805 and 1814 respectively. A slow process of linguistic anglicisation then set in, as on all the formerly French and Spanish Caribbean islands.

Texas was part of Mexico but was subjected to what was essentially an American invasion. The area had been gradually infiltrated by large numbers of American settlers, who eventually became sufficiently numerous that, in 1836, they began a war against Mexico. They achieved 'independence' for the area, as the Republic of Texas, but this turned out to be a deplorable development for many different peoples. In the new 'Republic', unlike in Mexico, it became perfectly legitimate to keep slaves: this was a right which was guaranteed under the new Texas constitution, which also barred Native Americans from becoming citizens. The independent status of Texas was never agreed to by Mexico; and when Texas was admitted into the United States of America in 1846, this provoked the Mexican–American War or, as the Mexicans viewed it, the *Intervención estadounidense en México*. The war ended in 1848, with the Americans victorious. After the defeat, Mexico was compelled to cede not only Texas to the USA but also California, Nevada, Utah, Arizona, New Mexico and the parts of Colorado which were not already under US control.

After the acquisition of California from Mexico, the US government signed a treaty setting aside 7.5 per cent of California's land area for the indigenous Native American population, but it was never ratified because the US Senate, in a ballot which was kept secret, voted it down, with not a single senator voting in favour. In 1851, the governor of California then announced that a war of extermination would be waged against any Indians remaining to the west of the Sierra Nevada mountain range, until they became extinct. Over the rest of the nineteenth century, the state of California basically waged war on Native Americans in what is now known as the 'Californian Genocide', with many of the few survivors being forcibly turned into indentured labourers.

THE BLOODY ISLAND MASSACRE

The Bloody Island Massacre occurred on 15 May 1850 on an island in Clear Lake, California, about 65 miles (105 kilometres) to the north-west of Sacramento. A number of the indigenous Pomo, who were speakers of the Pomoan language Eastern Pomo, had been enslaved by two settlers, Andrew Kelsey and Charles Stone, who in 1847 had acquired a cattle ranch where they kept several hundred local Pomo men as slave labourers. The Pomo were starved and prevented from fishing for themselves; and Kelsey and Stone abused the Pomo women and children sexually, with any resistance being countered with whipping. After one young man was whipped and then shot in the head and killed, the Pomo men turned on Kelsey and Stone and killed them both. In retaliation for these two killings, the US Cavalry were sent in, and 200 Pomo men, women and children were slaughtered on the island, which they had tried to escape to. The Americans employed gunfire, including even heavy artillery, and bayonets. The Cavalry Captain is reported to have said afterwards that "the island became a perfect slaughtering pen".[6]

In 1846, the Oregon Treaty was signed by Britain and the USA, confirming the location of the border between the USA and Canada at its present-day location along the northern edge of Washington State. North of that border, Vancouver Island became an official British colony in 1849; and the Canadian colony of British Columbia was founded in 1858.

Then, further north still, in 1867, Alaska was sold by Russia to the USA, which it now formed a discontinuous part of, separated from the rest of the nation by western Canada. This arrival of English in Alaska represented the furthest extent of the expansion of the language northwards from its original homeland.

The Enslaved

After the outlawing of the slave trade by Britain in 1807, the Royal Navy was active in the Atlantic and Caribbean running down the slave ships of other nations, liberating the Africans and taking them to Freetown.[7]

A further instance of the eastward movement of English back across the Atlantic then occurred with the repatriation of African Americans to Liberia, beginning in 1820. Programmes of this type were often motivated by white Americans' racist

---

[6] Garsha (2015).   [7] Sierra Leone officially became a British colony in 1808.

reluctance to live alongside free Blacks and were opposed by Black American leaders. Nevertheless, the American Colonization Society of Virginia dispatched shiploads of free Black emigrants from New York to West Africa, and by 1821 the Society had acquired land from the local ruler near to Monrovia, the present-day capital of Liberia which is named after the US President James Monroe,[8] who supported the initiative. The 'colonists' suffered badly from attacks by the local people, who resented the settlements on their land, as well as from disease and malnutrition, and the mortality rate was enormous. But more settlements continued to be founded, and more land was occupied by American colonisation societies, sometimes by force. In 1838, the different settlements were combined into the Commonwealth of Liberia; and in 1847, at the direction of the Colonisation Society, independence was declared.

The descendants of the Americo-Liberian settlers remain African American English in language and culture to this day; and until 1980, although a minority demographically, they constituted the dominant group politically and economically in the country. The linguistic situation concerning English in Liberia today is rather complex, but the elite continue to speak a variety of English in which the input from African American English is still very apparent.[9]

In the 1820s, there was a similar African American settlement of former slaves in the Dominican Republic, where communities of English speakers still remain (see also Chapter 10).

About 8 per cent of the population of Costa Rica are English-speaking descendants of nineteenth-century black Jamaican immigrant workers. And there are similar communities in Panama. We will discuss these three Caribbean-area communities further in Chapter 10.

The Dispossessed

The Lewis and Clark Expedition passed through territories occupied by speakers of many different language varieties from many different language families, including Algonquian, Penutian, Numic, Siouan and Salishan.

In most of non-Maritime Canada east of the Rocky Mountains, varieties of the Eskaleut language, Inuit, were spoken in the northern zones, with Central Algonquian languages – particularly Chippewa/Ojibwa and Cree – and the Siouan languages Dakota-Lakota in the south (see Chapter 11). In the west and north-west, it was mainly Na-Dene languages which predominated (as also in neighbouring Alaska).

[8] Monroe is a Gaelic-language name, originally Bun-Rotha or Mun-Rotha, 'man from Ro', referring to the River Roe in Northern Ireland.

[9] Singler (2004, 2008).

After the Mexican War, speakers of large numbers of languages found themselves for the first time living in the USA – in Texas, California, Nevada, Utah, Arizona, New Mexico and the newly annexed parts of Colorado. Many of them were actually European-origin Spanish speakers: in modern New Mexico, there are still several communities of *Hispanos*, descended from the settlers from Spain who arrived in the area in the 1500s, 300 years before the Americans. They today speak a variety of Spanish which is distinctively different from the Spanish of Mexico.

But most of the newly annexed peoples were speakers of Native American languages. One of the principal groups of Native Americans involved were the Comanche. The Comanche were originally the same people as the Shoshone, and their language, like the Shoshone as spoken by Sacajawea, is a Numic language. The Comanche are descended from members of the Shoshone tribe who were amongst the first indigenous people to acquire horses and to learn how to ride and breed them. They also developed the ability to fight on horseback. Thus equipped, in the late 1600s they moved out of the Shoshone homelands in the northern Great Basin and onto the Great Plains. The Shoshone and the Comanche, and their Numic dialects, gradually diverged from one another and ultimately came to be regarded as separate peoples, and as distinct languages. The Comanche subsequently ranged widely across the Plains, from Saskatchewan to Mexico, and Wyoming to Kansas, and came to control a vast area of the Plains known to the Spanish settlers as the Comanchería. At the start of the Mexican War, the Comanchería, which has been referred to as the Comanche Empire,[10] covered much of Texas, Oklahoma and New Mexico – where there was considerable interaction with the Hispanos – as well as parts of Kansas and Colorado.

Languages which were members of a number of other language families were also found in the area, including Kerean languages; Kiowa-Tanoan languages; Yuman languages; Uto-Aztecan languages, including Hopi; and Zuni (a language isolate).

Alaska today has the highest proportion of Native Americans of any American State, roughly 15 per cent. The surviving indigenous languages of Alaska are members of four different language families: Eskimo-Aleut (Eskaleut), Na-Dene, Haida and Tsimshian languages.

The Dispossession

The 'Trail of Tears' is the name, derived from the Cherokee, which has been given to the forced displacements of Native American peoples by the US government. It was an appalling series of acts of ethnic cleansing which took place between 1830 and 1850, after the Indian Removal Act had been passed by the US Congress. The passage of the Act was by no means unanimous, and there was some considerable

---

[10] Hämäläinen (2008).

political opposition to it, with Davy Crockett from Tennessee being one notable opponent. Native Americans were also quite naturally extremely opposed to being removed from their ancestral lands, and there were many battles with would-be settlers. Around 60,000 Cherokee, Chickasaw, Choctaw, Muscogean Creek and Seminole people were eventually driven from their homelands, often by the US Army itself, with 25 million acres (10 million hectares) of land in North Carolina, Tennessee, Georgia, Alabama, Mississippi and Florida being subject to this ethnic cleansing. The Native Americans were forced across the Mississippi River and moved on to so-called Indian Territory, basically what is now the State of Oklahoma. Many of the Cherokee were infamously forced to walk more than 1,000 miles in atrocious conditions, with insufficient provisions and clothing, and many thousands of Indians of all groups died of disease, starvation and exposure (or were murdered by white Americans) along the way or after arrival. The survivors were then left to cope as best they could in unfamiliar terrain, much of which was already occupied by Native Americans with very different languages and cultures who were not necessarily very welcoming.

Another of the deplorable ways in which the spread of the English language was effected in North America was through the institution of the boarding school. In the USA, 'American Indian Boarding Schools' were originally established by Christian missionaries. Until the early 1900s, in a centuries-long process of cultural genocide, Native American children were forcibly taken away from their homes and communities and held in residential schools, where they were compelled to adopt Christianity and to abandon their languages and cultures, which were denigrated and ridiculed. They were punished for speaking their own native languages; forced to abandon their native clothing and hairstyles; and given English-language names which they were obliged to use. Sometimes, children from different tribal and linguistic backgrounds were deliberately mixed together in the same school to further reduce their opportunities for using their native languages. If the children were young enough, they would actually lose their native languages altogether and would be unable to communicate with their parents and families, if and when they were reunited. There were many deaths in the schools, and more recent investigations have shown that there were many cases of physical, sexual and mental abuse in these church-run institutions.

The Truth and Reconciliation Commission of Canada/*Commission de vérité et réconciliation du Canada* has also found that the former policy in that country of forcibly removing aboriginal children from their families for compulsory schooling in the Indian Residential School system can also most accurately be described as cultural genocide. The commission's report has documented widespread physical and sexual abuse at government-sponsored residential schools which indigenous children, including Inuit, were forced to attend. The schools, which operated from 1883 until as recently as 1998, were financed by the federal government but were largely run by churches and were responsible for the deaths of at least 3,000 pupils over that 100-plus-year period through neglect or mistreatment.

Summary

As a result of revolution, purchase, negotiation, violent conquest, slavery and genocide, the continental USA finally reached its modern geographical limits. English-speaking powers were now in control not only of the whole east coast of North America from Labrador to Florida but also of the whole west coast from the Arctic Ocean down to the USA–Mexico border between San Diego and Tijuana.

This expansion had taken the English language from a situation where, in 1763, it had occupied the eastern seaboard of North America but not very much more, to a situation just over 100 years later in which its territory extended right to the shores of the Pacific Ocean.

That 250 years of spread of native English speakers, following on from the Jamestown and Cuper's Cove settlements, had occurred at the expense of very many indigenous North American languages, and to a lesser extent of Spanish and French and the other languages of other European colonists.

FURTHER READING

Greenberg, Amy. 2012. *A wicked war: Polk, Clay, Lincoln, and the 1846 U.S. invasion of Mexico*.

Hinton, Alexander, Andrew Woolford & Jeff Benvenuto (eds.). 2014. *Colonial genocide in indigenous North America*. Durham, NC: Duke University Press.

Laramie, Michael. 2021. *Queen Anne's War: the second contest for North America 1702–1713*. Yardley, PA: Westholme.

9 Across the Equator: Into the Southern Hemisphere, 1800–1900

St Helena

For its first 5,000 years and more, the language which became English and its descendants remained firmly geographically anchored in the Northern Hemisphere. Like the expansion into the Western Hemisphere, the first expansion of English as a native language into the Southern Hemisphere did not take place until the seventeenth century, but in this case only in an extremely modest way. In 1659, English arrived on the small, remote island of St Helena, which lies about 15° south of the equator in the South Atlantic Ocean, about 1,100 nautical miles (2,000 kilometres) from the coast of Angola, western Africa, and 1,300 nautical miles (2,400 kilometres) from the coast of Brazil. Today, it is a British colony with a population of about 6,000.

The hitherto uninhabited island was first discovered in 1502 by the Portuguese, but the English had learnt of it before the end of the century – there is some suggestion that Sir Francis Drake sighted the island during his pioneering 1577–80 round-the-world voyage – and it became a port of call for ships travelling from Europe to Asia around the Cape of Good Hope. In 1659, the English East India Company took possession of it. As is well known, the island, which is only 10 miles by 6 miles square (16 kilometres by 10 kilometres) in area, was the place where the defeated Napoleon Bonaparte was confined from 1815 after the Battle of Waterloo until his death, aged fifty-one, in 1821. The English of St Helena is very distinctive and is best described technically as a *creoloid*.

LANGUAGE NOTES

A creoloid is a variety which has been subject to a certain amount of simplification and mixture, but where a degree of continuous native-speaker tradition has been maintained throughout. As a result of language contact, a creoloid has experienced regularisation and admixture but has not undergone the reduction associated with full pidginisation (nor therefore the expansion associated with creolisation). Such a language will in its linguistic characteristics resemble a post-creole – a creole which has undergone decreolisation – but will be different in its history: a creoloid remains at all times intelligible to speakers of its

cont.

source language; and it maintains throughout its development a community of native speakers. A good example of a creoloid is the South African language Afrikaans, which is historically a form of Dutch but has undergone a certain amount of simplification and admixture in the southern African multilingual contact situation.

Australia

There was no further movement of the English language across the equator for more than 100 years. Then, the 1780s saw another very significant English-language expansion which penetrated much further across the equator than to St Helena and in fact to about 34°S.

A certain amount of exploration of northern Australia had been carried out by Dutch, Spanish and English seafarers in the 1600s. But then, in 1770, the Englishman Captain James Cook explored and mapped the whole of the east coast, naming it 'New South Wales' and claiming it for Britain.

The southward expansion of the English language itself was then actually brought about rather soon afterwards as a result of events elsewhere. Not all the seventeenth- and eighteenth-century English-speaking arrivals on the East Coast of America had arrived of their own free will. Between 1615 and 1700, about 2,500 English convicts were transported to the American colonies; and then during the 1700s at least another 50,000 British convicts arrived, in spite of opposition from the American colonists themselves. About half of the criminals were sent to Virginia, but Maryland and Georgia also became favoured destinations.[1] Many of the convicts were transported for a fixed period but were often unable to return home after their sentences had been served because they were unable to pay for the transatlantic crossing back to Britain.

It was not just a coincidence, then, that the British New South Wales penal colony was founded during the reign of King George III in 1788, soon after the conclusion of the 1775–83 American War of Independence or American Revolutionary War (see Chapter 8). American independence had deprived the British government of the use of its American colonies as a destination for the transportation of convicted criminals; and they now therefore embarked instead on a programme of sending convicts to the faraway coast which had been charted by Captain Cook.

The 'First Fleet' of eleven convict and accompanying vessels arrived in the area of what is now Sydney from Portsmouth, England, on 20 January 1788, after a voyage of more than eight months. The sailing fleet transported 537 male convicts, 180 female convicts, 191 male guards, 19 male officers and about 100 officers' wives and children to the Australian east coast.

---

[1] Many convicts were also sent to Bermuda.

This voyage from the south coast of England to the east coast of Australia was by far the longest single journey the English language had ever undertaken during its centuries-long expansion. From London to Sydney, via the Cape of Good Hope, was a sea voyage of more than 13,000 nautical miles (24,000 kilometres). It marked the beginnings of the anglophone nation-state of Australia. But it also marked the beginning of the eventual extermination of most of the several hundred indigenous Australian languages which were spoken there at that time. The Second Fleet of prisoners arrived in 1789 and the Third Fleet in 1791. Free settlers from England then started arriving in Australia from 1793 onwards.

LANGUAGE NOTES: THE LONG JOURNEY OF IRISH

Most of the early convicts who arrived with the First Fleet had been sentenced to transportation for petty crimes by courts in southern England, but thereafter it seems that a proportion of the convicts who arrived were not native-English speakers. More than 30 per cent of convicts transported by the Second Fleet were Irish, at a time when more than half the population of Ireland were still Gaelic speakers. So Irish, too, was now making a long journey of its own.

The distinctively Australian variety of English which we are familiar with today initially emerged from the mixing together of English dialects from different parts of the British Isles, as they arrived from 1788 onwards, although it was dialects from the south-east of England which predominated in the mixture.[2]

The development of a new, unified colonial dialect out of a mixture of different metropolitan dialects is now known, in normal circumstances, to take approximately two generations.[3] We can therefore suppose that Australian English, which now has about 20 million native speakers, was first formed in the speech of those born in the period 1790–1840, and we would therefore expect to find the first adolescent speakers of this fully fledged variety from about 1855 onwards. In fact, the first complaint about 'an Australian dialect' (which they obviously found highly disagreeable) came from the New South Wales School Commission report of 1854–5, tallying very well with our hypothetical date.

Pitcairn and Norfolk Island

The end of the eighteenth century also saw another – minor but extremely intriguing – case of the spread of English into the Southern Hemisphere. This time the site of the expansion, as much as 13,000 nautical miles (24,000 kilometres) from

---

[2] Corrigan (2020).   [3] Trudgill (2004).

England, was way beyond Australia, in the remoteness of the Eastern Pacific Ocean (Map 9.1). The location was the small, extremely isolated volcanic island of Pitcairn, which is located about 1,200 nautical miles (2,200 kilometres) south-east of Tahiti and 300 nautical miles (550 kilometres) south-east of Mangareva in the Gambier Islands, French Polynesia.

As is rather well known, the modern population of Pitcairn are descended from the mutineers of the British ship HMS *Bounty*. The British Royal Navy had dispatched the *Bounty* to Tahiti to collect breadfruit plants to be transported to the Caribbean, where plantations of the fruit were planned. This was the result of a suggestion from Sir Joseph Banks, the scientist who had taken part in Captain James Cook's first great voyage of 1768–71, which visited Tahiti in 1769.

The mutiny occurred in 1789, one week before the start of the French Revolution. After a lengthy and apparently idyllic stay in Tahiti, the crew of the *Bounty*, led by the first mate Fletcher Christian, mutinied when their voyage from the Pacific back to England via the West Indies had reached Western Polynesia. The despotic Captain, William Bligh, and eighteen of his loyal crew members, were put into a small boat by the mutineers and set adrift in the South Pacific, not far from the Tongan island of Tofua. After a remarkable journey, they eventually made it to Jakarta, Indonesia, from where they were eventually able to return to England.

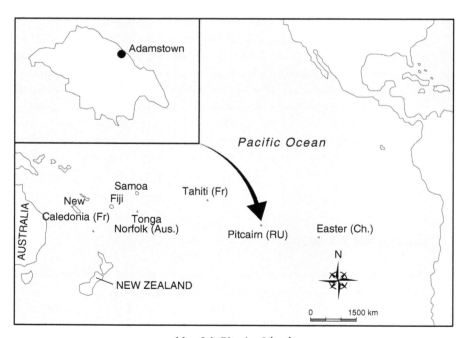

Map 9.1 Pitcairn Island

Under the captaincy of Fletcher Christian, the mutineers headed back to Tahiti, where they picked up a number of the local women, who were clearly an important part of their motivation for returning, as well as a few local men. Fearing discovery and execution at the hands of a vengeful Royal Navy, they soon headed off again towards the east. The *Bounty* with its crew of mutineers reached Pitcairn in 1790, where they had decided that they would have the best chance of remaining undiscovered and safe, not least because they knew that the location of Pitcairn was incorrectly indicated on the Royal Navy charts: Pitcairn had been 'discovered' by British navigators in 1767.

In the interests of not being visible from the sea to passing vessels, at least one of the mutineers then decided to literally burn their boat, and the *Bounty* sank. The mutineers now had no way of leaving this island, less than 2 miles square, which had no timber suitable for the construction of seagoing vessels because of deforestation resulting from former Polynesian habitation. Pitcairn seems to have been inhabited by Polynesian people for at least some centuries, from approximately AD 900 until perhaps as late as the 1400s; and it appears to have been this deforestation and general environmental degradation which had led to the collapse and departure of the original Mangarevan Polynesian population.

The community of mutineers and their families survived undiscovered on Pitcairn for eighteen years until they were found by American whalers in 1808. Extraordinarily, by the time of this discovery, John Adams was the only adult male still alive out of the original nineteen.

The Royal Navy themselves did not make contact with the islanders until 1814, twenty-five years after the setting adrift of Captain Bligh and his loyalists. It was then decided that they would take no action against Adams, who was now approaching fifty. He died in 1829, aged sixty-one, on the small island where he had lived for nearly forty years, very far indeed from his childhood home in London.

The landfall of the anglophone mutineers on Pitcairn represented the end of the longest ever journey taken by the English language to reach a location where it is still natively spoken today: Pitcairn is located around 17,000 nautical miles (31,500 kilometres) from England by sea.

Some of the descendants of the mutineers still live on Pitcairn, but most of them are now to be found a great distance away on Norfolk Island, which lies between northern New Zealand and southern New Caledonia. By 1856, conditions on Pitcairn had become very difficult because of overpopulation, and the entire population of 193 were voluntarily relocated to uninhabited Norfolk, which was granted to them in perpetuity by Queen Victoria. A number of them, however, decided to return to Pitcairn a few years later, with the present-day Pitcairners being their descendants. Of the current Norfolk Island population of about 1,700, approximately half are descended from those first Pitcairnese settlers, and many of them still bear the surnames of the mutineers Fletcher Christian, John Adams, William McCoy, Matthew Quintal and Ned Young.

A majority of the original *Bounty* arrivals on Pitcairn, including all of the women, were native speakers of Tahitian or other related Eastern Polynesian languages. The mutineers communicated with each other in English. Fletcher Christian had grown up on the Isle of Man and may also have spoken some Manx Gaelic. John Williams was from Guernsey and knew Guernsey French. William McCoy and John Mills were Scots: Mills was from Aberdeen, and McCoy was probably also a Scots rather than Gaelic speaker. Matthew Quintal was from Cornwall but probably did not speak Cornish since it had rather few speakers left by that time (see Chapter 11), and in any case he came from Padstow, which was not in the far west of the county where the language survived the longest. Isaac Martin seems to have been an American. And Ned Young was from St Kitts in the West Indies: his native language was a form of Caribbean Creole.

At the time of the arrival of the mutineers, as already noted, there was no surviving indigenous population, and so no indigenous language. The linguistic outcome of the mutiny is therefore of considerable interest. All the mutineers apart from Adams, and all the Tahitian men, had been murdered or had otherwise died by 1808, leaving behind a population of nine Polynesian women and twenty-plus children. It was amongst these children that a fascinating new English-based language developed, out of interaction between the English of the mutineers and the Tahitian of the children's mothers.

This linguistic outcome of the colonisation was a variety which was derived mainly from English but also from Oceanic Eastern Polynesian languages. The Polynesians who had joined the mutineers gradually shifted, over time, to speaking English, but it was a form of English heavily affected by having been learnt by adult native Polynesian-language speakers. The modern Pitkern-Norf'k language, as it is now called, is the intriguing outcome of the way in which that small group of children combined the resources of the Tahitian language with the English dialects which they heard around them, to shape their own community language. The endpoint was a language variety which is best described as an English-based creoloid.[4]

LANGUAGE NOTES

In 2016, the self-governing status of the Norfolk Islanders was unilaterally abolished by the Australian government, against the wishes of a majority of the islanders and also, we can assume, Queen Victoria. The islanders' case for the restoration of their independence has been taken to the United Nations, and signs have been displayed on

cont.

[4] Mühlhäusler (2020).

the island in Pitkern- Norf'k with slogans such as *Auwas hoem, auwas chois!* 'Our home, our choice' and *Du we giw up, we gwen win!* 'Don't give up, we're going to win!'. A majority of the words in modern Pitkern-Norf'k come from some form of English, but there are also many Tahitian items such as *whawhaha* 'conceited' and *ama'ula* 'clumsy', as well as words whose origin is uncertain, such as *salan* 'people' and *aklan* 'us'.

The Nineteenth Century

The beginnings of the 1800s saw the continuation of the spread of English across Australia, with further British settlements along parts of the east, south and west coasts of the continent. An English-speaking community was founded on the island of Tasmania in 1803 and became a separate colony in 1825. In 1827, another anglophone settlement was established on the south-west coast of western Australia, which then gave the British government a reason, as they saw it, to claim the whole of Australia for the British Crown. The Swan River Colony, in the area of what is now Perth, Western Australia, was founded in 1829. And the anglophone settlements of South Australia and Victoria date from the 1830s, with South Australia, which unlike the other colonies was never a penal settlement, officially becoming a colony in 1836, and Victoria in 1851. Queensland officially became a colony in 1859.

Tristan da Cunha

During the course of the nineteenth century, native anglophone settlement was also extended to a significant number of other Southern Hemisphere locations. One of the most remarkable examples of this further expansion took place in 1816, on the island of Tristan da Cunha, which is in the South Atlantic about halfway between southern Africa and South America. It is said to be the most remote permanently inhabited settlement in the world, the nearest other habitation being on St Helena, which is about 1,100 nautical miles (2,000 kilometres) away to the north (Map 9.2).

Uninhabited Tristan was first sighted in 1506 by the Portuguese explorer Tristão da Cunha. A British garrison was dispatched there in 1816 because of fears that it might be used as a base for an attempt to rescue Napoleon from his incarceration on St Helena, and the archipelago of which Tristan is part was formally annexed to Britain. It remains a British dependent territory today. When the garrison left again in 1817, as fears about a possible rescue of Napoleon abated, three soldiers asked to stay; and during the rest of the 1800s they were joined by shipwrecked sailors, a few European settlers and six women they had invited to come from St Helena. By 1886, the population was 97 and latest figures indicate a population of about 250.

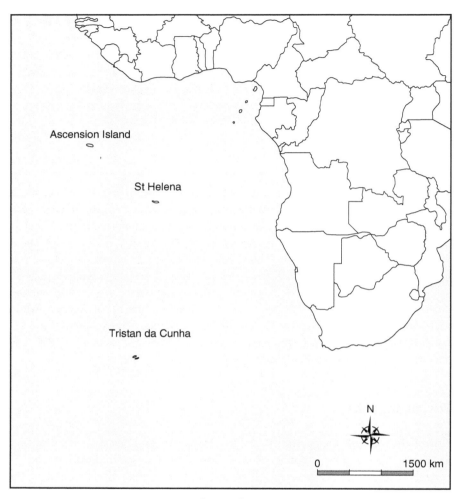

Map 9.2 St Helena and Tristan da Cunha

LANGUAGE NOTES

The variety of English spoken on Tristan is a remarkable outcome of both dialect contact and language contact.[5] It has a number of different dialect features from different parts of the British Isles and the USA, but it also has a number of features which are clearly due to language contact. It is probably, for instance, the only variety of native-speaker English to use 'double past tense marking' or 'past tense infinitive' constructions, as in *he didn't want*

cont.

[5] Zettersten (1969); Schreier and Lavarello (2003).

to went. Since this is normally a feature only of foreign learners' English, it makes sense to ascribe it to language contact. This could have been contact, in that very small community, with a small number of speakers of European languages who arrived on the island – Danish, Dutch, Italian – and/or with the creoloid variety brought by the women from St Helena.

South Africa

The second major Southern Hemisphere anglophone settlement after Australia occurred in South Africa, beginning on the Cape in 1820 just after Queen Victoria had come to the British throne, following on from an original Dutch settlement in the 1650s.[6] This was followed by anglophone settlement in Natal in 1824 – though the first major influx there took place in the period 1849–51 when between 4,000 and 5,000 British people arrived. There was also another influx, to the Transvaal, after 1867 as a result of the discovery of diamonds there.

South African English currently has about 3 million native speakers, with very many more South Africans who speak it as a second language. Like Australian English, South African English is the outcome of dialect contact: the initial English-speaking immigrants came from London, Ireland, Lancashire, Yorkshire and Scotland. According to Professor Len Lanham, South African English is derived from "at least 20 regional (geographical) dialects – out of a welter of English dialects there grew up in a remarkably short space of time a form of English which was not identical with any one of them but presented a unique set of dialectal features deriving probably from several British dialects".[7] We can suppose that South African English was formed by those born between 1820 and 1870, and we would therefore expect to find the first adolescent speakers of a new focussed colonial variety in about 1885. Professor Lanham allotted a primary role to the Eastern Cape as "the cradle of South African English", pointing out that "even Natal had, in its earliest years, a preponderance of Settler descendants from the Eastern Province".[8]

The Falkland Islands

The next settlement of English speakers in the Southern Hemisphere began in 1834, when Britain established sovereignty over a third colony in the South Atlantic Ocean, the Falkland Islands. Like St Helena and Tristan da Cunha, these islands had

---

[6] A relatively small number of English speakers had already arrived in the Western Cape from Britain in 1795.

[7] Lanham (1967: 104).   [8] Ibid.

previously been uninhabited by any indigenous population. The capital, Port Stanley, is 420 nautical miles (780 kilometres) east of the South American mainland. There are two major islands in the archipelago, East Falkland and West Falkland. At around 51°S, the Falklands mark the southernmost point of expansion of English as a native language in its centuries-long movement across the world.

Of the approximately 3,000 inhabitants of the Falklands today, roughly 80 per cent live in Port Stanley. Anglophone immigration has been almost entirely from England and Scotland, although there have been some arrivals from Ireland also. The population in 1850 was about 400, and by 1900 it had reached 2,000. As in Australia, New Zealand and South Africa, a distinctive and unified new local variety of English – which bears some resemblance to the other Southern Hemisphere Englishes – developed out of dialect mixture and appears to have been established in Stanley and parts of East Falkland by the end of the nineteenth century, making it a little older than New Zealand English. On West Falkland, which was not settled until the 1860s and where the population is very small, individual communities may still preserve various individual British Isles varieties unmixed because of immigration from a single British Isles location.

New Zealand

The third major Southern Hemisphere English-speaking settlement, after Australia and South Africa, was in New Zealand, which had started to be visited by native English speakers from Britain and Australia, many of them sealers and whalers, towards the end of the 1700s. The English language, however, did not start arriving as a significant force until 1840 onwards, when large groups of immigrants began to arrive, so a little later than on the Falklands.

The crucial period for the formation of New Zealand English was thus between 1840, when the first significant numbers of New Zealand–born anglophones were born, and 1890. We would therefore expect to find the first adolescent speakers of New Zealand English in about 1905, and indeed it was in the early 1900s that public complaints begin to be made about New Zealand English pronunciation. New Zealand English currently has about 4 million native speakers.

The Chatham Islands of New Zealand, which are about 430 nautical miles (800 kilometres) east of the mainland, represent the westernmost point of native English-speaking settlement in the world, 176°W, even if the first English speakers to arrive did so by traveling eastwards. The indigenous population were the Eastern Polynesian-speaking Moriori, who are thought to have arrived from the New Zealand mainland in around 1500.

LANGUAGE NOTES

The Englishes of Australia, South Africa, the Falkland Islands and New Zealand have a number of characteristics which distinguish them collectively from Northern Hemisphere varieties. Many British people are unable to tell an Australian from a New Zealander by their speech; and Falkland Islanders are often mistaken for Australians or South Africans. These similarities are due to the fact that all four varieties are the result of dialect mixture and because they arose out of similar mixtures of similar dialects in similar proportions occurring at similar times. A useful analogy would be that if you bake cakes from roughly the same ingredients in roughly the same proportions in roughly similar conditions for roughly the same length of time, you will get roughly similar cakes.

Palmerston

There is also another little-known native anglophone colony in the South Pacific which dates from the nineteenth century. This is Palmerston, a coral atoll in the Cook Islands, about 270 nautical miles (500 kilometres) north-west of Rarotonga, which was visited by James Cook in 1774. All the islanders are descended from one Englishman, William Masters or Marsters, a Gloucestershire ship's carpenter who arrived in July 1863. He eventually acquired three or four Cook Island wives from Penrhyn (Tongareva), who were native speakers of Tongarevan, and ultimately more than twenty children. He insisted that they should all speak English as their first language, which their descendants still do. The English that is spoken today has clearly been influenced by Tongarevan.[9]

Hawai'i

The first Europeans who are known to have landed on the Polynesian Hawai'ian islands were Captain James Cook and his crew, who landed on the island of Kaua'i in 1778. On his return to the islands later in 1778, Cook was killed in a confrontation with Hawai'ians.

Christian missionaries from the USA started arriving in the archipelago in the 1820s and were soon followed by American and European traders, whalers and colonists. Hawai'i was illegally annexed by the USA in 1898 – with the agreement of the elite American colonists, even if of no one else. In 1993, the 1883 coup was

---

[9] Hendery (2015).

officially recognised as having been illegal by the US government under President Bill Clinton, and the Congress issued an Apology Resolution.

LANGUAGE NOTES

Hawai'ian Pidgin developed out of interaction, on the multilingual sugar plantations and elsewhere, between native Hawai'ian-language speakers, English speakers and other immigrants, including speakers of Tagalog and Ilocano and other languages of the Philippines as well as Portuguese, Cantonese, Japanese and Korean. It became a valuable lingua franca and started being acquired by children born into multilingual families, thus evolving into a creole, and then spread as the language of the wider community. It is clearly an English-based creole but has considerable admixture from the other languages which contributed to its formation. Today, it has well over half a million native speakers, plus perhaps 400,000 more who speak it as a second language. In spite of the fact that it is technically a creole, it is still most usually called 'Hawai'ian Pidgin'.

The Dispossessed

As we have already noted, St Helena, Tristan da Cunha and the Falkland Islands never had indigenous populations; and Pitcairn was uninhabited at the time of the arrival of the first English speakers. No one was dispossessed on these islands. But this was not at all true of the other Southern Hemisphere settlements.

Australia had between 200 and 300 aboriginal languages at the time of the first European settlement; and the ancestors of the speakers of these languages are now thought to have arrived in Australia as much as 50,000 years before the arrival of English.[10] Today, many of the languages are already extinct and, of those that survive, some are spoken by decreasing handfuls of elderly people. A few remain vigorous: the Western Desert Language has about 5,000 speakers. But most are spoken by very small communities of speakers and are very vulnerable.

THE SKULL POCKET MASSACRE

In 1884, a number of Queensland policemen, each armed with a rifle and a revolver, surrounded a group of indigenous Yidindji who were camped in a hollow to the north of Yungaburra, in the northern part of the state. At dawn, by arrangement, one of the

cont.

---

[10] Dixon (2019).

policemen fired a shot from one side of the camp into the middle. The defenceless Yidindji then tried to escape by rushing out of the other sides of the camp, where they were shot down as they ran, an easy target. The children were slaughtered with knives. The police then moved on to the nearby Mulgrave River, where they shot and killed further groups of indigenous people, including some who had already been wounded in the earlier raid. Some years later, a whole case of skulls from Skull Pocket, as it had become known, were loaded up and taken away as specimens. Details of the massacre were revealed in 1938 by one of the participants.

For some of the Australian languages which are highly vulnerable, and even for some that are extinct, revitalisation programmes are under way in an attempt to assist communities to continue their native-speaker traditions, to develop writing systems and to encourage the acquisition of literacy. But the effects of the invasion of English-speaking peoples and their diseases, together with the displacements and massacres of indigenous people by the colonisers, and the deliberate destruction of aboriginal cultures and languages – not least through schemes which took aboriginal children away from their families and put them into residential schools where they were forbidden to speak their own languages (see also Chapter 8) – all combined to destroy many of the legacies of millennia of linguistic and cultural development in Australia.

The most dismal story of all comes from Tasmania where, after what can only be called wars between the indigenous peoples and the colonialists, the indigenous Tasmanians were either killed by disease, removed to offshore islands or hunted to their deaths in a genocidal process which was so extensive that relatively little is now known about their cultures and languages. By 1850, only forty-seven indigenous people had survived from an original population of many thousands. In her paper 'The riddle of Tasmanian languages', Professor Claire Bowern suggests that there were probably originally twelve different Tasmanian languages belonging to a number of different language families.[11] They are not known to have been related to the languages of mainland Australia.

LANGUAGE NOTES

Kriol is an Australian English–derived creole language which is spoken natively by about 10,000 aboriginal people in northern areas of Western Australia, Northern Territory and Queensland, and by even more second-language speakers. The name Bamyili Creole is

cont.

---

[11] Bowern (2012).

sometimes used to refer to certain dialects. Here is a version of the Lord's Prayer in Kriol (note that *melabat* translates as 'we/us'):

Dedi langa hebin, yu neim im brabli haibala,
en melabat nomo wandim enibodi garra yusum yu neim nogudbalawei.
Melabat wandim yu garra kaman en jidan bos langa melabat.
Melabat askim yu blanga gibit melabat daga blanga dagat tudei.
Melabat bin larramgo fri detlot pipul hubin dumbat nogudbala ting langa
*   melabat,*
en melabat askim yu blanga larramgo melabat fri du.
Melabat askim yu nomo blanga larram enijing testimbat melabat brabli
*   adbalawei.*

The indigenous languages of the whole of southern Africa were all Khoesan languages. These are a group of languages which were once spoken from Angola in the west to Swaziland in the east and the Cape in the south. They have not been shown to constitute a single genetically related language family, although they are all famously characterised by their usage of click sounds as consonants. Three independent genetic groupings are currently recognised: Northern, Central and Southern Khoesan.

Many Khoesan languages have died out, not least because their communities of speakers, some of them traditionally hunter-gatherers, have themselves died out. Others are severely endangered. Those that remain are now confined mostly to Botswana and Namibia, with some speakers in Angola and South Africa. The strongest of the surviving languages is the Central Khoisan language Nama, which is spoken mainly in Namibia, where it has official status. It has around 100,000 speakers, which is probably more than the rest of the thirty or so other surviving Khoesan languages put together. Like the Australian languages, the Khoesan languages merit the label 'indigenous' more than most. All the evidence suggests that they have been in southern Africa for very many millennia indeed. Speakers of the other group of South African pre-colonial languages, members of the Bantu language family, started arriving on what had hitherto been Khoesan territory only comparatively recently and were not fully established in the far south-east of the continent until about AD 400, at about the same time that West Germanic speakers were becoming established in eastern England. The major Bantu languages of South Africa include Zulu, Xhosa, Tswana and Sotho, which all have millions of speakers.

In New Zealand, the Eastern Polynesian language Maori had already been in place for between 400 and 800 years – nobody is entirely sure – by the time that English started arriving in the mid-nineteenth century. There were perhaps 200,000 Maori in New Zealand at that time, and many of the earliest

European colonialists became more or less fluent in Maori. Considerable numbers of Maori words are now current in and known to most speakers of New Zealand English although, with a few exceptions such as *mana* 'honour, prestige, authority, status, charisma', they are mostly employed only in connection with indigenous flora and fauna and Maori cultural practices. Recent work has also suggested that there is now a distinctively Maori form of the New Zealand English accent; but language contact between Maori and English had a much greater effect on the former than on the latter.

Today, the Maori language is one of the two official languages of New Zealand, alongside English, and has a considerable symbolic and ceremonial presence. Nevertheless, the future of the language is less than secure. Relatively few Pakeha – European-origin New Zealanders – have any fluency in the language now; and for many of the younger Maori who can speak it, it is a second language, often very influenced by English, and they do not necessarily have many opportunities to use it.

The Hawai'ian Islands had first been settled in around AD 400 by Polynesians who had travelled there across 2,000 nautical miles (3,700 kilometres) of ocean from the Marquesas Islands. After European contact, the Polynesian Hawai'ian kingdom was recognised around the world as an independent nation-state, until 1893 when in a shameful episode the monarchy was overthrown in a coup carried out by the American colonists. These people had increased steadily throughout the nineteenth century in numbers, power and the wealth generated by the sugar-based economy, all to the detriment of the indigenous Hawaiian-speaking population. Queen Lili'uokalani, the last Hawai'ian monarch, was deposed, imprisoned and forced to abdicate at gunpoint.

The diseases that the missionaries and other outsiders brought with them had already tragically reduced the Polynesian population of Hawai'i to about 50,000 in 1850, probably less than 20 per cent of what it had been at the beginning of the century. And then, the Hawai'ian language, which is closely related to Maori, itself came under attack. English was made the official language of education on the islands and, although Hawai'ian was still the majority language, children were discouraged from speaking it and, in a sad but familiar story, were punished for doing so at school.

Today, the status of Hawai'ian has very much improved, and it is now an official language of the state alongside English. There is some publication and broadcasting in Hawai'ian, and serious efforts are under way to revive the language. But there are now only about 2,000 fluent native speakers out of a total population of about 1.5 million, which is not of course totally unconnected with the fact that native Hawai'ians now constitute only about 10 per cent of the population. There are reported to be, however, several thousands of people who can use Hawai'ian as a second language. And on the westernmost and privately owned isolated island of Ni'ihau, the mostly native Hawai'ian population of rather fewer than 200 continue to use Hawaiian almost exclusively on a daily basis.

The Enslaved

By 1673, nearly half of the inhabitants of St Helena were imported slaves, initially mostly people who had been snatched from East Africa and Madagascar; thereafter from West Africa, including especially the Cape Verde Islands and the Gold Coast; and then India and Madagascar. The importation of slaves was banned in 1792, and all slaves were freed between 1826 and 1836. The current anglophone population is largely of mixed British, East Asian, South Asian and African descent.[12]

The Polynesian Moriori people of the Chatham Islands suffered worse than most as a result – to an extent, an indirect result – of the expansion of English speakers into the Southern Hemisphere. There were no natural materials on the Chathams that lent themselves readily to the construction of oceangoing vessels, and the Moriori people remained there in total isolation for several centuries after their (possibly accidental) arrival from mainland New Zealand in about 1500. During that time, their language and New Zealand Maori became significantly different from one another, though they still remained somewhat mutually intelligible. The Moriori had also developed a pacifist culture in which the only form of fighting permitted was duels between individuals which were stopped as soon as any blood was drawn.

As with the New Zealand mainland, the Chathams had started to be visited by English speakers from Britain and Australia, many of them sealers and whalers, in the late 1700s. They brought diseases with them; and large numbers of Moriori had already died from imported diseases when, in 1835, the islanders suffered a genocidal invasion by about 1,000 Maori, arriving from New Zealand in a hijacked British vessel, with guns and bent on colonisation. The Moriori maintained their tradition of pacifism, and those who were not killed by the Maori were either removed from the islands or enslaved. Moriori were even forbidden by the Maori invaders to have children with each other. In the space of three decades, the indigenous population fell by 90 per cent to a few more than 150, and the language had died out by the end of the century. Slavery was ended by the British administrators in 1870, but by then no younger people were learning Moriori.

FURTHER READING

Belich, James. 2007. *Making peoples: a history of the New Zealanders from the Polynesian settlement to the end of the nineteenth century*. Auckland: Penguin.

---

[12] Wright (2013).

Clements, Nicholas. 2014. *The black war: fear, sex and resistance in Tasmania*. Brisbane: University of Queensland Press.

Fitzsimmons, Peter. 2019. *Mutiny on the Bounty*. London: Constable.

Winchester, Simon. 2003. *Outposts: journeys to the surviving relics of the British Empire*. London: Penguin.

10 Some Turning Back: English in Retreat

Professor Hugh Brody tells us that when the French explorer Jacques Cartier first arrived on the coast of Labrador in 1534 he was

dismayed by its desolate qualities and lack of soil. He called it 'frightful and ill-shaped ... the land God gave to Cain'. The Europeans who attempted to settle there found themselves living on fish and game, and using the land more as hunters than as farmers. To this day there are the descendants of Europeans living along the North Atlantic coast, in tiny villages and 'outports', as the Newfoundlanders call them, who wear the clothes and speak the language of the Inuit.[1]

So, although the tale of English spreading around the world, killing off other languages as it goes, is a spectacular and sad story, it is not the whole story – or at least not quite. There have been a few cases, like that of the Inuit-Métis as told by Hugh Brody (see also Chapter 8), where English has first of all established a presence on the territory of a particular indigenous language, only to be replaced in the long term by that indigenous language as native anglophones have abandoned their mother tongue.

English Yields to Indigenous Languages

In the sixteenth century, in the whole of the Americas, there were several thousand languages spoken between Arctic Alaska and Greenland in the north and the southernmost languages in the world in Tierra del Fuego, in southern Chile and Argentina. Now, as we have already seen, most of the languages of North America, where they are threatened by English and French, are likely to be extinct within a hundred years. And the future is not much brighter for the languages of Central and South America, where very many of them are endangered by Spanish and Portuguese.

But, in one small area of the continent, there has been a remarkable reversal of this tragic pattern of English killing off indigenous languages. In Paraguay, English is today actually being replaced by a Native American language. The language in question is Guaraní, the main indigenous language of Paraguay which, uniquely in

---

[1] Brody (2002: 229–30).

the Americas, is spoken by most of the population and has official status in the country.

One of the most appallingly bloody wars ever fought was the War of the Triple Alliance (in Spanish *La Guerra de la Triple Alianza*, Portuguese *A Guerra da Tríplice Aliança*), also called the Paraguayan War. This tragic conflict took place in the years from 1864 to 1870, with Paraguay fighting against an alliance formed by Brazil, Argentina and Uruguay (Map 10.1). The war had absolutely catastrophic consequences for Paraguay: its forces were utterly defeated, and a Brazilian army of occupation remained in the country until 1876.

During this war, Paraguay suffered a colossal number of casualties, both military and civilian. There is a great deal of uncertainty about the figures but, according to the *Encyclopedia Britannica*, out of a total population of rather more than half a million Paraguayans, only 220,000 remained alive at the end of the hostilities, including only 28,000 adult men as compared to 106,000 women.

The presence of the English language in Paraguay came about as a result of a subsequent Paraguayan government attempt, in the aftermath of the war, to respond to this depopulation by encouraging European settlement. In one response to this invitation, a colony of English-speaking people arrived in Paraguay from

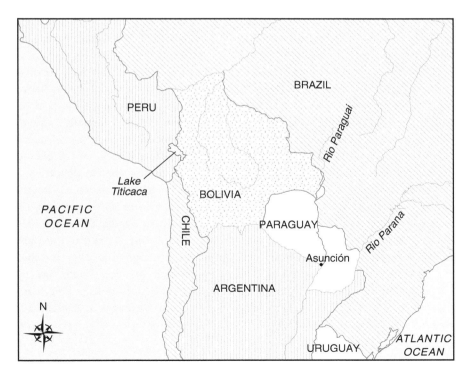

Map 10.1 Paraguay

Australia; and a utopian colony of around 400 English-speaking people was established in 1892.

The process started in Australia, during the Great Shearers' Strike in Queensland of 1891. During the strike, more than 10,000 agricultural workers downed tools and demanded the nationalisation of private property. An Englishman from Bristol, William Lane, was one of the main leaders of this strike movement. He and others wanted to establish an egalitarian society as an example for others around the world to follow, and he led a group of Australians to Paraguay in 1892 with the plan of setting up a socialist community there.

Lane himself stayed in Paraguay for only seven years and died in New Zealand in 1917, but the community he founded survived. Many of the descendants of these 'New Australia' colonisers can still be found, a century later, in and around the town of Nueva Londres (formerly Nueva Australia), where they still bear English-language surnames and remember their Australian origins and customs. But, over the decades, members of the community have gradually become assimilated into mainstream Paraguayan society, including through intermarriage, and large-scale language shift is taking place.[2]

Although there are two major official languages in Paraguay, Spanish and Guaraní, Guaraní is the majority language, as noted, and so as a consequence this is the language which the descendants of the Australian settlers are now shifting to: English is being lost as a native language, as younger members of the originally Australian community become native speakers of Guaraní. In a kind of revenge of the colonised, English is being killed off by a Native American language.

Elsewhere, there are very few examples of the retreat of English which are quite as dramatic as this case of English yielding to Guaraní; but the fate of the mediaeval colonial anglophones in Ireland was also rather dramatic. The descendants of the twelfth-century Anglo-Norman invaders of Ireland shifted gradually, and on a very large scale, from English to Gaelic during the period between the thirteenth and fifteenth centuries, to the extent that English more or less died out completely, except for the south-eastern area of Forth and Bargy, as described in Chapter 6.

During the Black Death, which arrived in Ireland in 1348, many of the Anglo-Normans retreated to the Pale, the fortified zone centred on Dublin, taking the English language with them. Those who did not retreat gradually adopted the Gaelic language and Gaelic culture of the island and, during the rest of the 1300s and after, began to intermarry with the Irish people on a large scale. They and their children ultimately became Gaels. The Anglo-Norman aristocrats who became Gaelicised in this way were subsequently known as the 'Old English'; and in any conflicts which occurred they generally sided with the Irish against England and never converted to Protestantism.

---

[2] Perez-Inofuentes (2015).

The English authorities in London and Dublin became so disturbed by this Gaelicisation process that they passed a law known as the Statutes of Kilkenny, aimed at people of English origin, which made it illegal for them to speak Irish Gaelic, intermarry with the Irish or wear Gaelic-style clothing. The Statutes, however, had no real effect, not least because the power of Dublin and the English Crown in Ireland continued to weaken during the 1400s. By 1500, Ireland was in many respects, and in very many areas, more or less self-governing; and the English language had disappeared from nearly all of the island. Having obtained a good foothold in Ireland, the English language survived for a few centuries but then all but died out again.

Demography versus Prestige

This pattern of a ruling class of colonisers succumbing to the language of the lower-class colonised is one which has been repeated many times, if only rarely in the case of English. In spite of the power and prestige attached, in England after 1066, to the same conquering Norman ruling class who invaded Ireland in the following century, their Anglo-Norman language was dead and gone as a spoken language in Britain 300 years later. Their Anglo-Norman French had been rather different from the French of Paris. We still have traces of it in modern England: the phrase *Le Roy le veult* 'the King desires it' continues to be used at Westminster to show that His Majesty has assented to parliamentary bills. And we still use occasional French-style noun-adjective phrases like *heir apparent* and *court martial*. Although the Normans were the ones in charge, there were very many more English speakers than French. When it comes to competition between languages, demography usually wins out over prestige, and so in the end it was the English language which prevailed.

When, moreover, the Normans in England abandoned their native French for English, they were doing something which they had already done once before. They had originally been Northmen, Scandinavian Vikings who had arrived in northern France speaking Old Danish. But only a few generations after taking control of Normandy, they shifted to French, the language of the majority of the population.

Similarly, during the Germanic diaspora, the Visigothic people who we discussed in Chapter 2 invaded Iberia in the early AD 400s, bringing their East Germanic language with them. They took control of most of Spain and Portugal, as well as of parts of south-western France; and they founded a kingdom there which lasted until the early AD 700s, when it succumbed to the Moorish invasion from North Africa. But, well before that, many of the Visigoths had succumbed linguistically to the power of numbers and abandoned their language in favour of the varieties of Late Spoken Latin which later became Catalan, Spanish and Portuguese.

Some of the West Germanic–speaking Franks, who we have noted above as being in conflict with the Frisians, underwent the same fate. Originally inhabiting the east bank of the Rhine, they started expanding west across the river in the fifth century and gradually took control of the Rhineland, the Low Countries and northern France – which bears that name because it was the kingdom of the Franks. In those regions where the ruling Franks remained a demographic minority – the areas which are now France and southern Belgium – they eventually switched from speaking Germanic Franconian to the Latin-derived language of the Romano-Celtic population, which later became Old French. Some of the linguistic characteristics which distinguish French from the Romance varieties of southern France are thought by some scholars to be due precisely to this Frankish influence in the north.

The tendency is for human beings to speak like the people around them who they have most contact with, not like the rich and the powerful; and it is rather normal for powerful alien elites to end up speaking the language of the indigenous common people.

English Yields to Major Languages

There are also today a number of places in the world where English as a native language is under the threat of extinction, not in the face of relatively small indigenous languages such as Irish Gaelic and Guaraní but because of major world languages like Japanese, Spanish, Portuguese and French.

Japanese

One very striking example of English as a native language under threat concerns the almost certainly least-known anglophone community in the world. These are the inhabitants of the Bonin Islands (Japanese *Ogasawara-gunto*) which lie in the northern Pacific Ocean, about 520 nautical miles (960 kilometres) to the south-east of Japan and rather further than that to the north of the Northern Marianas Islands of Micronesia (Map 10.2).[3]

These originally uninhabited islands were discovered by the Spanish navigator Ruy López de Villalobos in 1543. They were nominally claimed by the USA in 1823 and by Britain in 1825. But the spread of native English into the Northern Pacific started occurring in 1830 when the Bonin island of Chichijima (or Peel Island) was first settled, totally unofficially, by fifteen people: five seamen – two Americans,

---

[3] One of the islands of the Bonin Islands chain is Iwo Jima, famous as the site of one of the crucial battles of World War II.

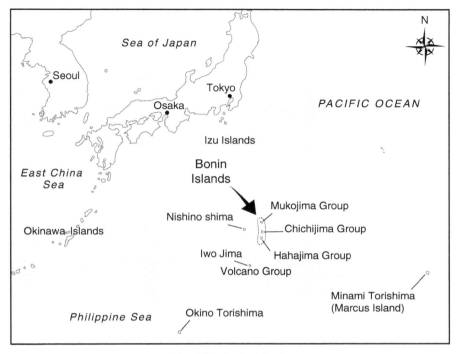

Map 10.2 Bonin Islands

one Englishman, one Dane and one Italian; and ten Hawaiians, five men and five women. They had to communicate in English because it was the only language which all of them could manage even if, in some cases, not very well. This community was later gradually joined by whalers, shipwrecked sailors and drifters of many different origins, leading to the development of a unique blended form of English.

The settlers lived far beyond the control of any national government for a couple of generations, until the islands were claimed by Japan in the 1870s. Within a few years of this claim, the original settlers and their children and grandchildren, who never numbered more than about 100 in total, were outnumbered by incoming Japanese settlers. But the 'Westerners', as these English-speaking people of mixed European and Pacific Island descent came to be called, continued to retain a sense of their own unique identity, which lasted even throughout World War II and until the present day. There are today two main centres of habitation, the principal one on Chichijima, the original settlement on the main island of Ogasawara, with a much smaller one on the island of Hahajima, about 26 nautical miles (48 kilometres) to the south. The current population of the islands is about 2,000.

The language history of the Bonins is complex. Austronesian languages which were brought to the islands after 1830 included languages from the Philippines and Bougainville, together with Malagasy, Rotuman, the Polynesian languages Hawaiian, Tahitian and North Marquesan, and the Micronesian languages Carolinian, Kiribati, Ponapean and Chamorro. There were also speakers of varieties of Chinese. And some of the most influential men on the island were native speakers of the European languages English, Portuguese, German, Italian, French and Danish. But, from the very beginning, as we have seen, English was used as the lingua franca in the settlement, and it became the first language of all the children born on the island.

The form of English spoken on the Bonins is remarkable not only linguistically but also in terms of its research history. It was totally unknown to the international community of English linguistics scholars until it was discovered in the 1990s – and 'discovered' is an entirely appropriate word here – by Daniel Long. Professor Long is an American linguist who teaches Japanese dialectology in Japan. He was alerted to the possible presence of an anglophone community on the Bonins by a Japanese television documentary. This showed an interview, in fluent native Japanese, with an elderly man on the Bonins who looked to be of European origin and whose name was the very un-Japanese Abel Savory. This led Long to investigate the history of the islands and then to take the 28-hour boat trip from Tokyo to Chichijima, where he encountered Mr Savory in the street, spoke to him in English and got a reply from him in English. The rest is linguistics history: more or less everything we know about Bonin Islands English is due to Long and his pioneering work.

Long has shown that contact between the three original English speakers and speakers of the other European and Pacific Island languages led to the development of an English-based creoloid (see Chapter 9), which became the basilectal variety in the community. At the same time, Mainstream English, as spoken by the Americans and the Englishman, continued to be spoken natively, and a dialect continuum developed between the acrolectal Mainstream Bonin English and the basilectal Bonin English Creoloid.

As late as the 1950s, there were Bonin Island Westerners who were English monolinguals: Mr George Webb (1870–1951) was more or less incapable of speaking Japanese in spite of the fact that he had lived on Japanese territory through the late 1930s, when the use of English was the object of increasing suspicion and oppression on the part of the Japanese authorities.

During the course of the twentieth century, however, Mainstream Bonin English and Bonin English Creoloid both became progressively weaker in terms of proportions of speakers and of speakers' linguistic abilities. The mainstream variety did receive a boost from 1945 when, following the defeat of Japan in World War II, the islands were administered by the US Navy, who allowed only the Westerners to remain. The presence of American military personnel, and the provision of exclusively English-medium education, greatly strengthened the position of English. In

1968, however, the islands were returned to Japanese authority by the USA, and ethnically Japanese settlers from the pre-war era were allowed to return, along with their mainland-born offspring. Together with new settlers from the mainland, they now once again became the majority.

Our best source of information about Bonin Islands English comes from recordings which were made in 1971 by Dr Mary Shepardson (1906–97), an American anthropologist. She interviewed many of the Westerners, but the longest of the interviews was with Charles Washington (1881–1972), known as Uncle Charlie. He was born in 1881 and had Japanese nationality. He was educated on the Bonins at Japanese government schools which at that time were bilingual, teaching in both English and Japanese.

At the age of seventeen, Charlie left Ogasawara on a whaling ship and during the next forty years he participated in ten or so voyages of about a year each, whaling and sealing. At home with his children, Charlie only ever spoke Japanese, but he spoke English with other islanders, especially when they were employing it as an in-group language in the presence of Japanese people.

The phonology of Mainstream Bonin English shows rather clearly that its original source was the English of the area of Boston, Massachusetts, which was where one of the original settlers, Nathaniel Savory, Charlie's grandfather, came from.[4]

Spanish

During the late nineteenth century, there was large-scale expansion of native-speaking anglophones out of some of the Caribbean islands, notably Jamaica, across to eastern coastal areas of Costa Rica, focussing on Limón. They arrived in order to work on the construction of a railway to transport coffee from the interior highlands of Costa Rica to the coast. The first ship with migrants from Jamaica arrived in Limón, Costa Rica, in 1872. The number of Jamaican workers in Limón increased rapidly, and by 1873 there were already more than 1,000 Jamaican workers in the port. They had little contact with the Spanish-speaking centre and Pacific coast of the country and had their own English-medium schools with teachers from Jamaica.

Today, there is an unusual situation in the country in which the mother-tongue English which is very widely spoken in eastern Costa Rica generally has lower social status than Spanish, the official language. Spanish is spoken natively in Costa Rica by people who are mostly of European origin. The anglophones, on the other hand, are people of African origin who have in the past experienced considerable

---

[4] See Trudgill (2010).

racial discrimination. Until 1949, they were by law actually not allowed to travel any further inland from the coast than a certain fixed point in the highlands.

Younger English speakers are now all bilingual in Spanish and English – necessarily so, because they are required to speak Spanish in school – and recent reports suggest that English is giving way to Spanish to a certain extent, as is also happening on the anglophone Colombian islands and coastal areas of Nicaragua (see Chapter 7). However, it seems to have become clear to many anglophone Afro-Costa Rican families on the Caribbean coast that it is an advantage today, especially in tourist areas, to be bilingual in Spanish and English. Together with the distinctive culture the community has maintained,[5] this may well help English to survive as a native language.

A similar situation obtains in Panama, where English is spoken natively by minorities in three different regions. The first is Bocas del Toro, where an anglophone community was founded by people who had left the Colombian island of San Andrés in 1827. The other two areas are in the largest cities, Panama City and Colón, where anglophones of Jamaican origin have been in residence since the mid-1800s: as in Costa Rica, people from the Caribbean immigrated to Panama to assist in the building of the Panama Railway and then the Panama Canal. Anglophones make up about 14 per cent of the total population of Panama, but younger speakers are all bilingual, and a shift to Spanish is taking place.

The Dominican Republic is basically monolingual Spanish-speaking, but several regions of the country were settled in the 1820s by some 6,000 American ex-slaves, who immigrated there through arrangements between the Haitian rulers of Santo Domingo and American church and philanthropic agencies. One such settlement is situated on the peninsula of Samaná. The anglophones there refer to themselves as 'Americans' and still speak English natively, some of them to the apparent total exclusion of Spanish even in the third and fourth generations. Most of them cite Philadelphia, New York and New Jersey as the places of origin of their forbears. Linguistic research has been carried out here which is of considerable historical importance for an understanding of the origins of African American Vernacular English.[6] However, there is now considerable pressure on the community to shift to Spanish, and in the long run English may well not survive.

Portuguese

At the end of the American Civil War, in 1865, thousands of Americans from the defeated South left the USA. Some went to Mexico and the West Indies, and some even made it as far as Japan and Egypt, but the largest number of those who departed, perhaps as many as 40,000 of them, went to Brazil, where they founded

---

[5] Just one example: they play cricket.   [6] Jones and Tagliamonte (2004).

a number of settlements. The best known of these is called Americana and is located about 90 miles (150 kilometres) north-west of São Paulo. Today, it has about 200,000 inhabitants.

The language of the community was for many decades a Southern variety of American English, and older people continued to speak a conservative form of English with its roots in, particularly, Georgia and Alabama.[7] This conservative Southern US English is of considerable interest for the reconstruction of the history of English in the southern USA. Gradually, however, the community has become bilingual in English and Portuguese, and most younger people are as comfortable in Portuguese as in English, if not more so. It is rather clear that, if it has not already done so, English will give way to Portuguese soon.

French

A number of the small anglophone communities in the predominantly French-speaking Canadian Province of Quebec are also under threat from a lack of institutional support and consequent language shift.[8] Not the least of these is found in the Magdalen Islands (Map 10.3). These are an island chain located between Prince Edward Island and Newfoundland, about 130 nautical miles (240 kilometres) from the mainland of Quebec. Of the 13,000 inhabitants, about 600 live in two small anglophone communities located at either end of the chain, at Old Harry and Grosse-Ile in the north-west and Entry Island in the south-west. Unsurprisingly, in view of their location, the variety of English spoken in these communities resembles that of Newfoundland, Cape Breton Island, Nova Scotia and Prince Edward Island.

LANGUAGE NOTES

One notable feature of rural Atlantic Canadian English is, unusually in a worldwide anglophone context, the pronunciation of word-final /t/ as a released, aspirated stop, often including the slit-fricative variant associated with Irish English varieties.[9] This is true of the English of Newfoundland, Cape Breton Island, Nova Scotia, Prince Edward Island and the anglophone Magdalen Islands of Quebec. It is presumably not a coincidence that varieties in the British Isles where this is usual are those of Ireland and the Scottish Highlands, as well as of Liverpool, England, which experienced heavy Irish immigration.

---

[7] As described by Montgomery and Melo (1995).   [8] Warren and Oakes (2011).
[9] See Wells (1982); Pandeli et al. (1997).

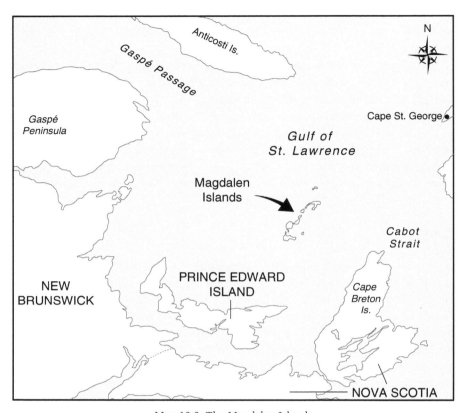

Map 10.3 The Magdalen Islands

FURTHER READING

Brody, Hugh. 2002. *The other side of Eden: hunter-gatherers, farmers and the shaping of the world*. London: Faber.

Trudgill, Peter. 2010. *Investigations in sociohistorical linguistics: stories of colonisation and contact*. Cambridge: Cambridge University Press.

11 Meanwhile . . . Britain and the British Isles from 1600

This story of English retreating and being replaced by another language as the mother tongue of a particular area is very much not the main story of this book. We can see, if we now return to the island of Britain and study the dynamics of the situation in the original homeland of the English language, that the major continuing story from 1600 onwards is the by now very familiar one of the retreat, not of English, but of all the other languages it came into contact with.

The Retreat of Welsh

In 1600, even as English was slowly becoming established as the dominant language in several parts of the world which were very remote from the island where it had first come into being, back in Britain itself there were still several regions which were not yet at all English-speaking.

This was true even of parts of England. At the time of the compilation of the Domesday Book by the Norman conquerors in 1085–6, much of the English county of Herefordshire was still Welsh-speaking, and it was necessary for the surveyors to employ interpreters. Even five centuries later, in 1600, the Archenfield/*Ergyng* part of the county, on the west bank of the River Wye/*Afon Gwy*, continued to be Welsh-speaking, and indeed it remained predominantly Welsh-speaking until the middle of the eighteenth century. The area still has a number of Welsh-language place names today, including Bagwyllydiart, Llangarron and Pontrilas.

The Battle of Orewin Bridge took place between the armies of England and Wales, near Builth Wells in mid-Wales, in 1282. After three large English armies under Edmund Mortimer had invaded Wales, the Prince of Wales, Llywelyn ap Gruffudd, led a Welsh army towards Builth, in an attempt to defend the centre of the country. However, he was defeated and killed by the English during the battle, and something like 2,000 Welsh men were reported to have been killed.

This defeat marked the beginning of the end of Wales as an independent nation. The country came under English military and political control to varying extents and was in effect close to being a colony. However, it was King Henry VIII's Acts of Union of 1536 and 1542 which effectively united Wales with England and also definitively established the location of the Wales–England border. In doing so, the Acts sealed the status of a number of Welsh-speaking regions as officially being part of England. In addition to the Archenfield area of Herefordshire, Shropshire too now contained several Welsh-speaking regions, notably the areas around Oswestry/*Croesoswallt* and the Clun Forest/*Colunwy*. Even during the twentieth century there were many English families of long-standing residents in the Oswestry area who were Welsh-speaking; and still today Welsh has a significant presence amongst local people in and around the town, with Welsh-language signage, a Welsh bookshop and Welsh-speaking school pupils.

In Scotland, by 1600, Welsh/Cumbric had been lost from Galloway and the Scottish south-west, as well as from the Lake District and the rest of north-western England. Wales itself, on the other hand, was still more or less entirely

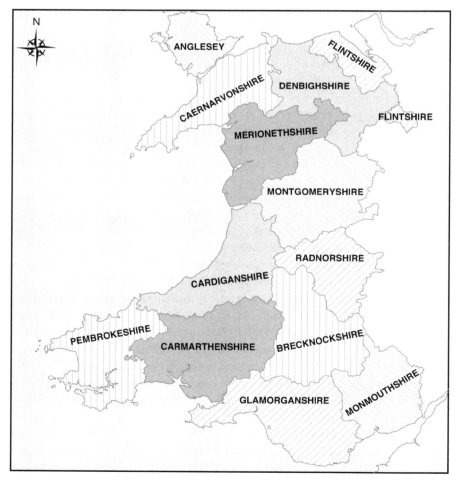

Map 11.1 Wales

Welsh-speaking, with the exception of the areas south of the Landsker Line (see Chapter 6) which had already been anglophone for several centuries.

Yet from the beginning of the seventeenth century, a slow process of language shift set in, with the English language spreading into Wales (see Map 11.1) from the east, both through demic diffusion – in-migration from England – and transcultural diffusion (language shift from Welsh to English on the part of Welsh people). This was especially true of the lower-lying areas of eastern Wales, with the valleys of the rivers Severn, Wye and Dee – which all rise in Wales but reach the sea in England – acting as particularly significant conduits. During the 1700s, Welsh mostly disappeared from the county of Radnorshire, which lay just to the west of the borders of Herefordshire and Shropshire. And by about 1750, eastern Montgomeryshire, which also bordered on Shropshire, was almost totally anglophone, as were also the far east of Flintshire, Denbighshire, Breconshire and Monmouthshire, as well as parts of the south coast of Glamorganshire.

Today, Welsh has a large and thriving community of native speakers and is particularly strong in the western areas of Wales furthest from England. There is no reason for complacency about its future, even so. West Germanic English continues to penetrate into Celtic territory in stealthier ways than in earlier centuries, notably in the form of peaceful but potentially deadly in-migration to the more attractive areas of Wales by monolingual incomers from England.

LANGUAGE NOTES: THE LONG JOURNEY OF WELSH

In order to find communities of native Welsh speakers today who are unable to speak English, one has to travel to Patagonia, to the Chubut Valley of southern Argentina, where there are some thousands of native Welsh speakers who are, however, also bilingual in Spanish. English was not the only British language to set off on a long journey around the world. Welsh is spoken in Patagonia as a result of mid-nineteenth-century immigration from Wales. The capital of the Patagonian province of Chubut is called Rawson, a name which is clearly not Spanish or Amerindian – the town is named after the Argentinian Guillermo Rawson, whose father was an American. Other Patagonian settlements have Welsh-language names like Porth Madryn (Puerto Madryn in Spanish) and Trelew, formed from the Welsh word *tre* or *tref* 'village, town' and Lewis, the name of the town's founder, Lewis Jones. The motivation for establishing a Welsh colony in South America was very much a linguistic one. The original proposal by Michael Jones, a Congregationalist minister from Bala in North Wales, was specifically to set up a colony where the Welsh language and Welsh culture could be preserved, away from the influence of English. In the end, it seems that something like 2,000 Welsh-speaking people emigrated to Chubut between 1865 and 1914. In the province today, there are three bilingual schools, and Welsh speakers now number about 5,000. Any of them who travel to Wales to take part in Eisteddfodau there are, of course, very welcome

cont.

in themselves, but they are also popular because their presence requires British Welsh speakers to refrain from switching into English, which they mostly don't speak. In twentieth-century Canada, in 1974, there were also two small Welsh colonies of mainly elderly and middle-aged Welsh speakers, in Ponoka, Alberta, and Bangor, Saskatchewan, founded in 1902. Some of these speakers were the descendants of Welsh colonists who had arrived from Chubut.

The Retreat of Cornish

The other British variety of Brittonic, Cornish, had successfully survived the incursions of the Anglo-Saxons for many centuries, but by 1600 it was in a considerably weakened position: the geographical base of Cornish had been shrinking for centuries. As we saw in Chapter 3, the Saxons had totally taken control of Devon by about AD 800, turning the River Tamar, which is today the border between Devon and Cornwall, into the Celtic-Germanic language frontier. And migration of Brittonic speakers across the English Channel to Brittany had also been going on since the Germanic invasions of Britain first began in the 400s, thus reducing the population base of Brittonic speakers on the south-western peninsula.

The River Tamar remained the linguistic frontier until perhaps the end of the 1200s, but thereafter Cornish was slowly pushed back towards Land's End, though it lasted longer on the mainland than it did on the Isles of Scilly. As with Wales, the spread of English resulted both from demic diffusion – in-migration – and trans-cultural diffusion – language shift, some of which was due to official repression and lack of legal and ecclesiastical recognition (Map 11.2).

In Truro, the capital of Cornwall, Cornish had mostly been lost by the middle of the seventeenth century; but in the far south-west of the county the language did not totally disappear as a viable native community language until the late eighteenth century. There would not, though, have been many monolingual Cornish speakers for several generations before that. The last Cornish speaker who had no English was reported to be a woman called Chesten Marchant, who died in 1676 at Gwithian, 15 miles (24 kilometres) west of Truro, although we cannot have any real confidence about the accuracy of this report.

Tradition has it that the last native speaker of Cornish was Dolly Pentreath. She lived in Paul, close to Mousehole in the far south-west of Cornwall, which is no more than 8 miles (13 kilometres) from Land's End, and died in Paul, aged eighty-five, in December 1777. She was certainly the best known of the last fluent speakers of Cornish. But the language did not simply disappear from the face of the earth when Dolly Pentreath passed away. What truly happened was certainly a good deal more complicated than that. Modern linguistic studies of language death show that

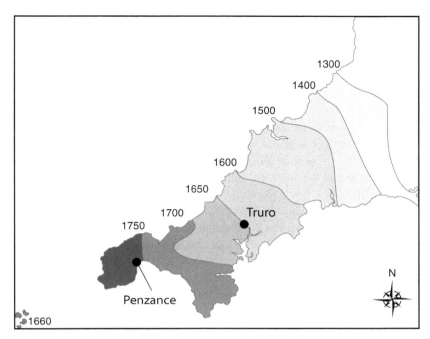

Map 11.2 Retreat of Cornish

it is typically a gradual process which involves many different stages. Fluent speakers like Dolly Pentreath live alongside and eventually give way to less than fluent speakers and then, as time passes, to semi-speakers, then poor speakers who can nevertheless understand quite well, and finally community members who simply know a few words and phrases. But according to Dr Ken George,[1] Cornish had ceased to be used as a means of communication by 1800 at the latest.

In modern times, there has been a rather successful revival of interest in the language, and indeed some revival of the language itself, with some families bringing up their children speaking Cornish; and the number of people able to conduct a conversation in Cornish is increasing all the time. As with any revival of a language which has died out, however, it is not at all clear how similar modern spoken Cornish is to the language of the eighteenth- and nineteenth-century native speakers or how the language would have been spoken naturally today if a continuous native speaker tradition had been maintained. But, in a positive sign, UNESCO have changed their classification of Cornish from 'extinct' to 'severely endangered'.

When, probably some time around 1800, Cornish did eventually die out as a native speaker community language, the total linguistic germanicisation of

---

[1] George (2010).

England had been achieved.[2] To go to completion, this process had taken 1,300 years, from the date of the first landings on the east coast of England by the peoples of the continental North Sea littoral, the Jutes, Angles, Saxons and Frisians.

The Retreat of Gaelic

In Scotland, from its initial foothold in Argyll, Gaelic had penetrated into most of the centre and north of Scotland by 800 at the expense of Brittonic Celtic Cumbric and Pictish. There was then further Gaelic expansion, even at the expense of English/Scots; and in the eleventh century, the whole country had become Gaelic-speaking, with just a few exceptions. These were the North Germanic Norse–speaking areas of the Hebrides and Northern Isles; the West Germanic English/Scots–speaking Lothians in the far south-east; and the Brittonic Celtic Cumbric–speaking area of the south-west, although in many cases these languages were also spoken alongside Gaelic.

By the middle of the fifteenth century, however, Scots had pushed northwards and westwards from its long-established south-eastern base and was now spoken over all of Lowland (southern, central and eastern) Scotland as far as the Grampian Mountains. However, Gaelic did continue to be spoken alongside English in some of the formerly Brittonic areas of the south-west for perhaps another 100 years or so. In 1600, Gaelic was still very strong and was still being spoken everywhere from the Grampians northwards and westwards, apart from Norse Caithness, Orkney and Shetland. It was still also spoken in Galloway, in the south-west of Scotland, though most of eastern Scotland now spoke Scots.

The Gaelic-speaking areas of the Scottish Highlands then gradually started becoming anglicised in the eighteenth century. One significant factor here was the defeat of the 1745 Highland uprising against the German Hanoverian monarchy, in support of the restoration of the Stuart dynasty. The campaign was led by the Stuart 'Young Pretender' known as Bonnie Prince Charlie, the grandson of James II who had been deposed in 1689. Prince Charles Stuart and his army of Highlanders were eventually defeated by the British army in 1746 at the Battle of Culloden, near Inverness, during which thousands of Highlanders were killed. Many more were also hunted down and slaughtered in the weeks which followed the battle.

Another significant factor was the infamous, genocidal Highland Clearances which started taking effect after 1750. These involved the forced and often violent evictions of inhabitants from the villages and settlements of the Highlands and

---

[2] I acknowledge that the description of Cornwall as part of England is controversial for some Cornish people who regard themselves as not being English, but legally and administratively it is currently one of the counties of England.

Western Isles by large landowners, and continued off and on until the middle of the nineteenth century. The Duke of Sutherland, for example, evicted thousands of families from his vast holdings of land and burnt down their homes. The purpose of these Clearances was to rid the land of the Gaelic Highlanders, who had been relying on it for subsistence farming and as a base for activities such as fishing, in order to introduce large-scale sheep farming instead. They led to misery, poverty, starvation and death, as well as to considerable depopulation. They tragically helped to destroy traditional Gaelic society, which had already been weakened by laws banning the speaking of the Gaelic language and the wearing of tartan, and led to considerable emigration, to the Lowlands as well as to North America and Australia. Today, the only regions which remain strongholds of native Gaelic speakers are the Hebridean islands, notably the Outer Hebrides.

Although Scotland is not yet monolingual English/Scots-speaking, there is sadly no particular reason to be especially optimistic about the long-term survival of Gaelic. Even if it does survive – and many efforts are being made at various levels to ensure that it does – English has clearly achieved a permanent presence over the whole of the country. In 1,300 years, English has spread from being a language with a small foothold in the south-east of Scotland to being the one language which is spoken all over the country, with bilingualism in English and Gaelic being increasingly confined to geographically peripheral areas.

LANGUAGE NOTES: THE LONG JOURNEY OF SCOTTISH GAELIC

Like Welsh, Gaelic also travelled far around the world. Especially after the Highland Clearances, Gaelic speakers emigrated in very large numbers, one result being that Gaelic was extensively spoken for some decades in Australia and New Zealand. During the eighteenth and nineteenth centuries, significant Scottish Gaelic-speaking colonies were also established in Newfoundland and elsewhere in Canada, notably the Maritime Provinces, which received maybe as many as 50,000 Gaelic-speaking refugees from the Scottish Highlands and Islands. It was estimated that in the whole of Canada there were about 250,000 speakers in the late 1800s. Gaelic was for many decades the major language of Cape Breton Island, Nova Scotia, where, sadly, there may now be no more than about 1,000 native speakers left, although several schools do have Gaelic language programmes, and it is also taught at University College of Cape Breton in Sydney, the major town. Scottish Gaelic colonies also established themselves in the three eastern counties of Nova Scotia (Guysborough, Pictou and Antigonish), on Prince Edward Island, in the Codroy Valley in south-west Newfoundland, in Compton County, Quebec, in southern Ontario (Stormont, Dundas and Glengarry counties south-east of Ottawa and in Middlesex County west of London) and on each side of the Manitoba–Saskatchewan border.

The Isle of Man was first settled by Goidelic speakers from Ireland at about the same time as western Scotland, during the fifth century AD. The Manx language – a close relative of Scottish and Irish Gaelic – then survived periods of Norse and Scottish dominance until the island came under the control of England during the 1400s, although even today it is not officially part of the United Kingdom. Gradual linguistic anglicisation began in the fifteenth century, and the last native speaker of Manx died in the 1970s. Attempts at revival are under way, but clearly English has come to stay.

The same thing is true of Ireland. After the recolonisation of Ireland by English speakers during the sixteenth century (see Chapter 6), and by Scots speakers in the seventeenth century,[3] there has been a gradual decline in the usage of Irish Gaelic as a native language to the extent that today it has relatively few mother-tongue speakers, mostly in the far west of the country – and this in spite of the official status which the language has had for many decades in the Republic of Ireland, and despite its large number of second-language speakers and the many official steps which have been taken to encourage its survival.

THE RATHLIN ISLAND MASSACRE

The Enterprise of Ulster was an initiative undertaken by Queen Elizabeth I to encourage English settlement in Ireland: English aristocrats were granted large areas of eastern Ulster. The Gaelic-speaking Irish used Rathlin Island, off the north-east coast of Ireland, as a base for their armed resistance to the Enterprise and sent their women and children and other non-combatants to the island for safety. The massacre took place in July 1575, when English forces under Sir Francis Drake and Sir John Norreys stormed the island's castle, using cannons to break down the walls. The Irish had no choice but to surrender. The Irish fighters were all killed, and the English also hunted down and slaughtered the women and children, as well as the elderly and the sick, about 400 civilians in all.

It is probably fairly safe to say that there are no monolingual native Celtic speakers over the age of five anywhere in the British Isles today; and only in Wales does an indigenous Celtic language survive at all strongly. The processes of linguistic contact and competition between the Celtic and Germanic language families, which began along an east–west front in northern Germany 3,000 years ago, thus continue to this day to be a dynamic feature of the modern European linguistic landscape.

---

[3] Corrigan (2010).

The Retreat of Norn

The North Germanic Norn language had been lost from Caithness during the 1400s; and in 1600 it was already under threat in Shetland and Orkney. Following the coming of the first Viking settlers to Orkney and Shetland in the 800s, the Northern Isles had remained Scandinavian-speaking for many centuries, as we saw in Chapter 6. But, although the Northern Isles were essentially part of Norway until 1468–9, the Danish-Norwegian monarchy then handed them over to Scotland in lieu of a dowry for Princess Margaret of Denmark, on the occasion of her marriage to the Scottish King James III.

A process of scotticisation then very gradually set in. Scottish law rather than Scandinavian law started being enforced in 1611; immigration from Scotland increased; and the Scots language began to be used in church – the Society for the Propagation of Christian Knowledge and their schools are often blamed for accelerating the death of Norn. In 1700, there were very few monolingual Norn speakers left; and by 1750 Scots had replaced Norn in Orkney. It lasted rather longer in Shetland but had been replaced there by Scots by the mid-nineteenth century.

One of the last redoubts of the language seems to have been the northernmost Shetland island, Unst – which is in fact the most northerly inhabited territory in the British Isles – where the supposedly last speaker of Norn, Walter Sutherland, died in the hamlet of Skaw, the UK's northernmost settlement, in about 1850. The name Skaw comes from Old Norse *skagi* 'headland'. The modern Norwegian word is *skage*; and Skagen 'the cape', which is what the northernmost tip of Jutland is called in Danish, is known as the The Skaw to English-speaking seamen.

Other sources, though, claim that the Norn language lasted even longer on the remote island of Foula (from Old Norse *fugl-ey* 'bird-island' – there is also an island called Fugloy in the Faroes). Foula lies 20 miles out into the Atlantic, to the west of the rest of the Shetland archipelago.

LANGUAGE NOTES

The modern dialect of Shetland is a dialect of Scots, but large numbers of Norn words have survived in this variety. Many seabirds, for instance, are still referred to by their Norn names. A *longie* is a guillemot, from Old Norse *langvé* (the modern Norwegian is *lomvi*); a *maa* is a seagull (the Old Norse was *már*); a *shalder* is an oystercatcher, from Old Norse *tjaldr* (*tjeld* in modern Norwegian); and a *skarf* is a cormorant, from Old Norse *skarfr* (modern Norwegian *skarv*). Other everyday Norn words survive: *de haaf* means 'the deep sea', from Old Norse *haf* 'ocean', modern Norwegian *hav*; and *bigg* signifies 'to build' (the modern Icelandic is *byggja*). It is a tragedy that this British Scandinavian language died, but at least some of it survives in the vocabulary of the modern Shetland Scots dialect.

The Retreat of Insular Norman

As we saw in Chapter 6, the Channel Islands/*Les Îles Anglo-Normandes* were also settled by Old Norse speakers, but they did not remain Old Norse–speaking for anything like as long as Shetland. The Normans, as noted, were originally Scandinavians, and the names of many of the islands are of Old Norse origin. The *-ey* ending of Alderney, Guernsey and Jersey is the Old Norse word for 'island', modern Norwegian *øy*.

The islands lie about 70–85 nautical miles (130–160 kilometres) (Map 11.3) off the south coast of England and are very much closer to the Cotentin Peninsula of Normandy in France, about 12 nautical miles (22 kilometres). The Channel Islands are not officially part of the United Kingdom but are rather dependencies of the British Crown, as they have been since 1066, when the ruler of the Duchy of Normandy, William the Conqueror, seized the crown of England. In fact, today they form two different British Crown dependencies: the Bailiwick of Jersey; and the Bailiwick of Guernsey, which consists of Guernsey, Herm, Sark and Alderney, plus the smaller islets of Jethou and Brecqhou.

Brittonic Celtic speakers arrived on these already Romano-Celtic islands from England in the fifth century, as part of the same wave of emigration which led to the

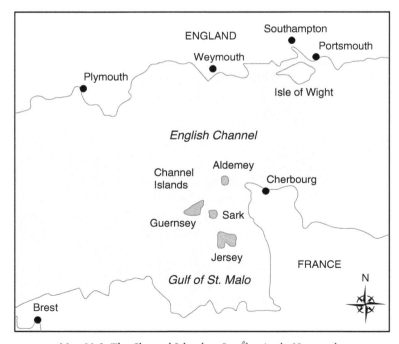

Map 11.3 The Channel Islands – *Les Îles Anglo-Normandes*

British settlement of mainland Brittany. But then Vikings started arriving in the Channel Islands in the ninth century, just as they did on the nearby coasts of mainland Normandy. They were mostly from Denmark and were Old Norse–speaking.

LANGUAGE NOTES

Channel Island Norman French originally came in three main variants: the Alderney dialect *Auregnais*; the Guernsey dialect *Guernsiais*, divided into Northern and Southern subdialects; and the Jersey dialect, *Jèrriais*, divided into the Eastern, Western and Sark or *Serquiais* subdialects, with Western *Jèrriais* and *Serquiais* being especially closely related. Norman dialect pronunciations found in the archipelago include *chent* /ʃã/ 'hundred' (French *cent*); *ka* /ka/ 'cat' (French *chat*); and *mè* /mɛ/ 'me' (French *moi*). The original Germanic initial /h/ in words such as *hache* 'axe' is still pronounced, for example /haʃ/.

The linguistic history of the islands was subsequently identical to that of Normandy. Language shift from Old Norse to Old French took place quite early on, probably late in the tenth century; and the Normans who invaded England in 1066 were no longer Norse-speaking but speakers of Norman French. Like mainland Normandy, the islands were Norman French-speaking in 1066 and they remained so for many centuries, until very recently. Norman French had died out in England, as well as in Ireland, by 1400. But it continued to be spoken for at least another five centuries and more on the Channel Islands. By 1600, the Channel Islands were still very much Norman-speaking, though there was a significant presence of French as well.

The three major dialects of Channel Islands Norman were those of Guernsey, Alderney and Jersey-Sark. The dialects survived strongly until the nineteenth century, when immigration from England set in, particularly to Jersey. Many people became trilingual in Norman, French and English, and there are still such speakers today. On Alderney, Norman French died out soon after 1900, being replaced by English. By 1960, estimates suggested that there were about 10,000 Norman speakers out of a population of 60,000 on Jersey, but today that figure is probably closer to 2,000. And in the 1980s, there were also about 10,000 speakers on Guernsey, with only a few hundred left today. On the island of Sark, on the other hand, nearly 100 per cent of the indigenous population were still Norman speakers until at least the 1990s. Now, there are perhaps 20 native speakers out of a population of 500. Most of these Norman dialect speakers did not, and do not, speak French, switching to English when communicating with outsiders.

The Ingvaeonians Who Stayed Behind: The Frisians from 1700

The expansion of the languages ancestral to English, and then of English itself, has for the last 4,000 years been associated with the triggering of language shift, of which the shift away from Norman French is only one of very many examples: the story of the expansion of English is mostly also a story of language death, with indigenous languages dying out after contact.

Frisian has not been responsible for the death of any other language in any significant way. On the contrary, Frisian has itself been subject for centuries to the sorts of pressures – in this case from Flemish-Dutch, Low German and German – which have led to language shift and language loss. As we have seen in earlier chapters, although Frisian was formerly spoken along the North Sea coast all the

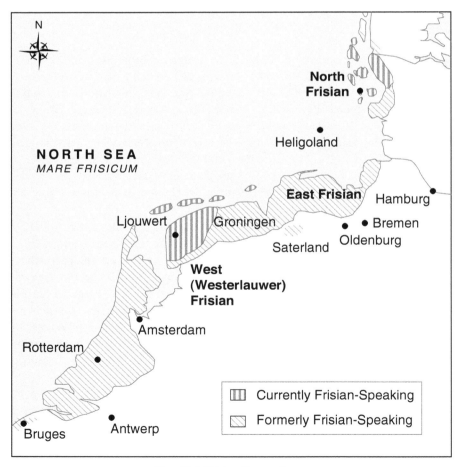

Map 11.4 Frisian then and now

way from where Antwerp now is, in northern Belgium, to what is now the German–Danish border in northern Schleswig, including the offshore islands, Frisian is now spoken only in three small relic areas, each with its own Frisian language (Map 11.4). These are West Frisian, which is spoken in the province of Friesland in the Netherlands, including the islands of Schiermonnikoog and Terschelling; East Frisian, which is spoken in the Saterland west of Oldenburg, in Germany; and North Frisian, which is spoken along the west coast of Schleswig in Germany and on the offshore islands of Sylt, Föhr, Amrum, the Halligen Islands and Heligoland (North Frisian *Hålilönj*; German *Helgoland*).

The geographical extent of the language loss since the time of Frisian's greatest expansion can be seen from Map 11.4. Only the areas with dark hatching are to any degree Frisian-speaking today, with the strongest area being West Friesland, where there has been a revival of the West Frisian language in recent times. The language is now used in the schools and courts in the province; and in the town of Ljouwert (Dutch Leeuwarden), The Frisian Academy/*It Fryske Akademy* is a significant and influential presence.

FURTHER READING

Davies, Janet. 2014. *The Welsh language: a history*. Cardiff: University of Wales Press.

Doyle, Aidan. 2015. *A history of the Irish Language: from the Norman invasion to independence*. Oxford: Oxford University Press.

Filppula, Markku, Juhani Klemola & Heli Paulasto. 2008. *English and Celtic in contact*. London: Routledge.

Watson, Moray, & Michelle MacLeod (eds.). 2010. *The Edinburgh companion to the Gaelic language*. Edinburgh: Edinburgh University Press.

12 Transcultural Diffusion: The New Native Englishes

The most recent chapter in the story of the geographical spread of mother-tongue English around the world is a tale of transcultural diffusion. It is a story of places in the world which native English has spread to, not through the arrival from elsewhere of native speakers, as in the settlement of Australia, but through the transformation of communities of non-native English speakers into native-speaking communities, through language shift.

We saw in Chapter 1 that languages can move from place to place without people themselves actually moving – that is, without demic diffusion. *Transcultural diffusion* implies the acquisition of cultural phenomena by one group from another, most often a geographically or socially neighbour-ing group, without any migration taking place. The fact that Indo-European spread outwards geographically from the Pontic-Caspian steppe certainly did indicate that Indo-European speakers themselves migrated to other places. But it does not necessarily mean that that is what happens in all cases. Languages can spread from one location to another by means of a gradual process whereby people acquire the language of their neighbours and other people they come into contact with and, eventually, also abandon their own.

There are many such examples. The spread of the Roman Empire, until it extended across the whole of southern Europe from the Atlantic shore of Portugal to the Black Sea coast of the Balkan peninsula, eventually led to the whole of that area (with the one major exception of the Greek- and Albanian-speaking southern Balkans) being occupied by speakers of Latin and, subse-quently, the Romance languages which are descended from Latin. But that was not because the region was totally overrun by Latin-speaking Roman soldiers and colonisers. Latin became the indispensable language of communi-cation between the different ethnic groups who met and mingled with one another under Roman rule. And the language achieved such importance and utility that people started speaking it even to their children, abandoning their native languages and shifting to Latin instead. This language shift eventually led to the Portuguese, Spanish, Catalan, French, Romansh, Italian and Romanian languages coming into being across that whole area of southern Europe.

Singapore

This same kind of process can be seen to be in progress today in different parts of the world where English is not a recent arrival but where it is its status as a native language that is a recent phenomenon, as in the case of Singapore.

Singapore is one of the most recent territories to be added to the list of those geographical spaces where English is spoken natively by a significant proportion of the population. But it has never experienced settlement by large numbers of native English speakers from Britain or anywhere else. Insofar as it is becoming native English-speaking, this is because of language shift.

Singapore is the major island at the southern end of the Malay Peninsula, separated from the mainland by the Johor Strait which is less than 1 nautical mile (1.9 kilometres) wide at its narrowest point. The early inhabitants of the Peninsula were speakers of Austroasiatic languages; and the descendants of some of these languages are still spoken by many of the aboriginal peoples who remain on the Peninsula. These peoples are known by the Malay term *Orang Asli* 'Original People', and their twenty or so languages form a subgroup within the Austroasiatic family which are classified by linguists as Aslian languages.[1] One group of Orang Asli people, known as the Orang Seletar, live on the shores of the Johor Strait today, but they now speak their own distinctive form of Malay rather than their ancestral Aslian language.[2]

LANGUAGE NOTES: AUSTROASIATIC LANGUAGES

Like the Aslian languages, the Munda languages of northern India also belong to the Austroasiatic family, as do Cambodian and Vietnamese. The languages of the Nicobar Islands are also Austroasiatic (Map 12.1). In addition to Vietnamese and Cambodian, the other major Austroasiatic languages today are the Mon language of Thailand and Burma and the Munda language Santali, which has more than 7 million speakers mainly in India but also in Bangladesh, Nepal and Bhutan.

Languages from this family were possibly once spoken over a great deal of mainland Southeast Asia, including the areas which are now Malaya, Cambodia, Laos and Vietnam and immediately neighbouring areas of China, Thailand, Burma and Bangladesh. Other languages families later intruded from the north, cutting different Austroasiatic-speaking areas off from one another. These intruders included Tibeto-Burman languages like Burmese, and Kra-Dai languages including Thai. There was also seaborne intrusion from the south in the form of Austronesian languages, such as Malay.

[1] Benjamin (2013).   [2] Anderbeck (2012).

Map 12.1 Austro-Asiatic languages

Several millennia after Austroasiatic languages first came to be spoken on the Malayan Peninsula, but at some point before 500 BC, seafaring Austronesian-speaking people also started settling there. Their arrival on the Peninsula was the result of a millennia-long migration which had led Austronesian-language speakers from Taiwan, via settlement in the Philippines and Indonesia, to Southeast Asia. The island of Singapore and the surrounding areas came in time to be dominated by speakers of the particular Austronesian linguistic variety which later became Malay; and a form of Malay then remained the main language of local people in Singapore for very many centuries.

Much later, during the 1500s and 1600s, there was also some immigration to Singapore and the rest of the Malay Peninsula by people from southern China. Many of them were speakers of Hokkien Chinese. But this did not ultimately give rise to a permanent linguistic presence of Chinese on the island. Intermarriage between the minority of new Chinese incomers and the majority indigenous Malay people led to the development of a distinctive hybrid culture and to the ethnogenesis of the ethnic group who are now known as Peranakans. And Peranakans have traditionally spoken a form not of Chinese but of Malay, albeit one which is characterised by the presence of many words from Hokkien.

LANGUAGE NOTES: AUSTRONESIAN LANGUAGES

The Austronesian language family is very remarkable in many ways. These languages – there are more than 1,200 of them – are spoken over an area which stretches halfway across the globe, from the Malagasy language, which is spoken in Madagascar, to Rapanui, the Polynesian language of Easter Island, in the far eastern Pacific – a distance of more than 11,000 nautical miles (20,400 kilometres) from east to west.

At the northern and southern extremities of the language family's range, there are two further Polynesian languages – Hawai'ian and New Zealand Maori – which are spoken 3,800 nautical miles (7,000 kilometres) apart.

It was then another two centuries or so before the domination of the Singapore linguistic scene by Chinese languages actually began. Singapore was established as a British trading port in 1819, under the governorship of Sir Stamford Raffles; and waves of traders and labourers then began to emigrate from southern China to Singapore, as it rapidly became an increasingly successful entrepôt and trading centre. By as early as 1826, there were more Chinese on the island than Malays.

LANGUAGE NOTES: CHINESE

Chinese is not a single language but a group of related though mostly not mutually intelligible languages. The main Chinese languages found in Singapore today are Hokkien, which has the largest number of speakers, Teochew, Cantonese, Hakka and Hainanese.

The homeland of the Hokkien speakers was in south-eastern Fujian. The Teochew people came from the Chaozhou area of the province of Guangdong/Canton, while the Cantonese speakers came mainly from south-western Canton, by the Pearl River Delta where Hong Kong is situated. The Hainanese homeland is on the large southern Chinese island of Hainan.

Today, the official languages of Singapore are Malay, Mandarin Chinese, Tamil and English. The Malays are recognised as the indigenous people of Singapore, in spite of the fact that speakers of Aslian languages had actually got there first, and Malay is officially the national language. The Chinese have long been the biggest group of inhabitants on the island, but it is surprising that Mandarin should have been selected because it was not one of the Chinese languages brought to Singapore by any group of immigrants, and it had no native speakers there. Tamil, which is a Dravidian language spoken in south-eastern India and parts of Sri Lanka, is the native language of about three-quarters of the 10 per cent of the Singaporean population who are of Indian origin: Tamils are the largest ethnic group of Indian origin in Singapore. And English is of course the language of Great Britain, which was the colonial power until 1963.

Singapore became a fully independent nation-state upon seceding from the Malaysian Federation in 1965. Like Latin in the Roman Empire, English became the main lingua franca in Singapore – the language used for wider communication between speakers from different communities. Because it is now the main language of education, and the language of the government and the legal system, English has for many Singaporeans become their primary language (the language they use most), even if it is not their first or native language, which is again what initially happened with Latin in southern Europe two millennia ago. Now, more and more younger Singaporeans, growing up in households where English is the primary language of the older generations, have English as their native language, or one of their native languages, having spoken it since infancy.

The geographical spread of English as a native language around the world has now, then, come to include, through language shift, the Asian island nation of Singapore. Most of the inhabitants of Singapore are not currently English native speakers, but the increasing numbers who do speak it natively are not descended from immigrants who arrived from some native English-speaking country but have acquired the language in situ.

LANGUAGE NOTES: SINGAPORE ENGLISH

Singaporean English is characterised by a number of distinctive discourse particles not found in other varieties of English, some of them derived from Chinese. These tend to be used in functions which in other varieties might be signalled by intonation and/or syntactic devices. For example, *lah* is a particle signifying informality, solidarity and emphasis: *Please lah come to the party* 'Please do come to the party!'.

Models of English

There are three types of nation-state in the world in terms of their relationship to the English language. Firstly, there are nation-states in which English is a native language (ENL), where most or a large proportion of the people speak English natively, as they do in Australia, Canada and England. Secondly, there are countries where English is a foreign language (EFL), as is the case with Poland, Japan and Brazil. These are places where people do not speak English natively and where, if they do speak it at all, they have learnt it at school and use it to speak to foreigners. And, thirdly, there are places where English is a second language (ESL). In ESL countries such as Pakistan, Ghana, Kenya, the Philippines and Fiji, English is typically not spoken as a mother tongue, but the language has some form of governmental or other official status; it is used as a means of communication within the country, at least amongst the educated classes, and it is widely employed in the education system, in the newspapers and in the media generally.

The distinction between ENL, EFL and ESL polities is a dynamic one, and a number of varieties of English have an interesting history of transition from EFL to ESL and on to ENL status. As we have just seen, in recent decades ENL has spread to Singapore, not through the arrival of English speakers as such but through the transitioning of Singaporean English from ESL to ENL status as children grow up acquiring the non-native second-language English of their parents' generation as their native language.

Language Shift Varieties

'Shift varieties' of native English occur rather widely around the world. As was pointed out in Chapter 6, until the nineteenth century most of the people in most of Ireland were native speakers of Irish Gaelic. But then a process of language shift set in, whereby the population for the most part gradually abandoned Irish, with the consequence that today Irish people are generally native speakers of English. This, however, has meant that some traces of Gaelic have been left behind in the modern English of Ireland. These traces were originally EFL or ESL features resulting from English having been learnt, post-childhood, by people whose native language was Gaelic. These originally non-native features have now simply become established as integral to the native-speaker English of Ireland.

Irish English can thus be characterised technically as a *shift variety* of English, meaning that it is the result of a relatively recent process of language shift. As elsewhere, the shift from Gaelic to English in Ireland was the result both of *demic* and of *transcultural* diffusion: demic diffusion because many English and Scots speakers did indeed cross the Irish Sea from Britain to Ireland and settle there; and transcultural diffusion because increasingly large numbers of Irish-speaking people over the decades gradually abandoned the speaking of Irish and became English speakers instead, acquiring the language directly or indirectly from the immigrants from Britain. Gaelic was then less and less frequently and less success-fully passed on to subsequent generations, until the community's original native language was mostly lost – except for the traces it left behind in the newly developing variety of English. The whole island of Ireland became a geographical space where English was spoken natively instead of, or as well as, Irish.

And insofar as Singapore is, or is going to be, an ENL polity, Singaporean English is, or then will also be, a shift variety.

LANGUAGE NOTES

We saw earlier that Shetland Scots contains many lexical items which have been borrowed from the original Scandinavian Norn of the islands. Many language-shift varieties of English also have grammatical features which are due to the influence of the substratum language (see also Chapter 1). We saw in Chapter 6 that the Irish English grammatical construction exemplified in *Im after reading the paper* 'I've just read the paper' is a calque (loan translation) from Irish. Guernsey English frequently makes reinforcing use of disjunctive personal pronouns as in *I can't say, me* and *The older I get and the more I learn, the more I know I don't know nothing, me* on the pattern of French *je ne peux pas dire, moi*.[3] Manx English similarly has *They'd money at them* 'they had (plenty) of money' modelled on Gaelic possessive constructions. And Scottish Highlands and Islands English makes frequent use of Gaelic style clefting, as in *It was always Gaelic I spoke at home*.

The same kind of scenario applied also in the creation and development of distinctive varieties of English in Wales, Cornwall, the Scottish Gaelic-speaking area of Scotland, the Northern Isles (Orkney and Shetland) and the Isle of Man. Recall, indeed, that in Chapter 5 we discussed the possibility that mediaeval English itself was a language shift variety, resulting from the acquisition of Old English as a foreign language by Brittonic Celtic speakers. Elsewhere in the world, as we saw in Chapters 7 and 8, North America became English-speaking for the most part because of the large numbers of English speakers from the British Isles who emigrated to the continent, bringing their own language with them. But another, albeit much smaller factor, was language shift on the part of Native Americans, who abandoned, often under duress, their native languages and began to speak English, with the consequence that large numbers of Native Americans are now monolingual English speakers. Nevertheless, for many such people their English retains features carried over from Native American languages, because of the way in which their forbears learnt it as a foreign language.

[3] Ramisch (1989).

As we also saw in Chapter 9, English first came to Australia with the arrival of convicts and guards from England in 1788; and English as spoken by most Australians today is a clear example of an ENL variety. But many Aboriginal Australians are now speakers, in many cases native speakers, of a shift variety of English which shows signs of its original formation through being spoken by learners of EFL who were native speakers of indigenous Australian languages.

LANGUAGE NOTES: ABORIGINAL ENGLISH

Aboriginal kinship systems are very different from European systems, and these differences have carried over into Aboriginal English. *Mother* in Aboriginal English may refer not only to your female parent but also to her sisters, and *father* may apply to your father's brother as well as your father. *Son* and *daughter* may correspondingly therefore also have a wider range of meaning than in other forms of English. And *brother* and *sister* can be used of certain relatives who would elsewhere be called *cousins*.

When English speakers first started arriving in New Zealand in large numbers, in the mid-nineteenth century, many of them acquired some considerable competence in Maori. However – and sadly – the numbers of such people declined as the Maori became increasingly outnumbered by English speakers, and as we saw in Chapter 9 the survival of Maori as a native language is now endangered. Modern New Zealand English, however, has acquired many Maori words, to the extent that visiting overseas English speakers may require occasional lexical assistance – when reading a newspaper, for instance – though most such words are employed mainly in a Maori cultural context. There seem to be few or no grammatical features derived from Maori in any form of contemporary New Zealand English. But there is a significant variety of English which has been labelled Maori Accented English by New Zealand linguistic scientists: phonological features due to the influence of Maori do appear in the English of a number of Maori people, including speakers who do not actually know their ancestral language.

In South Africa, there are, as we saw in Chapter 9, millions of native English speakers who descend from families of British Isles origin. There is also a population of people of Indian origin who speak English as a first language. But today there are, too, people in communities which were not originally native English-speaking at all but are now becoming so. Many members of the younger generation of middle-class Black Africans often have English as at least their primary language; and their variety of English has been labelled *Black South African English* by South African linguistic scientists. These speakers have shifted to English from southern African Bantu languages, the major ones being Tsonga, Venda, Sotho, Tswana, Zulu, Xhosa, Swazi and Ndebele.

Native English in India

India is a very typical example of an ESL country: English has a very major role as a second language there, and millions of Indians speak, write, read and listen to English on a daily basis. The majority of them are not native speakers and have some language of the South Asian subcontinent such as Bengali or Tamil as their mother tongue. Nevertheless, there are now, as in Singapore, an increasingly large number of Indians who are native speakers of English. Although they constitute well under 1 per cent of the population, they still number in the millions. This is perhaps particularly true of children who have grown up in households where the older generation do not have an indigenous language in common and therefore communicate mainly in English.

However, English has to an extent been spoken natively in India for a very long time – and much longer than in Singapore. The beginnings of the Eurasian Anglo-Indian community date back to the 1600s, with the arrival of large numbers of single British men on the subcontinent working as administrators and soldiers, as the East India Company and other British interests exerted increasing control over India. There was subsequently considerable intermarriage with local women, producing Eurasian or Anglo-Indian children.[4] By the nineteenth century, however, increasingly racist attitudes meant that mixed-race people were no longer accepted as part of the colonial expatriate community and, most often, if and when the men returned to Europe, the women and children were left behind: soldiers were specifically and cruelly required to return to Britain and abandon their mixed-race families.

In time, Eurasians came to form a community in their own right. They were distinguished from other Indians by being Christian and by having English as their native language. They also developed distinctive forms of dress, as well as a distinctive cuisine and set of naming practices. When Indian independence came about in 1947, there were about 300,000 native anglophone Anglo-Indians but, because of subsequent emigration, the community has today become considerably smaller. There are also Anglo-Indian communities in Bangladesh; and there are, or were, similar native anglophone groups in Burma.

FURTHER READING

Deterding, David. 2007. *Singapore English*. Edinburgh: Edinburgh University Press.

Mesthrie, Rajend (ed.). 2008. *Varieties of English, vol. 4: Africa, South and Southeast Asia*. Berlin: Mouton de Gruyter.

Trudgill, Peter, & Jean Hannah. 2017. *International English: a guide to varieties of English around the world*. London: Routledge.

---

[4] 'Intermarriage' is a convenient shorthand term for relationships which did not always involve actual marriage, though many did.

Epilogue: Sixteen Hundred Years On

The expansion of English has been a remarkable phenomenon, but there have been many losers. And, indeed, there is an important sense in which we are all the losers: the loss of linguistic diversity from the world as a result of the expansion of English has been what can only be described as a language-ecological disaster.[1]

Today, English is still spoken as a native language in the same areas of eastern England where it first came into being, and where I am writing this 1,600 years later. But, in the meantime, it has spread right across the world. The most remote anglophone communities on earth are to be found in the middle of the Atlantic Ocean, on Tristan da Cunha, which lies 1,505 nautical miles (2,787 kilometres) from the South African coast; and in the middle of the Pacific Ocean, on Palmerston Island in the Cook Islands, which is 430 nautical miles (800 kilometres) from Rarotonga, the main island of the Cooks.

The northernmost permanent native English-speaking communities in the world are to be found in Arctic Canada and Alaska. Utqiagvik/Barrow, Alaska, where the Eskaleut language Inupiaq is also spoken, is situated at 71°N. There are no permanent settlements speaking any language at all anywhere between Barrow and the North Pole. The southernmost permanent native English-speaking communities in the world are located in New Zealand: the formerly Maori-speaking settlement of Oban on Stewart Island/Rakiura, situated off the southern end of New Zealand's South Island, at 47°S; and on the Falkland Islands. The capital of the Falklands, Stanley, on East Falkland, lies at 51°S: you can travel in a straight line from there to the South Pole without encountering any other permanent human settlement at all.

English as a native language truly has spread, as I wrote in the Prologue to this book, "to the furthest ends of the earth".

---

[1] It is, of course, not just the expansion of English which has been involved in this process. Other languages, including Spanish, Portuguese, French, Russian, Chinese, Malay-Indonesian and Arabic have also been particularly involved.

References

Chapter 1: The Language Which Became English

Ammerman, Alberti, & Luca Cavalli-Sforza. 1971. Measuring the rate of spread of early farming in Europe. *Man* 6, 674–88.

Braunmüller, Kurt. 2008. Das älteste Germanische: offene Fragen und mögliche Antworten. *Sprachwissenschaft* 33, 373–403.

Hawkins, John. 1990. Germanic languages. In B. Comrie (ed.) *The major languages of Western Europe*. London: Routledge, 58–66.

Kallio, Petri. 2003. Languages in the prehistoric Baltic Sea region. In Bammesberger & Vennemann (eds.) *Languages in prehistoric Europe*. Heidelberg: Winter, 227–44.

Lehmann, Winfred. 1961. A definition of Proto-Germanic: a study in the chronological delimitation of languages. *Language* 37, 67–74.

Mailhammer, Robert. 2011. The prehistory of European languages. In B. Kortmann & J. van der Auwera (eds.) *The languages and linguistics of Europe: a comprehensive guide*. Berlin: Mouton de Gruyter, 671–82.

Mitxelena, Koldo. [1961] 1990. *Fonética histórica vasca*. San Sebastián: Diputacion Foral de Gipuzkoa.

Prokosch, Eduard. 1939. *A comparative Germanic grammar*. Philadelphia: University of Pennsylvania Press.

Ringe, Don. 2006. *From Indo-European to Proto-Germanic: a linguistic history of English* vol. 1. Oxford: Oxford University Press.

Schrijver, Peter. 2001. Lost languages in Northern Europe. In C. Carpelan, A. Parpola & P. Koskikallio (eds.) *Early contacts between Uralic and Indo-European: linguistic and archaeological considerations*. Helsinki: Mémoires de la Société Finno-Ougrienne, 417–25.

Schrijver, Peter. 2003. Early developments in the vowel systems of North-West Germanic and Saami. In Bammesberger & Vennemann (eds.) *Languages in prehistoric Europe*. Heidelberg: Winter, 195–226.

Schrijver, Peter. 2018. Talking Neolithic: the case for Hatto-Minoan and its relationship to Sumerian. In G. Kroonen, J. P. Mallory & B. Comrie (eds.) *Proceedings of the workshop on Indo-European Origins held at the Max Planck Institute for Evolutionary Anthropology, Leipzig, December 2–3, 2013. (Journal of Indo-European Studies* Monograph 65.) Leipzig: Max Planck Institute for Evolutionary Anthropology.

Vennemann, Theo. 1994. Linguistic reconstruction in the context of European prehistory. *Transactions of the Philological Society* 92, 213–82.

Vennemann, Theo. 2003. Languages in prehistoric Europe north of the Alps. In Bammesberger & Vennemann (eds.) *Languages in prehistoric Europe*. Heidelberg: Winter, 319–32.

Wiik, Kalevi. 2003. Finnic-type pronunciation in the Germanic languages. *The Mankind Quarterly* 44, 43–90.

Chapter 2: The First Movement South

Ahlqvist, Anders. 2010. Early Celtic and English. *Australian Celtic Journal* 9, 1–17.

Crystal, David. 1992. *An encyclopedic dictionary of language and languages*. Oxford: Blackwell.

Green, Dennis. 1998. *Language and history in the early Germanic world*. Cambridge: Cambridge University Press.

Hawkins, John. 1990. Germanic languages. In B. Comrie (ed.) *The major languages of Western Europe*. London: Routledge, 58–66.

König, Ekkehard, & Johan Van der Auwera (eds.). 1994. *The Germanic languages*. London: Routledge.

Kuhn, Hans. 1955–6. Zur Gliederung der germanischen Sprachen. *Zeitschrift für deutsches Altertum und deutsche Literatur* 86, 1–47.

Laker, Stephen. 2002. An explanation for the changes *kw-, hw-* > *χw-* in the English dialects. In Markku Filppula, Juhani Klemola & Heli Pitkänen (eds.) *The Celtic roots of English*. Joensuu: Joensuu University Press, 183–198.

Laker, Stephen. 2008. Changing views about Anglo-Saxons and Britons. In Henk Aertsen & Bart Veldhoen (eds.) *Six papers from the 28th Symposium on Medieval Studies*. Leiden: Leiden University, 1–38.

Lewis, Henry, & Holger Pedersen. 1937. *A concise comparative Celtic grammar*. Göttingen: Vandenhoeck & Ruprecht.

MacAulay, Donald. 1992. *The Celtic languages*. Cambridge: Cambridge University Press.

Musset, Lucien. 1993. *The Germanic invasions: the making of Europe 400–600* A D. New York: Barnes & Noble.

Ó Siadhail, Micheál. 1989. *Modern Irish: grammatical structure and dialectal variation*. Cambridge: Cambridge University Press.

Ringe, Don. 2006. *From Indo-European to Proto-Germanic: a linguistic history of English* vol. 1. Oxford: Oxford University Press.

Ringe, Don, & Ann Taylor. 2014. *The development of Old English: a linguistic history of English* vol. 2. Oxford: Oxford University Press.

Schumacher, Stefan. 2009. Lexical and structural language-contact phenomena along the Germano-Celtic transition zone. In S. Zimmer (ed.) *Kelten am Rhein II: Philologie. Sprachen und Literaturen*. Mainz: von Zabern, 247–66.

Sims-Williams, Patrick. 2006. *Ancient Celtic place-names in Europe and Asia Minor*. (Publications of the Philological Society 39). Oxford: Blackwell.

Vennemann, Theo. 2002. On the rise of 'Celtic' syntax in Middle English. In P. Lucas & A. Lucas (eds.) *Middle English from tongue to text*. Berne: Lang.

Vennemann, Theo. 2003a. Languages in prehistoric Europe north of the Alps. In Bammesberger & Vennemann (eds.) *Languages in prehistoric Europe*. Heidelberg: Winter, 319–332.

Vennemann, Theo. 2003b. *Europa Vasconica-Europa Semitica*. Berlin: Mouton de Gruyter.

Wischer, Ilse. 2011. On the use of *beon* and *wesan* in Old English. In U. Lenker, J. Huber & R. Mailhammer (eds.) *Verbal and nominal constructions in the history of English: variation and conventionalisation*. Amsterdam: John Benjamins, 217–36.

Chapter 3: A View from the Celtic Island

Adams, James. 2003. *Bilingualism and the Latin language*. Cambridge: Cambridge University Press.

Adams, James. 2007. *The regional diversification of Latin 200 BC–AD 600*. Cambridge: Cambridge University Press.

Baldi, Philip, & Richard Page. 2006. Review of Vennemann *Europa Vasconica-Europa Semitica* (2003). *Lingua* 116, 2183–220.

Jackson, Kenneth. 1953. *Language and history in Early Britain*. Edinburgh: Edinburgh University Press.

Mitchell, Bruce, & Fred Robinson. 2011. *A guide to Old English*. Oxford: Wiley-Blackwell.

Morris, John. 2004. *The age of Arthur: a history of the British Isles from 350 to 650*. London: Phoenix.

Patterson, Nick, Michael Isakov, Thomas Booth, T. et al. 2021. Large-scale migration into Britain during the Middle to Late Bronze Age. *Nature* 601, 588–94. https://doi.org/10.1038/s41586-021-04287-4.

Rhys, Guto. 2015. Approaching the Pictish language: historiography, early evidence and the question of Pritenic. PhD thesis, Glasgow University.

Schrijver, Peter. 2002. The rise and fall of British Latin: evidence from English and Brittonic. In M. Filppula, J. Klemola & H. Pitkänen (eds.) *The Celtic roots of English*. Joensuu: Joensuu University Press, 87–110.

Schrijver, Peter. 2007. What Britons spoke around 400 AD. In N. Higham (ed.) *Britons in Anglo-Saxon England*. Woodbridge: Boydell, 165–71.

Chapter 4: The North Sea Crossing

Barnes, Michael. 2012. *Runes: a handbook*. Woodbridge: Boydell & Brewer.

Hines, John. 1984. *The Scandinavian character of Anglian England in the pre-Viking period*. London: British Archaeological Reports.

Holman, George. 1962. The Frisians in East Anglia. In Holman *Sentiments and activities: essays in social science*. Glencoe: Free Press, 189–206.

McMahon, Robert. 2011. Variation and populations. In W. Maguire & A. McMahon (eds.) *Analysing variation in English*. Cambridge: Cambridge University Press, 237–60.

Munske, Horst H., Nils Århammar, Volker Faltings et al. (eds.) 2001. *Handbuch des Friesischen/Handbook of Frisian studies*. Tübingen: Niemeyer.

Nielsen, Hans Frede. 1998. *The continental backgrounds of English and its insular development until 1154*. Odense: Odense University Press.

Trudgill, Peter. 1986. *Dialects in contact*. Oxford: Blackwell.

Chapter 5: Anglo-Saxons and Celts in the British Highlands

Ahlqvist, Anders. 2010. Early Celtic and English. *Australian Celtic Journal* 9, 1–17.

Durkin, Philip. 2023. Norse borrowings in the OED: a fresh examination. In R. Dance, S. M. Pons-Sanz & B. Schorn (eds.) *New perspectives on the Scandinavian legacy in medieval Britain*. Turnhout: Brepols.

Ekwall, Eilert. 1960. *The concise Oxford dictionary of place-names*. Oxford: Oxford University Press.

Emonds, Joseph, & Jan Terje Faarlund. 2014. *English: the language of the Vikings*. Olomouc: Palacký University Press.

Filppula, Markku. 2003. More on the English progressive and the Celtic connection. In Hildegard Tristram (ed.) *The Celtic Englishes III*. Heidelberg: Winter, 150–68.

Hoekstra, Jarich. 1995. Preposition stranding and resumptivity in West Germanic. In Hubert Haider, Susan Olsen & Sten Vikner (eds.) *Studies in comparative Germanic syntax*. Dordrecht: Kluwer, 95–118.

Holmberg, Anders, & Jan Rijkhoff. 1998. Word order in the Germanic languages. In Anna Siewierska (ed.) *Constituent order in the languages of Europe*. Berlin: Mouton de Gruyter, 75–104.

Keller, Wolfgang. 1925. Keltisches im englischen Verbum. *Anglica: Untersuchungen zur englischen Philologie* vol. 1. Leipzig: Mayer & Müller, 55–66.

Kuhn, Hans. 1955–6. Zur Gliederung der germanischen Sprachen. *Zeitschrift für deutsches Altertum und deutsche Literatur* 86, 1–47.

Laker, Stephen. 2008. Changing views about Anglo-Saxons and Britons. In H. Aertsen & B. Veldhoen (eds.) *Six papers from the 28th Symposium on Medieval Studies*. Leiden: Leiden University Department, 1–38.

Lutz, Angelika. 2009. Celtic influence on Old English and West Germanic. *English Language and Linguistics* 13, 227–49.

Lutz, Angelika. 2010. Why is West-Saxon English different from Old Saxon? In H. Sauer & J. Story (eds.) *Anglo-Saxon England and the continent*. Tempe: Arizona Center for Mediaeval and Renaissance Studies, 113–38.

Mittendorf, Ingo, & Erich Poppe. 2000. Celtic contacts of the English progressive? In Hildegard Tristram (ed.) *The Celtic Englishes II*. Heidelberg: Winter, 117–45.

Morris, John. 2004. *The age of Arthur: a history of the British Isles from 350 to 650*. London: Phoenix.

Riemsdijk, Henk van. 1978. *A case study in syntactic markedness: the binding nature of prepositional phrases*. Breda: Ridder.

Tristram, Hildegard (ed.). 2003. *The Celtic Englishes III*. Heidelberg: Winter.

Tristram, Hildegard. 2004. Diglossia in Anglo-Saxon England, or what was spoken Old English like? *Studia Anglica Posnaniensia* 40, 87–110.

Tristram, Hildegard. 2006. Why don't the English speak Welsh? In N. Higham (ed.) *Britons in Anglo-Saxon England*. Woodbridge: Boydell, 192–214.

Vennemann, Theo. 2000. English as a 'Celtic' language: Atlantic influences from above and below. In Hildegard Tristram (ed.) *The Celtic Englishes II*. Heidelberg: Winter, 399–406.

Vennemann, Theo. 2001. Atlantis Semitica: structural contact features in Celtic and English. In Laurel J. Brinton (ed.) *Historical linguistics 1999: Selected papers from the 14th*

International Conference on Historical Linguistics. Amsterdam and Philadelphia: John Benjamins, 351–69.

White, David. 2002. Explaining the innovations of Middle English: what, where, and why? In Markku Filppula, Juhani Klemola & Heli Pitkänen (eds.) *The Celtic roots of English*. Joensuu: Joensuu University Press, 153–74.

Chapter 6: Across the Irish Sea

Århammer, Nils. 2001. Grundzüge nordfriesischer Sprachgeschichte. In Horst H. Munske, Nils Århammar, Volker Faltings et al. (eds.) *Handbuch des Friesischen/Handbook of Frisian studies*. Tübingen: Niemeyer, 744–66.

Corrigan, Karen. 2010. *Irish English, vol. 1: Northern Ireland* (Dialects of English 5). Berlin: de Gruyter.

Dolan, Terence, & Diarmaid Ó Muirithe. 1996. *The dialect of Forth and Bargy Co. Wexford, Ireland*. Dublin: Four Courts.

Ebert, Karen Heide. 1971. *Referenz, Sprechsituation und die bestimmten Artikel in einem nordfriesischen Dialekt (Fering)*. Bredstedt: Nordfriisk Instituut.

Jellema, Dirk. 1955. Frisian trade in the Dark Ages. *Speculum* 30, 15–36.

Kallen, Jeffrey. 2013. *Irish English, vol. 2: The Republic of Ireland* (Dialects of English 9). Berlin: de Gruyter.

Owen, Wyn, & Richard Morgan. 2008. *Dictionary of the place-names of Wales*. Llandysul: Gomer.

Samuels, Michael. 1972. *Linguistic evolution: with special reference to English*. Cambridge: Cambridge University Press.

Chapter 7: Atlantic Crossing

Cadigan, Sean. 2009. *Newfoundland and Labrador: a history*. Toronto: University of Toronto Press.

Campbell, Lyle. 1997. *American Indian languages: the historical linguistics of Native America*. Oxford: Oxford University Press.

Davidson, William. 1974. *Historical geography of the Bay Islands, Honduras: Anglo-Hispanic conflict in the Western Caribbean*. Birmingham, AL: Southern University Press.

Goddard, Ives. 1997. Pidgin Delaware. In Sarah Thomason (ed.) *Contact languages: a wider perspective*. Amsterdam: Benjamins, 43–98.

Goddard, Ives. 2000. The use of pidgins and jargons on the east coast of North America. In Edward Gray & Norman Fiering (eds.) *The language encounter in the Americas 1492–1800*. New York: Berghahn, 61–78.

Gray, Edward, & Norman Fiering (eds.). 2000. *The language encounter in the Americas 1492–1800*. New York: Berghahn.

Hickey, Raymond. 2005. English dialect input to the Caribbean. In Raymond Hickey (ed.) *Legacies of colonial English: studies in transported dialects*. Cambridge: Cambridge University Press, 326–60.

Holm, John. 1978. The English creole of Nicaragua's Miskito Coast. PhD thesis, University of London.

Holm, John (ed.). 1983. *Central American English*. Heidelberg: Julius Groos.

Holm, John. 1994. English in the Caribbean. In Robert Burchfield (ed.) *The Cambridge history of the English language, vol. 5: English in Britain and overseas – origins and development*. Cambridge: Cambridge University Press, 328–81.

Jarvis, Michael. 2010. *In the eye of all trade: Bermuda, Bermudians, and the maritime Atlantic world, 1680–1783*. Chapel Hill: University of North Carolina Press.

Mithun, Marianne. 1999. *The languages of native North America*. Cambridge: Cambridge University Press.

O'Neil, Wayne. 1993. Nicaraguan English in history. In C. Jones (ed.) *Historical linguistics*. London: Longman, 279–318.

Palmié, Stephan, & Francisco Scarano (eds.). 2011. *The Caribbean: a history of the region and its peoples*. Chicago: University of Chicago Press.

Rountree, Helen. 1990. *Pocahontas's people: the Powhatan Indians of Virginia through four centuries*. Norman: University of Oklahoma Press.

Taylor, Christopher. 2012. *The Black Carib wars: freedom, survival, and the making of the Garifuna*. Jackson: University Press of Mississippi.

Trudgill, Peter. 2019. Bermudian English as a North American dialect: a note on the segmental phonology. www.researchgate.net/publication/330180330.

Williams, Jeffrey. 2010. Euro-Caribbean English varieties. In Edgar Schneider, Daniel Schreier, Peter Trudgill & Jeffrey Williams (eds.) *The lesser-known varieties of English: an introduction*. Cambridge: Cambridge University Press, 136–57.

Williams, Jeffrey, & Michael Aceto (eds.). 2003. *Contact Englishes of the Eastern Caribbean*. Amsterdam: Benjamins.

William, Jeffrey, & Caroline Myrick. 2015. Saban English. In Jeffrey Williams, Edgar Schneider, Peter Trudgill & Daniel Schreier (eds.) *Further studies in lesser-known varieties of English*. Cambridge: Cambridge University Press, 144–64.

Wilson, Samuel. 1997. *The indigenous people of the Caribbean*. Gainesville: University of Florida Press.

Chapter 8: Onwards to the Pacific Shore

Bakker, Peter. 1997. *A language of our own: the genesis of Michif, the mixed Cree French language of the Canadian Métis*. Oxford: Oxford University Press.

Bickerton, Derek. 1975. *Dynamics of a creole system*. Cambridge: Cambridge University Press.

Campbell, Lyle. 1997. *American Indian languages: the historical linguistics of Native America*. Oxford: Oxford University Press.

Craton, Michael, & Gail Saunders. 1992–8. *Islanders in the stream: a history of the Bahamian people*. 2 vols. London: University of Georgia.

Faragher, John. 2005. *A great and noble scheme: the tragic story of the expulsion of the French Acadians from their American homeland*. New York: Norton.

Fleming, Thomas. 2003. *The Louisiana Purchase*. Hoboken, NJ: Wiley.

Garsha, Jeremiah. 2015. 'Reclamation Road': a microhistory of massacre memory in Clear Lake, California. *Genocide Studies and Prevention: An International Journal* 9, 61–75.

Granberry, Julius, & Gary Vescelius. 2004. *Languages of the pre-Columbian Antilles*. Tuscaloosa: University of Alabama Press.

Gray, Edward, & Norman Fiering (eds). 2000. *The language encounter in the Americas 1492–1800*. New York: Berghahn.

Hackert, Stephanie. 2004. *Urban Bahamian Creole: system and variation*. Amsterdam: Benjamins.

Hämäläinen, Pekka. 2008. *The Comanche empire*. New Haven, CT: Yale University Press.

Higman, Barry. 2011. *A concise history of the Caribbean*. Cambridge: Cambridge University Press.

Holm, John. 1994. English in the Caribbean. In Robert Burchfield (ed.) *The Cambridge history of the English language, vol. 5: English in Britain and overseas – origins and development*. Cambridge: Cambridge University Press, 328–81.

Mithun, Marianne. 2001. *The languages of native North America*. Cambridge: Cambridge University Press.

Peckham, Howard. 1964. *The colonial wars 1689–1762*. Chicago: University of Chicago Press.

Perdue, Theda, & Michael Green. 2007. *The Cherokee nation and the trail of tears*. London: Penguin.

Prescod, Paula (ed.). 2015. *Language issues in St Vincent and the Grenadines*. Amsterdam: Benjamins.

Singler, John. 2004. Liberian Settler English: morphology and syntax. In Bernd Kortmann, Edgar Schneider, Clive Upton, Rajend Mesthrie & Kate Burridge (eds.) *A handbook of varieties of English* vol. 2. Berlin: Mouton de Gruyter, 879–97.

Singler, John. 2008. Liberian Settler English: phonology. In Rajend Mesthrie (ed.) *Varieties of English, vol. 4: Africa, South and Southeast Asia*. Berlin: Mouton de Gruyter, 102–14. https://doi.org/10.1515/9783110208429.1.102.

Williams, Maria Shaa Tláa (ed.). 2009. *The Alaska native reader: history, culture, politics*. Durham, NC: Duke University Press.

Woodger, Elin, & Brandon Toropov. 2004. *Encyclopedia of the Lewis and Clark Expedition*. New York: Facts on File.

Yakpo, Kofi. 2013. Pichi. In Susanne Michaelis, Philippe Maurer, Martin Haspelmath & Magnus Huber (eds.) *The survey of pidgin and creole languages* vol. 1. Oxford: Oxford University Press, 194–205.

Chapter 9: Across the Equator

Bowerman, Sean. 2008a. White South African English: phonology. In Rajend Mesthrie (ed.) *Varieties of English, vol. 4: Africa, South and Southeast Asia*. Berlin: Mouton de Gruyter, 164–76.

Bowerman, Sean. 2008b. White South African English: morphology and syntax. In Rajend Mesthrie (ed.) *Varieties of English, vol. 4: Africa, South and Southeast Asia*. Berlin: Mouton de Gruyter, 472–87.

Bowern, Claire. 2012. The riddle of Tasmanian languages. *Proceedings of the Royal Society* 279, 4590–5.

Britain, David, & Andrea Sudbury. 2010. Falkland Islands English. In Edgar Schneider, Daniel Schreier, Peter Trudgill & Jeffrey Williams (eds.) 2010. *The lesser-known varieties of English: an introduction.* Cambridge: Cambridge University Press, 209–23.

Burchfield, Robert (ed.). 1994. *The Cambridge history of the English language, vol. 5: English in Britain and overseas – origins and development.* Cambridge: Cambridge University Press.

Burridge, Kate, & Bernd Kortmann (eds.). 2008. *Varieties of English, vol. 3: the Pacific and Australasia.* Berlin: Mouton de Gruyter.

Clark, Ross. 1994. Moriori and Maori: the linguistic evidence. In Douglas Sutton (ed.) *The origins of the first New Zealanders.* Auckland: Auckland University Press, 123–35.

Corrigan, Karen. 2020. From Killycomain to Melbourne: historical contact and the feature pool. In Karen Beaman, Isabelle Buchstaller, Sue Fox & James Walker (eds.) *Advancing socio-grammatical variation and change: in honour of Jenny Cheshire.* London: Routledge, 319–40.

Dixon, R. M. W. 2019. *Australia's original languages: an introduction.* Sydney: Allen & Unwin.

Harlow, Ray. 2007. *Maori: a linguistic introduction.* Cambridge: Cambridge University Press.

Hay, Jennifer, Margaret Maclagan & Elizabeth Gordon. 2008. *New Zealand English.* Edinburgh: Edinburgh University Press.

Hendery, Rachel. 2015. Palmerston Island English. In Jeffrey Williams, Edgar Schneider, Peter Trudgill & Daniel Schreier (eds.) *Further studies in lesser-known varieties of English.* Cambridge: Cambridge University Press, 267–87.

King, Michael. 1989. *Moriori: a people rediscovered.* Auckland: Viking.

Lanham, Leonard. 1967. *The pronunciation of South African English.* Amsterdam: Balkema.

Lynch, John, Malcolm Ross & Terry Crowley (eds.). 2017. *The Oceanic Languages.* London: Routledge.

Mühlhäusler, Peter. 2020. *Pitkern-Norf'k.* Berlin: Mouton de Gruyter.

Sakoda, Kent, & Jeff Siegel. 2003. *Pidgin grammar: an introduction to the creole language of Hawai'i.* Honolulu: Bess Press.

Schreier, Daniel, & Karen Lavarello. 2003. *Tristan da Cunha: history, people, language.*

Schreier, Daniel, & Peter Trudgill. 2006. The segmental phonology of 19th century Tristan da Cunha English: convergence and local innovation. *English Language & Linguistics* 10, 119–41.

Schreier, Daniel, & Laura Wright. 2010. Earliest St Helenian English in writing: evidence from the St Helena Consultations 1682–1723. In Raymond Hickey (ed.) *Varieties in writing: the written word as linguistic evidence.* Amsterdam: Benjamins, 245–62.

Trudgill, Peter. 2004. *New-dialect formation: the inevitability of colonial Englishes.* Edinburgh: Edinburgh University Press.

Vossen, Rainer (ed.). 2013. *The Khoesan languages.* London: Routledge.

Wilson, Sheila. 2008. St Helena English: phonology. In Rajend Mesthrie (ed.) *Varieties of English, vol. 4: Africa, South and Southeast Asia.* Berlin: Mouton de Gruyter, 223–30.

Wilson, Sheila, & Rajend Mesthrie. 2008. St Helena English: morphology and syntax. In Rajend Mesthrie (ed.) *Varieties of English, vol. 4: Africa, South and Southeast Asia.* Berlin: Mouton de Gruyter, 535–45.

Wright, Laura. 2013. The language of slaves on the island of St Helena, South Atlantic 1682–1724. In Marijke van der Wal & Gijsbert Rutten (eds.) *Touching the past: studies in the historical sociolinguistics of ego-documents*. Amsterdam: Benjamins, 243–76.

Zettersten, Arne. 1969. *The English of Tristan Da Cunha*. Malmö: Gleerup.

Chapter 10: English in Retreat

Bailey, Guy, & Clyde Smith. 1992. Southern American English in Brazil, no? *SECOL Review*, 71–89.

Brody, Hugh. 2002. *The other side of Eden: hunter-gatherers, farmers and the shaping of the world*. London: Faber.

Holm, John. 1978. The English creole of Nicaragua's Miskito Coast. PhD thesis, University of London.

Holm, John (ed.). 1983. *Central American English*. Heidelberg: Julius Groos.

Jones, Megan, & Sali A. Tagliamonte. 2004. From Somerset to Samaná: pre-verbal did in the voyage of English. *Language Variation and Change*, 16, 93–126.

Long, Daniel. 2000. Evidence of an English contact language in 19th century Bonin Islands. *English World-Wide* 20, 251–86.

Long, Daniel, & Peter Trudgill. 2004. The last Yankee in the Pacific: Eastern New England phonology in the Bonin Islands. *American Speech* 79, 356–67.

Montgomery, Michael, & Cecil Melo. 1990. The phonology of the lost cause. *English World-Wide* 10, 195–216.

Montgomery, Michael, & Cecil Melo. 1995. The language: the preservation of southern speech among the colonists. In Cyrus Dawsey & James Dawsey (eds.) *The Confederados: Old South immigrants in Brazil*. Tuscaloosa: University of Alabama Press, 176–90.

Pandeli, Helen, Joseph F. Eska, Martin J. Ball and Joan Rahilly. 1997. Problems of phonetic transcription: the case of the Hiberno-English slit-t. *Journal of the International Phonetic Association* 27, 65–75.

Perez-Inofuentes, Danae. 2015. Anglo-Paraguayan English. In Jeffrey Williams, Edgar Schneider, Peter Trudgill & Daniel Schreier (eds.) *Further studies in lesser-known varieties of English*. Cambridge: Cambridge University Press, 219–35.

Trudgill, Peter. 2010. *Investigations in sociohistorical linguistics: stories of colonisation and contact*. Cambridge: Cambridge University Press.

Warren, Jane, & Leigh Oakes. 2011. Language policy and citizenship in Quebec: French as a force for unity in a diverse society? In Catrin Norrby & John Hajek (eds.) *Uniformity and diversity in language policy*. Bristol: Multilingual Matters, 7–21.

Wells, J. C. 1982. *Accents of English*. Cambridge: Cambridge University Press.

Chapter 11: The British Isles from 1600

Barnes, Michael. 1984. Orkney and Shetland Norn. In Peter Trudgill (ed.) *Language in the British Isles*. Cambridge: Cambridge University Press, 352–66.

Barnes, Michael. 1998. *The Norn Language of Orkney and Shetland*. Lerwick: Shetland Times.

Corrigan, Karen. 2010. *Irish English, vol. 1: Northern Ireland*. Edinburgh: Edinburgh University Press.

George, Ken. 2010. Cornish. In Martin J. Ball & Nicole Müller (eds.) *The Celtic languages*. London: Routledge, 488–535.

Jones, Mari. 2015. *Variation and change in Mainland and Insular Norman*. Leiden: Brill.

Liddicoat, Anthony. 1994. *A grammar of the Norman French of the Channel Islands*. Berlin: de Gruyter.

Millar, Robert McColl. 2007. *Northern and Insular Scots*. Edinburgh: Edinburgh University Press.

Nilsen, Kenneth. 2010. A'Ghàidhlig an Canada: Scottish Gaelic in Canada. In Moray Watson & Michelle MacLeod (eds.) *The Edinburgh companion to the Gaelic language*. Edinburgh: Edinburgh University Press, 90–107.

Paulasto, Heli, Rob Penhallurick & Benjamin Jones. 2021. *Welsh English*. Berlin: De Gruyter.

Ramisch, Heinrich. 1989. *The variation of English in Guernsey, Channel Islands*. Frankfurt: Lang.

Thomas, Alan. 1984. Cornish. In Peter Trudgill (ed.) *Language in the British Isles*. Cambridge: Cambridge University Press, 278–88.

Thomson, Robert. 1992. The Manx language. In Donald MacAulay (ed.) *The Celtic languages*. Cambridge: Cambridge University Press.

Watson, Moray, & Michelle MacLeod (eds.). 2010. *The Edinburgh companion to the Gaelic language*. Edinburgh: Edinburgh University Press.

Williams, Glyn. 1975. *The desert and the dream: a study of Welsh colonisation in Chubut 1865–1915*. Cardiff: University of Wales Press.

Chapter 12: The New Native Englishes

Anderbeck, Karl. 2012. The Malayic-speaking Orang Laut: dialects and directions for research. *Wacana* 14, 265–312.

Benjamin, Geoffrey. 2002. On being tribal in the Malay world. In Geoffrey Benjamin & Cynthia Chou (eds.) *Tribal communities in the Malay world: historical, cultural and social perspectives*. Singapore: ISEAS Publishing, 7–76.

Benjamin, Geoffrey. 2013. The Aslian languages of Malaysia and Thailand: an assessment. In Peter Austin & Stewart McGill (eds.) *Language documentation and description* vol. 11, 137–231.

Butcher, Andrew. 2008. Linguistic aspects of Australian Aboriginal English. *Clinical Linguistics and Phonetics* 22, 625–42.

De Klerk, Vivian, & David Gough. 2009. Black South African English. In Rajend Mesthrie (ed.) *Language in South Africa*. Cambridge: Cambridge University Press, 356–78.

Hawes, Christopher. 2013. *Poor relations: the making of a Eurasian community in British India 1773–1833*. London: Routledge.

Leap, William. 1993. *American Indian English*. Salt Lake City: University of Utah Press.

Maclagan, Margaret, Jeanette King & Gail Gillon. 2008. Maori English. *Clinical Linguistics & Phonetics*, 22, 658–70.

Mesthrie, Rajend. 2008. Black South African English: morphology and syntax. In Rajend Mesthrie (ed.) *Varieties of English, vol. 4: Africa, South and Southeast Asia*. Berlin: Mouton de Gruyter, 488–500.

Newmark, Kalina, Nacole Walker & James Stanford. 2017. The rez accent knows no borders: Native American ethnic identity expressed through English prosody. *Language in Society* 45, 633–64.

Ramisch, Heinrich. 1989. *The variation of English in Guernsey, Channel Islands*. Frankfurt: Lang.

Rooy, Bertus van. 2008. Black South African English: phonology. In Rajend Mesthrie (ed.) *Varieties of English, vol. 4: Africa, South and Southeast Asia*. Berlin: Mouton de Gruyter, 177–87.

Sidwell, Paul, & Mathias Jenny. 2015. *The handbook of the Austroasiatic languages* vol. 1. Leiden: Brill.

Tan, Ying-Ying. 2014. English as a 'mother tongue' in Singapore. *World Englishes* 33, 319–39.

Index

Ingram Content Group UK Ltd.
Milton Keynes UK
UKHW020055290623
424233UK00012B/103

9 781108 949576